Praise for Julia Roberts

I really got caught up in this book and became so involved with all the characters and their many twist and turns...exactly what I love for a good read! An impressive first novel
Lulu *international singing star*

Written in a very topical present day manner, in a way that many readers will recognise. Can't wait to read the next instalment! Well done, Julia Roberts!
Nicky Summer *Lifestyle Magazine*

'A slice of sheer escapism which packs an emotional punch'
Jemma Forte *novelist*

Julia Roberts' passion for writing began when, at the age of ten, after winning second prize in a short story-writing competition, she announced that she wanted to write a book. After a small gap of forty-seven years, and a career in the entertainment industry, Julia finally fulfilled her dream in 2013 when her first book, a memoir entitled *One Hundred Lengths of the Pool*, was published by Preface Publishing. Two weeks later she had the idea for her first novel, *Life's a Beach and Then…*, book one in the Liberty Sands Trilogy, which was released in May 2015. Julia still works full-time as a Presenter for the TV channel QVC, where she has just celebrated her twenty-second anniversary.

She now lives in Ascot with her 'other half' of thirty-eight years and occasionally one or other of her children and their respective cats.

You can find out more about Julia and her books on her Facebook page www.facebook.com/JuliaRobertsTV and her website www.juliarobertsbooks.co.uk

You can also follow her on Twitter @JuliaRobertsQVC

By Julia Roberts
One Hundred Lengths of the Pool
Life's a Beach and Then…
(book one in the Liberty Sands Trilogy)

If He
Really
Loved Me...

Julia Roberts

A ripped book

ISBN 978 0 9932522 3 5

Copy edited by Justine Taylor
Book cover illustration Angela Oltmann

Published by ripped

Book two in the

Liberty Sands Trilogy

PROLOGUE

Holly stirred. The gentlest of breezes rustled the glossy flat leaves of the badamier trees providing light relief from the warmth of the late afternoon Mauritian sun. As her eyes flickered open they rested on the empty buggy at her side, but before panic could set in over the whereabouts of her eighteen-month-old baby daughter Rosie, she spotted two familiar blond heads close together hard at work down by the shore. Rosie was picking up pieces of coral one by one and bringing them back to her helper who was building a fort with them. Even from twenty feet away Holly could hear her daughter's voice saying 'a du' as she handed each piece over. It was the little girl's way of saying thank you, which Holly much preferred to 'ta'. The chubby little legs, well protected from the sun by a generous layer of factor 50, were on the move again. Holly watched as Rosie stopped at the edge of the water but instead of bending down to choose her next piece of coral she was pointing at something and shouting excitedly in her baby voice, 'Ree, Ree!'

Harry was at her side in seconds and scooped her up in his arms. 'What is it, Rosie?'

At eighteen months Rosie had a very limited vocabulary. She could say mama, dada, a du and Ree, her name for her big brother, Harry. Whatever she had spotted in the water she had no word to describe it.

'What can she see, Harry?' Holly called out.

'It's just a shoal of fish, Mum. Go back to sleep.'

'I wasn't asleep,' Holly protested. 'I was just resting my eyes.'

'Of course you were,' Harry said as he released his wriggling sister back on to the sand to continue her coral search.

'Nice fort,' Holly said, changing the subject. 'Is it a scale model of something you and Robert are working on?'

'Very funny,' Harry said good-naturedly and then turned his attention back to his baby sister. 'I think Mummy has had too much sunshine, Rosie.'

'Mama,' the little girl said, reaching her hand in Holly's direction, clenching and unclenching her fist.

'We'll go and see Mummy in a minute, Rosie, let's finish our fort first.'

The two of them walked hand in hand towards the pile of stones, Harry talking one pace for each half dozen of Rosie's steps. Holly settled back on her sun-lounger to watch them, a warm feeling spreading through her entire body that had nothing to do with the sun that was starting its descent towards the sea. She had always loved the way the reflection on the water seemed to lead a path directly to the person observing it, sparkling and glittering on the way. As she reached up her hand to tuck a wayward strand of dark curly hair behind her ear, something else glinted and dazzled in the sunshine. Holly's breath caught in her throat as she admired the beautiful rings on the third finger of her left hand. There were three of them where two short years ago there had been none.

'Happy?' said a voice from behind her as two bronzed hands rested lightly on her shoulders and a kiss was planted firmly on the top of her head.

Holly turned her head slightly to gaze into the light green eyes that were full of adoration for her and said, 'I can't believe this is really happening to me...'

CHAPTER 1

Two years earlier

Holly closed and locked the door of her straw-roofed beach bungalow, descended the four wooden steps leading on to the soft white sand and headed towards the shoreline for her ten-minute walk to breakfast. She had never been to the Maldives before but had heard it described on many occasions as a 'no news, no shoes' destination, something she had been sceptical about before arriving on Kuremnu Island seven days ago. Holly had felt sure that the phrase didn't mean no shoes at all, so for the first couple of days she had carried her beaded flip-flops to the restaurant, slipping her feet into them at the entrance before going in. Once she realised that everyone else was embracing walking barefoot on the sandy restaurant floor she abandoned the practice for all meals except dinner. It didn't feel right to be wearing make-up and an evening outfit with nothing on her feet. The beaded flip-flops that she had packed for daytime use had come in handy, not so the wedge-heel gold sandals, which she hadn't bothered to unpack. They were now reunited with the rest of her belongings in the suitcase that had been collected from her veranda the previous evening by Muhammad, the house boy, for the first leg of her journey home.

The week had passed quickly and Holly had found little to complain about – the service, rooms and food had all been to a very high standard – but Holly had to admit that she wasn't in the least bit sad to be leaving this island paradise. Her job as a secret travel blogger for Soleil Resorts meant that she travelled alone, but she had never before felt so lonely on an assignment. Like most of the Maldivian holiday islands, the resort of Kuremnu took up the entire island, and there was no escaping loved-up honeymooners or older couples celebrating a lifetime spent together. In one of the blogs Holly had posted during the past week she had categorically stated that Kuremnu was not a destination for singles, not unless you had a masochistic streak. As if to underline her solitude, a young couple stopped on the shoreline fifty yards ahead of her to kiss, and beyond them another couple were walking hand in hand. It wasn't that Holly begrudged them their happiness, she wasn't even jealous of it, after all she had plenty to be thankful for, but she wasn't a member of their happy couples' club.

Everything had seemed so different four months ago when she had met and fallen in love with Philippe. After so long without a significant other, Holly had finally believed she had met her Mr Right. She paused mid-stride, allowing the warm turquoise water of the Indian Ocean to pool around her feet, her mind filled with images of his intense green eyes, slender Gallic nose and persuasive, hungry lips. She shook her head to remove the pictures.

How did I get it so wrong? she thought. Why couldn't I have learned from my previous mistake? Subconsciously she rested her hand on her slightly protruding belly. 'I don't mean you, little one,' she whispered. 'You're not a mistake, you're a blessing.'

Holly started walking again, the gentle waves lapping the hem of her colourful sarong. A hunger pang reminded her that she was later than usual for breakfast. Once she had got past the morning sickness of the first trimester Holly's appetite had returned with a vengeance and at times she really did feel like she was eating for two. She was quite surprised that none of the guests she had got chatting to over the past week had guessed that she was pregnant. Maybe they just think I'm chubby because I eat so much, Holly thought with a smile.

The day was already very warm and the clouds that had brought the rain of the last two days had now gone, leaving behind the most perfect blue sky. While the image of the Maldives was permanent sunshine and blue skies, and some travel agents did little to change that opinion, if you travelled in the rainy season, roughly equivalent to the British summer, you would expect to have some rain. This was different from the rain that Holly was used to back in England – warm and soft rather than cold and driving – and yesterday Holly had gone for a swim in the sea with the raindrops falling on the surface around her. Holly had written honestly about the weather, and it was exactly this honesty that had made her Liberty Sands blog so popular and driven people to the site. Holly's blog managed people's expectations, thus avoiding disappointment, and was seen as a refreshing change from other companies' blogs that just regurgitated the corporate line. Soleil Resorts were happy: they had seen a significant drop in complaints received – as well as an upsurge in bookings – since Holly had started writing her 'warts and all' blog for them.

Perspiration was beginning to trickle down the back of Holly's neck as she walked past the jetty towards the entrance of the main restaurant and some much-needed shade. The hotel staff were already setting up the welcome party at the head of the jetty for the next intake of guests. There were flower garlands to place over people's heads, a tray of glasses waiting to be filled with a fruity drink, and the bodu beru drums, made from bamboo and sting-ray hide, which would beat out a welcome to the new arrivals. In the first blog she had written the day after she arrived, Holly had mentioned what a nice touch it was. Fortunately for Holly, the 'no news' bit of 'no news, no shoes' was less accurate than the other part of the saying and most of the island resorts now embraced modern technology, although if she had actually been on holiday, as her fellow guests were, she would have viewed television and access to the Internet as an intrusion into the escape from reality that Kuremnu offered.

In a couple of hours, the sea plane would be discharging its latest cargo of holiday-makers, blinking like startled rabbits caught in headlights as they emerged from the cabin into the brightness of the midday sun and anxious to seek shade from the intense heat. As soon as they disappeared into the reception area clutching their welcome cocktail, Holly and the other departing guests would be ushered along the jetty to the waiting plane to fly them to Malé where they would check-in for their flights home. I'll be on my way to Heathrow in just a few hours, thought Holly, settling at the table indicated by Farhan, her waiter, and home before my birthday starts.

When she had received the dates for her latest assignment Holly had initially been disappointed that she wouldn't be spending her birthday in paradise but now she was glad that she would be back in the UK even if it rained, as it often seemed to in June these days. At least I won't be on my own, she thought. Her son Harry had invited her to spend the day with him in Bath where he was finishing his second year at university. Just the thought of seeing Harry caused her mixed emotions. Theirs was such a close relationship. There had only ever been the two of them after Harry's father, Gareth, had disappeared from Holly's life before the baby was born. She had never regretted her decision to keep her baby but there had been many times when she had wished there had been someone to share those special moments – Harry's first step, his first day at school, learning to ride his bike without stabiliser wheels – precious memories that only she had witnessed. And now history was set to repeat itself. She had fallen in love with Philippe – the first time she had allowed herself this emotion since Gareth had abandoned her – only to have her heart broken again. Philippe had no idea she was pregnant and she was going to keep it that way. She didn't want him back in her life because of some misplaced sense of duty. Harry was a different matter. He had been her entire life for twenty years but she had no idea how he would react to what she was about to tell him. She had already delayed longer than she had intended because Harry was in the middle of end-of-term exams but Holly knew she would have to have the talk with him when she returned from the Maldives.

'Can I get you some mint tea?' asked Farhan, bowing slightly as he spoke.

'You've got a good memory. That would be lovely,' Holly said, smiling. She guessed Farhan was probably about the same age as Harry. As she watched his retreating back she wondered what career path he might have chosen if he had been born somewhere else in the world. Maybe in England or America he would have gone to university to study architecture like her son. Or maybe he would have waited tables in a greasy spoon café, returning home after a twelve-hour shift to a tiny bedsit in a rough part of town. At least when the staff in Kuremnu had finished their work they lived in idyllic surroundings.

Farhan returned with a pot containing fresh mint leaves and boiling water. 'Would you like me to pour for you?' he asked.

'No thank you, I'll get my breakfast first. You've been here every day of my stay, do you have a day off soon?'

'I am going home tomorrow,' Farhan said, barely able to conceal his excitement.

'Home?' Holly queried. 'I thought this was home.'

'None of the staff live on the resort islands, we only work here. My home island is still in the Lhaviyani Atoll but it is a thirty-minute boat ride away, near the tuna cannery island. Did you go on the tour?'

Holly had, as she thought it would be good to put on her blog, with the added benefit of escaping the loved-up couples for a few hours. She had enjoyed the boat-ride in the colourful dhoni, a traditional Maldivian boat, but the moment they drew near to the island she began to regret her decision. There was an overwhelming stench of fish, which made her feel as nauseous as she had during her first few weeks of her pregnancy, and she was still surrounded by couples.

'How long will you stay at home for?'

'Usually it is only a week but my wife has just had our second baby so I am allowed to stay for a whole month.'

If Holly had been drinking her mint tea, she was pretty sure she would have choked on it after that revelation.

'You don't look old enough to be married, let alone a father of two,' Holly said.

'I'm twenty and my wife is nineteen,' he responded, somewhat defensively. 'I think people in England have children at this age too?'

Holly realised the absurdity of what she had said. Although she would be thirty-nine when her new baby was born, she herself had given birth to Harry at nineteen. At least this young couple were married and, judging by the look of pride in Farhan's eyes, happy.

'Of course,' said Holly, anxious to avoid offence. 'Was it a boy or a girl?'

'I have two beautiful girls but I love them anyway.' Holly raised her eyebrows but said nothing. 'Do you know what you are having?' he asked with an almost imperceptible glance at her rounded belly.

'N-not yet,' Holly stammered, thankful that she had been wearing the old gilt ring that Gareth had given her twenty years ago to back up her cover story of a grieving widow that she used to explain why she was travelling alone.

'Well, I hope you and your baby will have a happy life,' Farhan said, bowing slightly as he left Holly's table to attend to other guests.

Holly poured herself some mint tea and sipped it to calm her nerves. I'll definitely have to tell Harry about the baby when I see him on my birthday, she thought, if my bump is that obvious to a stranger.

Less than thirty minutes later, Holly emerged from the comparative cool of the restaurant, with its high ceilings and overhead fans, into a temperature already climbing towards thirty degrees. She deftly twisted her dark curly hair, now dry after her morning shower, into an elastic band before setting off on the post-breakfast walk around the island she had enjoyed every morning since her arrival on Kuremnu.

The island was larger than most in the Maldives but you could still circumnavigate it in under an hour. From the restaurant Holly headed along the beach to the northern-most tip of the island where the sand gave way to rocks and the lush vegetation draped in the water, making it difficult but possible to pass when the tide was low. It was only 9.30 a.m. but the sun was already high in the sky and as she had done on previous mornings Holly was tempted to stop for a drink at the small bar, The Outcrop, where very early risers could get a light breakfast of fruit and watch the sunrise. A quick glance at her watch told Holly that there would be no time for this particular indulgence if she was to have another shower before assembling in the Lionfish bar with the other guests who were leaving that day.

A smile spread across Holly's face as she remembered her reaction to her bathroom the night she arrived from England after a fourteen-hour journey. Muhammad had welcomed her to a beautifully appointed room with petals scattered on her bed and towels folded into the shapes of an elegant swan and her cygnet. Holly was tired. She had been anticipating slipping into a relaxing bath before dinner with water made silky to the touch by the addition of her favourite bath oils.

Muhammad had opened the door in the far corner of the room and said, 'And here is your bathroom.'

The door led outside to a small enclosed garden. A raised tiled area covered by a sloping straw roof housed the toilet, shower and washbasin. Although it was outside, it felt quite private but the bath was a different matter. It was standing isolated in the middle of the garden, completely open to the heavens.

'Well, this is different,' Holly had managed to say, trying not to show her disappointment.

After Muhammad had left, Holly sank on to the bed wondering what to do. She had really been looking forward to a soak, particularly as her ankles were swollen from the flight, but she was a private person and not given to displays of nakedness in public. The walls enclosing the garden didn't seem very high but then there were no two-storey buildings on the island, apart from the restaurant and nightclub, so she was pretty sure that no one would be able to see in, unless they climbed a tree or walked around on stilts. In the end her desire for total relaxation won over her fear of being seen naked but she had lowered herself carefully into the inviting bath water nonetheless, only releasing her towel at the last possible moment. As she had lain in the fragrant water with the skies gradually darkening to indigo, revealing a multitude of stars hidden from view in most of the light-polluted parts of the planet, Holly couldn't help wishing that she had been sharing the experience with Philippe. He would have made her feel completely at ease, as if this was the most natural thing in the world.

'Damn,' Holly swore, as she stubbed her toe on a partially sand-covered rock. Normally she was careful on this side of the island where the beach was punctuated by vegetation and rocky groynes designed to prevent sand erosion, but her thoughts had drifted to Philippe, making her lose concentration. After finding Rosemary's note while en route to the Seychelles, urging her to forgive Philippe, Holly had decided that she would give him a chance to explain his actions but only if he tracked her down, which Holly reasoned wouldn't be too difficult as they had a mutual friend in Rosemary's husband, Robert. But there had been no contact from Philippe, even though Robert had told her that he was back in the UK to promote his new book. Disappointment had turned quickly to anger, and the sense of betrayal returned with a vengeance when she started to read pre-release reviews on his 'new masterpiece', as one magazine put it. His true identity was still a mystery to most people but Holly had begun to hear rumblings in the book world that maybe the elusive Veronica Philips was not really a woman.

Holly could feel the familiar prickle of a blush rising from her chest to her face. The fewer people who knew how stupid and gullible she had been to fall for Philippe's charms the better. If her friend DD, who, as chance would have it, was also his publisher, ever found out that she was his muse for the new book, her other career as a copy editor for Ripped Publishing would be over. It wouldn't just be the embarrassment of facing DD after the revelations in Philippe's book, there was a strong possibility that DD would never trust her again.

Holly had passed the exclusive water bungalows, with their Jacuzzis and private sun decks, and was approaching her favourite part of the island. The south-western tip of Kuremnu was a wide sandy beach where holiday-makers congregated every evening, close to the aptly named Sunset Bar, to watch the orange globe of the sun slip gracefully over the horizon. Much as Holly had enjoyed taking part in this daily ritual, particularly as it gave her plenty of opportunity to mix with fellow guests, it was not the reason she loved this spot so much. When the tide was low, as it was now, a spit was revealed creating a silver pathway right out to the reef. It was a surreal feeling to be walking on sandbanks through the shallow turquoise lagoon with the midnight blue of the deeper water beyond the reef tantalisingly close. On one occasion Holly had been so lost in her own thoughts that she hadn't noticed the tide had turned and when she turned back from the reef the spit was already starting to disappear as she hurried back towards the safety of the shore as quickly as the soft sand would allow.

Despite not having enjoyed the assignment in the Maldives as much as she had hoped she would, Holly had to concede that it was the closest thing to paradise she had ever experienced. Sadly there was no time to walk out on the spit today and Holly reluctantly turned her back on it and headed back to her beach bungalow for the final time.

CHAPTER 2

The whole house shook from the slam of the front door and, over the sound of the vacuum cleaner, Harry could hear thundering footsteps on the uncarpeted stairs. Moments later Jack's face appeared at the living room door.

'Bloody hell, mate, am I in the wrong house?' Jack shouted over the noise.

'I told you my mum is coming down for her birthday on Sunday and I'm working at the pub all day tomorrow so I needed to make a start on the cleaning today. I couldn't work out why this thing wasn't picking anything up until I checked the bag,' Harry said indicating a black plastic bin liner in the corner of the room. 'It was full to bursting point and I think it will need emptying again when I've finished. When was the last time any of us cleaned up properly?'

'Christmas, wasn't it, after we had that little get together?' offered Jack, dodging the vacuum cleaner on his way to the kitchen which was housed in a large alcove to one end of the living room. 'Do you want anything?'

'Just an orange squash thanks. It's boiling in here

particularly with the oven on. What's it like outside?'

'Really sunny. I just met Amy for a quick coffee in the park and we had to sit in the shade because she burns so easily in the sun. She's gone back to work now. What's in the oven?' Jack asked, reaching to open the door. 'It smells really good.'

'Don't open it,' Harry said, panic-stricken. 'I'm making sponge cake for my mum and if you open the door it might sink in the middle.'

'I didn't know you could bake as well as cook, Harry. You've kept that one quiet.'

'I've never made a cake before. Mum usually makes her own birthday cake but she's out of the country until late tomorrow so it was either buying one or having a go at making one.'

'What is it you said your mum does that means she travels so much?' Jack asked. It was a question he'd asked dozens of times before and Harry always avoided answering but perhaps Jack was hoping that with the distraction of baking and cleaning Harry might just let it slip.

'I didn't say and I'm not about to,' replied Harry, finally turning the vacuum off and taking a long slurp of orange squash.

'Is she a spy?' Jack persisted.

Harry laughed. 'No, nothing like that but she has to keep her identity secret or she'll lose her job.'

'Doesn't she do something to do with books as well?'

'Yep, she's a freelance copy editor. She tidies up other people's books before they get published.'

'Wouldn't she like to write her own book one day? It must be really annoying if some writer is making loads of money and taking all the credit for a book that your mum has made readable.'

'Funny you should say that. I've been saving all my bar money to buy her a week at a writing retreat for her birthday. I hope she'll like it.'

At that moment the timer on Harry's iPad went off and the two of them raced over to the oven. Harry carefully pulled down the oven door and the two twenty-year-olds peered into the furnace to try and gauge if the sponge was cooked.

'Geez, your exam results weren't that bad were they?' said a voice they both recognized instantly as Hugo, one of their other flatmates.

'Funny,' said Harry, as he carefully slid the oven shelf out and gingerly prodded the chocolate sponge cake with his finger. 'It says in the recipe that it's supposed to bounce back when you press it in the middle. Do you think that's bouncing back, Jack?'

Not wanting to be responsible, Jack did what Jack always did, he passed the buck. 'What do you think, Hugo?'

Before Hugo had made it across the room Harry had removed the cake tin from the oven and placed it on the wire rack from the grill pan to start cooling.

'Not an expert in home baking, I'm afraid,' Hugo said. 'Mother never eats cake because she's terrified of getting fat and Pops is always at some fancy banquet or other so rarely eats at home. It smells awesome though.'

'Keep your hands off it, Hugo, it's a birthday cake for my mum.'

'I wonder if you two have any idea how lucky you are to have each other?' Hugo said, slumping down on to one of the sofas.

'What's up, mate?' Harry asked, flopping down beside him.

When the four of them had first begun sharing a flat at the beginning of their second year at Bath University, Hugo was the one that Harry had thought he would struggle to get along with most. Their backgrounds were so different. Harry had been brought up by his mum in a small terraced house in Reading with no spare cash for any of life's little luxuries. Hugo on the other hand was the only child of two members of the landed gentry whose estate in Gloucestershire was larger than the whole of Reading, but with considerably fewer houses. Hugo and Jack were on the same course so had become friends but Harry barely knew him.

On the day they moved in Hugo had held out his hand and said, 'I'm Hugo, pleased to meet you.'

Suppressing a laugh, Harry had asked, 'What do your mates call you, Hugo?'

Without so much as a raised eyebrow Hugo had replied, 'Hugo.'

Harry had instantly loved his honesty and dry sense of humour.

'I think my parents are going to get a divorce,' Hugo said flatly. 'Pops found out that Mother has been shagging her tennis coach and went berserk, even though he's been through ten secretaries in as many years if you get my drift. It was never the perfect marriage but I think this is just one step too far. I suppose there'll be an almighty row over money but at least there won't be a custody battle over me and I won't have to live with either of them, not that I ever have unless you count school holidays. Really,

Harry, you are so lucky to have just one parent and for her to absolutely adore you.'

Harry had never really considered himself to be fortunate for not having a father but he was well aware that the relationship he shared with his mum was rare and special.

'I'm sorry you've got all that shit to deal with, Hugo, especially at exam time. Let me know if I can do anything to help.'

'Me too,' added Jack. 'My folks got divorced years ago and it hasn't affected me.'

Hugo and Harry exchanged glances then burst out laughing. Jack responded by throwing cushions at them both.

CHAPTER 3

Holly could hear the sea-plane's throaty engines as she hurriedly crossed the last few metres of sand before entering the Lionfish bar for her 11 a.m. rendezvous. She glanced at her watch. It was only ten minutes past eleven but Holly was very conscious of the eyes of her fellow travellers casting disapproving glances in her direction. She hated being late, it was not one of the qualities she had admired in Philippe, but on this occasion it was worth it for the refreshing shower she had taken, after her walk around the island, before embarking on the long journey home.

Rather than joining any of the couples who were sat at tables around the bar, Holly walked over to the window and watched as the sea-plane bounced a couple of times on its ample floats before making continuous contact with the surface of the sea and slowly coming to a halt beside the jetty. The small door towards the rear of the plane opened and a member of Kuremnu's staff wheeled a small gangplank into place for the co-pilot to attach. Stooping, due to the height of the doorway, the passengers began to emerge for the start of their holiday in paradise. Most of them had had the foresight to carry a change of clothes in their hand luggage so were now attired in floral shorts or dresses and flip-flops. Holly smiled, knowing that the flip-flops would get very little action on Kuremnu.

The last couple off the plane however were dressed very differently. They were quite elderly and the gentleman was dressed in a suit with a wool overcoat. His companion was also wearing a wool coat and had topped off her look with a felt hat and umbrella. Initially Holly found it amusing. It looked like their intended destination was somewhere like Norway or Sweden but they had accidentally got on the wrong plane and ended up in the tropics. The smile playing at the corners of Holly's mouth disappeared as she watched the two of them struggling up the jetty to the welcome party in thirty-five-degree heat.

'Why don't they at least take their coats off?' Holly muttered under her breath.

'Miss Wilson,' a voice said, startling her slightly. She had been so engrossed in watching the elderly couple she hadn't noticed a waiter come up behind her with a tray of juice drinks. 'May I have your ticket and passport please,' he said. 'Please help yourself to some refreshment.'

Holly handed over her documents but declined the drink. She had forgotten from her previous pregnancy how often she needed to pee. There was no toilet on board the little sea-plane so it seemed wise to keep her fluid intake to a minimum until they reached Malé International.

A few moments later the waiter, Paresh, returned with Holly's documents.

'We are ready to board now, Miss Wilson. Please take all your hand luggage and follow the others,' he said, indicating a group of a dozen or so people leaving the bar.

Holly picked up her canvas beach bag and dusted the sand off its bottom before heading out into the bright sunshine a few paces behind her fellow passengers. She was still wearing flip-flops, however her trainers were in her bag. She had intended to put them on in the bar but had been too distracted by the elderly couple in their winter wear. I hope they are in their room with the air conditioning on full, Holly thought, wondering if their travel agent had been entirely honest with them about the temperatures in the Maldives in June.

Boarding the sea-plane was slow as only one passenger was allowed on to the gangplank at a time. As Holly neared the front of the queue she could see a sign that the pilot had probably thought was amusing when he had written it: THE MADNESS STARTS HERE. Not very reassuring for a nervous flyer, she thought, and then reprimanded herself for not having a sense of fun. She was the last person to board and as soon as she had crossed the threshold the co-pilot disengaged the ramp and closed the door before Holly was even in her seat. The interior of the plane was quite cramped and the tall co-pilot was bent almost double as he made his way up the aisle, checking that everyone had their seatbelts fastened as he passed, before sliding into the cockpit alongside his captain. In total, they would only be on the ground, or more accurately the sea, for about thirty minutes but that was the way the air taxi service could keep their flights so affordable, by packing in as many flights as possible.

'Ladies and gents,' the pilot said in a lazy Australian drawl, 'this is your captain and apparently you're all buckled in nicely so let's go flying. We should have you in

Malé in forty minutes provided there's no traffic.'

The announcement was rather less orthodox than the ones made on the bigger airlines, but there was something friendly and inclusive in his manner that Holly liked. She had become very used to flying in large aircraft since starting her job with Soleil resorts almost a year ago but this trip was the first time she had flown in a sea-plane and she had really enjoyed the experience on the way to Kuremnu even though she hadn't managed to get a seat near a porthole window so she hadn't had a very good view of the scenery below. Holly was always of the opinion that if a big plane went down, even over water, there was a zero chance of survival but this little plane had floats so, provided the pilot could get it on to the surface of the water, the survival odds were surely much greater.

There was no door to the flight deck just a tattered brown curtain, which although pulled across, allowed the passengers a pretty good view of the controls. Both the pilots were flicking switches and turning dials and the engine on the starboard side suddenly spluttered into life. Holly waited in anticipation for the port side engine to do the same but apart from a whirring noise nothing seemed to be happening. The two pilots exchanged words in hushed tones and then the port engine whirred again but still didn't cough into life.

'This is your captain again, and I'm sorry to have to tell you but this plane is going nowhere.'

A murmur ran through the cabin.

'I'll radio the controller in Malé and they'll send a replacement taxi out here as soon as possible. Don't worry, folks, you'll make your connecting flights and if not you'll just have to stay here another week.'

Nervous laughter from the passengers followed the announcement but a man sitting across the aisle from Holly called out in an angry tone of voice, 'I hope you're joking. I've got an important business meeting in London tomorrow.'

It saddened Holly that the man's tone was so unpleasant. The pilot was just making sure that his passengers were safe, there was no need to be so aggressive. He wasn't the only who needed to get home, Holly had a rather important meeting of her own on Sunday that she was anxious to keep.

'Trust me, mate, we want to see you on the plane to London as much as you want to be on it,' the pilot said, all warmth gone from his voice. 'Please remember to take all your hand luggage with you as you leave the plane.'

As she was the last person to board the tiny plane, Holly was the first one off and found herself leading the procession back to the Lionfish bar. This time she sat at a table and accepted a refreshing drink from Paresh. Holly was debating whether to email Harry to let him know that there was a possibility that she might not make her flight but decided to do it from Malé airport instead when she would know for definite whether her plans had changed. Instead she reached into her beach bag for her trainers. I might as well squeeze my feet back into them now if we're going to be pushed for time in Malé, she thought.

And that's when it happened. As she straightened up Holly felt a distinct fluttering in her belly. One hand shot up to her mouth and the other to the place just under her ribs where her unborn baby had given her the first evidence of its existence.

In the end the holidaymakers from Kuremnu had made their respective flights with time to spare. Holly had initially thought that the four-hour wait for the international flight to London was a little excessive but realised, after what had happened with their air taxi, that the holiday companies probably factored in the extra waiting time to cover all eventualities and to make sure the scheduled flights would not be delayed. The replacement sea-plane had arrived an hour after their aborted take-off and fifteen minutes later they were airborne.

Second time round, Holly was one of the first on to the plane and had managed to get a seat next to the porthole window, perfect for appreciating the view below. The Maldives from the air was a seemingly endless scattering of tiny islands surrounded by impossibly turquoise water, turning to inky blue beyond the reefs. The highest point above sea level was less than eight feet and for years scientists had warned that, as a result of global warning, in as little as thirty years the entire island nation might disappear under the same clear blue waters that currently attracted divers and holidaymakers from all over the world. What a tragedy that would be, thought Holly, particularly after the resilience the local people had shown in bouncing back from the devastation of the 2004 tsunami.

She had managed to stay awake for the entire forty-five-minute flight from Kuremnu to Malé but as soon as the seat belt sign had been turned off on the next stage of her journey Holly drifted off to sleep as she always did on long-haul flights.

CHAPTER 4

Since Rosemary's death, Robert had found that the only way to get through each day was to have a routine. Today, just as he had every day since his wife's funeral, he had cleared up his breakfast dishes before going into his office for the remainder of the morning to deal with email enquiries from the various contracts his company was working on and then, time permitting, he would settle at his drawing desk and do something creative.

For Robert that was the best bit about being an architect. Of course, he was more than capable of all the necessary mathematical calculations that went into designing buildings but that wasn't what he enjoyed doing. Robert liked nothing better than to sit at his desk with a blank sheet of paper and let his imagination run riot. The problem was that this morning he had been totally devoid of any inspiration. It was almost lunchtime and he hadn't managed so much as a doodle. In a changing world where so many of the young up-and-coming architects preferred to work almost entirely on computers, Robert was delighted that Holly's son, Harry, was more old school. When Robert had shown Harry some of his drawings for new projects that were in the pipeline, Harry had at first admired them and then, on a fresh sheet of paper, drawn some ideas of his own. Robert was really looking forward to Harry finishing his term at university so that the two of them could exchange ideas for the hotel project Robert was tendering for in Hong Kong. In truth, Robert realised he was also looking forward to some human company. The house, beautiful though it was, felt very big and lonely with just him rattling around in it.

Robert put his pencil down and gazed out of the window which he had opened enough to allow the aromas of roses and lavender and honeysuckle to permeate his office but not so much that a rogue gust of wind would scatter the pile of papers from his desk. He knew without looking that the top three letters were all from local estate agents whom he had approached to do a valuation on the house when he was feeling particularly sad and alone. Now they were hassling him, all eager to have such a fabulous listing on their books. Could I really sell this place? Robert pondered. In some respects it would feel like I was betraying Rosie.

The phone ringing cut into his thoughts.

'Robert Forrester,' he said into the mouthpiece in his most business-like tone.

'Hi Robert. It's Harry. How are you doing?'

Robert's tone changed immediately. 'Harry, my boy, how lovely to hear your voice. How did your exams go?'

'I haven't had any results yet but I think I did okay. Listen, it's just a quick call. I'm not sure if you know but it's Mum's birthday on Sunday and I thought you might want to send her a card?'

'Thanks for reminding me, Harry, I had completely forgotten. She let it slip last time I spoke to her on the phone and I should have made a note of it then. It's the sort of thing Rosie would have put on the calendar straightaway.' Robert paused slightly. 'I think your mum said she is going to celebrate in Bath with you isn't she?'

'Yes. She gets home from the Maldives tomorrow afternoon and then she is driving down to mine and staying over. I'm taking her to lunch and I've just finished baking her a birthday cake. It's my first attempt at a cake so I hope it will taste as good as it smells.'

'You're a braver man than me, Harry. I had to do most of the cooking while Rosie was ill but I never attempted a cake. I don't think sweet things appealed to her much towards the end...' Robert's voice tailed off.

'Are you coping all right, Robert?'

'Of course, of course, it's just that some days I feel so alone. When you rang I was sitting here wondering if I should put the house on the market.'

'Don't rush into any hasty decisions, Robert. You both loved that house so much and I would think you have a lot of happy memories there.'

'True. But we were thinking of selling it to move out to Mauritius. Did your mum tell you that my offer on Sunset Cottage was accepted?'

'No, she didn't mention it. Wasn't the Frenchman living there? Has he moved out or are you going to keep him as a tenant?'

Robert failed to notice the tension in Harry's voice. 'Philippe is back in England now. His new book is out in a couple of weeks and, judging by all the pre-launch publicity, it looks like it's going to be an even bigger success than his first. Such a shame that he and your mum couldn't work things out particularly with a baby on the way. Call me old-fashioned but I still believe every child should have a father.'

There was a pause on the other end of the phone.

'Are you still there Harry? I'm so sorry, that was a totally thoughtless remark. You've never known your dad and it hasn't done you any harm,' he blundered on, totally unaware of the bombshell he had just dropped.

'No offence taken. Actually, I was just looking for my diary so that we could arrange some dates for me to come over to yours but I must have left it downstairs. I'm in a bit of a rush now, Robert, but I'll call you after the weekend.'

'I look forward to it, Harry, and I'll pop out and get your mum a card,' Robert said, but Harry had already disconnected the call.

The shock was palpable. Harry could feel his heart pumping blood around his body as he sat on the edge of his bed staring at his mobile phone. Robert had definitely said, 'with a baby on the way'. His mum was pregnant.

Why didn't she tell me? We tell each other everything. How could she tell Robert before she told me? Harry felt confused and angry in equal measure. The smell of the chocolate cake he had left to cool in the kitchen wafted into his room, reminding him of the conversation he had with Hugo just fifteen minutes ago. Hugo's very words were, 'I wonder if you two have any idea how lucky you are to have each other?' There had always been just the two of them, that's why the bond between them was so strong, but now, if Robert was to be believed, the whole dynamic of their relationship was about to change.

Harry was in unfamiliar territory and he had no idea how he was supposed to feel. No one likes to think of their parents having sex, but for his mum to have had a whirlwind romance and fallen pregnant as a result was almost incomprehensible to Harry. The times she had nagged him about taking precautions, and now she was the one who had been caught out. Unless… unless she had deliberately tried to fall pregnant, he thought. That would make more sense of her breaking off the relationship with Philippe so suddenly for a reason she still wasn't prepared to discuss with him. Maybe with me getting older she's starting to worry about being on her own? But then why didn't she try to make the relationship with Philippe work rather than getting pregnant and repeating history by bringing the baby up on her own?

'I just don't understand,' Harry cried out to an empty room. For the first time in all of his twenty years Harry felt let down by his mother.

CHAPTER 5

'I thought you said your mum was coming here for her birthday,' Jack said, watching Harry carefully wrap aluminium foil around the still-to-be-iced chocolate cake. 'I was looking forward to seeing her again. She's always such a laugh and she and Amy get on like a house on fire. And weren't you supposed to be working today?'

'I swapped shifts with Mike and worked last night instead,' Harry replied.

'What about your lunch plans for tomorrow?' persisted Jack.

'I cancelled them,' Harry said, laying the wrapped cake on top of the clothes in his sports bag before zipping it shut.

'Are you okay, mate? You seem a bit grumpy.'

Harry's gregarious personality had earned him the nickname 'Happy Harry' among his university friends however he was anything but happy this morning and was making no attempt to hide it. Harry was tired and distracted. After finishing his swapped shift at the bar the night before, he had got back to the flat and gone straight to bed without looking into the lounge to see if any of his flatmates were still up. Harry didn't want to talk to anyone about anything, he just needed to think.

At 4 a.m., just before he finally fell asleep, Harry reached the conclusion that he didn't want to reveal to his mum that he knew about the baby over her birthday lunch at the restaurant, nor did he want to discuss it at the flat where they might be overheard. The best option was for him to drive home to Reading and surprise her with the birthday cake and some flowers. He wanted to give her the opportunity to tell him she was pregnant. He was still struggling to understand why she would tell Robert about the baby before she told him. It crossed his mind that maybe it was a confidence his mum had shared with Rosemary before she died and that Robert had merely overheard. Robert must have assumed that Mum had told me, thought Harry. A pretty fair assumption really.

'Sorry, Jack, I'm just a bit knackered,' Harry said, lightening his tone. 'I didn't get much sleep last night and for once it wasn't the sound of Hugo snoring! Your room is right next to his and yet it doesn't seem to bother you two. Anyway, I got to thinking that the last thing Mum should be doing after an eighteen-hour journey is getting in a car to drive down here. I thought I'd surprise her by being home before she gets back, so I need to get going.'

'Geez, you're so bloody thoughtful,' Jack said, 'I would never have thought of doing anything like that. Hang on a minute though cos Amy got your mum a card from us thinking she was going to be here. You can take it with you.'

Jack raced up the stairs to his room to fetch the card and as he handed it over Harry noticed it was Amy's writing on the envelope. Cards really are such a girl thing, he thought.

'Thanks, mate, she'll appreciate it,' Harry said, slipping it into the side pocket of his sports bag along with his own card. And she would appreciate it. Harry could still visualise the wooden shelf above the fireplace which each birthday for years had displayed a solitary card from him. Her dad was dead and her mother might as well be after she had refused to have contact with Holly since his funeral. There was no loving husband and very few friends, none of whom ever sent her a birthday card. With a bit of luck, Harry thought, there might even be three cards this year, if Robert had managed to get his in the post in time.

CHAPTER 6

Robert had only been settled at his desk for fifteen minutes, when he was disturbed by a knock on the front door. For a minute he toyed with the idea of not answering the knock, after all it was probably another overzealous estate agent who had got wind that he might be considering selling his beautiful Surrey home, Valley View. Whoever was at the door was persistent though. The knocking became louder and more prolonged.

Reluctantly, Robert rose from his desk and climbed the sweeping staircase. He inched the front door open, preparing an excuse in his head as to why he didn't want to talk to whoever was on the other side.

'Philippe!' Robert exclaimed, throwing the door wide open and uncharacteristically flinging his arms around the somewhat startled Frenchman. 'Why didn't you tell me you were coming? I nearly didn't answer the door. Come in, come in, it's so good to see you."

If Philippe was surprised by Robert's change in appearance since the last time he had seen him in Mauritius three months previously his facial expression didn't show it. 'Robert,' he said, returning the embrace, 'it's so good to see you too and I'm sorry it has taken me so long but there has been a lot to do with the book. That's for later though, most importantly how are you?'

'Getting by, I guess,' Robert said, a watery smile unable to reach his chocolate-brown eyes. 'Don't just stand there on the doorstep, come in and I'll make us some coffee.'

'This place is magnificent and the view is incredible,' Philippe said, pausing for a moment at the top of the stairs to really appreciate the view down the beautifully manicured garden at the height of summer bloom, to the wooded Surrey hillside beyond.

'I know. I've seen it hundreds, if not thousands, of times and I still can't believe that this place came on the market at exactly the moment Rosie and I were looking to buy. It's not hard to get inspiration and be creative when you're gazing out on a scene like that,' he said, disappearing into the kitchen. 'How would you like your coffee, Philippe?'

'Black, no sugar, please. When I'm writing I drink so much of the stuff to keep me awake I would probably bleed coffee if they cut me open.'

'And did you?' Robert asked, appearing at the kitchen door.

'What?'

'Did you bleed black coffee when they operated in Port Louis? You've never really explained what happened, Philippe. Were you in a road accident?'

It was a question that Philippe had expected at some point and although he had contemplated lying to Robert because he felt ashamed that a lack of control had led to the fight in the Dolphin Bar, he had decided to tell the truth. There had already been enough lies. 'Actually,

Robert, I'm afraid to say I got into a brawl in a bar.'

'Really?' Robert was taken aback. He had only known Philippe a year but had never heard him so much as raise his voice, let alone his fists. 'Well, I wasn't expecting you to say that. Were you drunk?' he asked.

'Hung-over, more like,' Philippe admitted. 'I had been very drunk the night before but that's not the reason for the fight. I had done something stupid and I thought the person I attacked had told Holly about it which made her finish things between us. Now I'm not so sure. I guess you could call it a crime of passion, of sorts. Actually, Robert, that's one of the reasons I'm here. Obviously I wanted to see you and make sure you are coping but I also need you to help me find Holly. The Plantation House hotel simply won't give me any details about her. I've tried, and so has my book editor, but they've remained tight-lipped, refusing to even give me her last name. Apparently they were visited by an undercover resort inspector so they are really twitchy and playing everything by the book at the moment. I know I've made a bit of a mess of things, Robert, but I've never felt this way about anyone in my life. I really love her. Will you help me? I know you're in contact with her.'

Robert didn't know what to say. The normally self-assured Philippe, with his 'love them and leave them attitude' towards women, looked vulnerable and slightly desperate. And Robert knew, more than any other living soul, how deep Holly's feelings towards him had been before whatever had happened had made her cease all contact with him. Rosemary hadn't divulged anything, saying that Holly would tell him about it in her own good time, but Holly hadn't confided in him yet and he was acutely aware of the promise he had made not to give Philippe her contact details.

Philippe was looking at him pleadingly. 'Please, Robert, I just want to try and explain what happened and hope that she'll forgive me. Have you seen her recently?'

'Not for a week or so, she's been busy with work,' he replied, careful not to mention that she had been away to yet another exotic location, 'but I did speak to Harry yesterday.'

'Harry?' questioned Philippe.

'Yes, Holly's boy...' Robert caught himself just in time. In his confusion, he had almost let it slip that Holly had a grown-up son. 'Erm, boy... f-friend,' he stammered. 'Well, not really a boyfriend as such, they've just been seeing each other,' he blundered on. 'I'll get the coffee,' he said, anxious to avoid further questioning.

Philippe felt like he had been struck a physical blow. Ever since he had regained consciousness in the hospital in Port Louis, he had been planning what he was going to say to Holly to try and win her back. He knew it wouldn't be easy, particularly as he was also going to have tell her he had been lying about the type of book he had been writing, but he had felt sure that his deep feelings for her were reciprocated and that once she found out she was the inspiration for his latest novel she would forgive him and they could start over. He couldn't believe he had so totally misread her. Had he simply been a holiday romance to be forgotten about the moment she arrived back home? Then he remembered the emails they had exchanged before his indiscretion. She had clearly been longing to see him again. He sank into the plush upholstery of the sofa and rested his head in his hands. 'I can't believe this is happening,' he muttered to himself. 'I can't believe I've let her slip away.' But looking at things from Holly's point of view, he realised that she was perfectly entitled to start seeing someone new after his appalling behaviour. He had just lived in the hope that once she set eyes on him again she would give him a second chance. Maybe this new relationship wouldn't last, he thought. Perhaps she was attracted to this new man merely because he has the same name as her late husband and she will discover that they are not right for each other.

Sitting on Robert's sofa, Philippe reached the decision that he wasn't going to give up on Holly without a fight. He wasn't normally a patient man but Holly was worth waiting for.

CHAPTER 7

The silver Toyota Prius pulled into the kerb and came to a halt outside the small Victorian terraced house that Holly had called home for the past fifteen years. Without glancing at the house, Holly handed over the fare to the cab driver before rummaging in her bag for the front door keys while he lifted her suitcase on to the pavement. Despite having slept for most of the twelve-hour plane journey from the Maldives, Holly felt overwhelmingly tired. Although she was really looking forward to seeing Harry, the thought of driving to Bath later that evening filled her with dread. I'm going to have to have a cat nap, she thought, putting the key in the lock. It didn't turn. Holly tried again. Still nothing, but when she turned the key in the other direction it locked.

Suddenly alert, Holly began to panic. Had she really forgotten to double lock the front door when she had left just over a week ago? The memory of a horrible incident that had occurred soon after she had moved in to this little house filled her mind. She had taken six-year-old Harry for a day out at the park. When they had arrived home, tired but happy, she had been unable to open the

Yale lock on the front door. Thinking it was broken, and not sure how she was going to get in, Holly had knocked at the door of her elderly next-door neighbour, Doug. He was a grumpy old man at the best of times but when he opened the door and saw Holly and Harry he had said, 'I presume you've come to apologise for the dreadful racket you were making earlier.' Holly had been about to protest their innocence and explain that they had been out all day when a cold fear gripped her heart. The reason she couldn't unlock the Yale lock was because someone had put the deadlock on from the inside, and Holly's fear was that they might still be there.

Once Doug understood the situation he invited Holly and Harry into his home and immediately called the police who had arrived twenty minutes later. They broke the lock to gain access only to find that the burglars had long gone, leaving through the sash-cord window in the back room, which was clearly how they had broken in as one of the panes of glass was smashed.

Fortunately, there had been nothing of any value for the burglars to take, apart from the contents of Holly's money box which didn't amount to much, so their efforts had been in vain. In their frustration, they had pulled everything out of the cupboards downstairs and the drawers upstairs creating a dreadful mess, and it was probably the noise that Doug had heard earlier.

Once the police and the emergency locksmith had left, Holly had fetched the spade and fork from the garden shed, jamming the handle of the spade under her bedroom-door handle and placing the fork at the side of the bed as a weapon. Harry hadn't really understood what had happened but he was really pleased at being allowed to sleep in his mum's big bed with her, something that was normally off limits. He was asleep as soon as his head hit the pillow but Holly didn't close her eyes all night, imagining she could hear sounds downstairs. She couldn't allow herself to show her fear in front of her young son, after all she was the only grown-up in his little world and he had to believe that she would keep him safe. The next day Holly had the additional lock added to the front door and locking bolts put on all the windows with money loaned to her by Doug from next door.

Holly had been so deeply engrossed in the awful memory that she let out a small scream as the front door of her home started to open.

'Whoa, Mum, calm down. It's only me.'

'Harry! You frightened the life out of me. What are you doing here? I thought I was coming down to yours for my birthday,' Holly managed to say, clinging on to her son until her trembling subsided.

'Change of plan, Mum. I knew you'd be knackered after your globe-trotting so I thought I'd save you the trip and surprise you by welcoming you home. Sorry if it was more of a shock than a surprise.'

'No, I'm the one that should be sorry, overreacting like that. You're so thoughtful, Harry. And you're right, I'm absolutely shattered. I could murder a cup of tea.'

'The kettle's already on. Do you want one of your hot fruity water drinks or should I make you a proper cuppa with loads of sugar? Isn't that meant to combat shock?' he added with a cheeky grin.

'Proper tea, I think, but hold the sugar and just a drop of milk,' Holly said, following her son into the hallway of her house, where he deposited her suitcase before

47

heading into the kitchen.

'Make yourself comfy, Mum,' he called over his shoulder.

Holly went into the compact living room, painted a pale shade of duck-egg blue, sank into her favourite armchair, kicked off her trainers and relaxed back closing her eyes. It was bliss. Her feet had protested at being squeezed back into shoes after a week of barefoot freedom, but after a twelve-hour flight, and the inevitable swelling that had caused, they were positively screaming to be set free. 'What time did you get here?' Holly asked, in a slightly raised voice so that Harry would hear her over the noise of the kettle boiling.

'Only a couple of hours ago,' Harry replied, 'just long enough to nip out to the florist and get you these.'

Without opening her eyes, Holly knew that her son was holding a bunch of white lilies. The pungent aroma had invaded her nostrils the moment he pushed the lounge door open.

'Shall I put them in the fireplace?'

'Oh Harry, they're gorgeous,' she enthused, opening her eyes to admire the display, 'but you shouldn't go spending so much money on me.'

'It's your birthday, Mum, I always buy you flowers,' he said with a slight shrug of his shoulders.

'Do you remember the first bunch of flowers you ever got me?'

Harry nodded. 'They were sweet peas. I bought them with my paper round money because you said you loved the smell of them.'

Holly's eyes began to mist at the memory. What she had told an eleven-year-old Harry was only partly accurate. True, she did love the scent but mostly because it reminded her of her dad. He had grown them every year of Holly's childhood. She remembered him soaking the small hard seeds that resembled miniature rabbit droppings in warm water overnight until they had swelled to twice their size. Then she would fish them out of the water one by one and hand them to her Dad to plant in their own little incubators made from the cardboard centres of toilet paper rolls. Once planted out the following Spring they would rampage over the double row of canes that traversed the tiny back garden of her childhood home in Nottingham. The fluttering, pastel-coloured blooms were still a favourite but, try as she might, she had never been able to grow them with the same success that her dad had.

As if he was reading her mind, Harry said, 'You know it's Father's Day tomorrow, as well as being your birthday?'

'How did you know I was thinking about your grandad?'

'I always know, Mum. I'll get our tea.'

Holly knew that the perfect opportunity had presented itself to tell Harry about the baby. She had been putting it off, making excuses, but she couldn't delay any longer. Nerves fluttered in her stomach, or was it the tiny being growing inside her urging her to declare its existence? How am I going to tell him? she thought. What should I say? The palms of her hands were starting to feel clammy as she struggled to think of the right words.

Harry was backing through the door holding two mugs of tea in one hand and the biscuit tin in the other. 'You were out of biscuits, Mum, so I got us some chocolate Hobnobs, our favourite. Well, when I say ours, I sort of mean mine,' he said, placing her mug on a bejewelled coaster that she had brought back from her recent trip to Dubai and sitting on the two-seater sofa opposite her. 'Are you okay? You look a bit pale.'

'Harry,' she faltered, 'th-there's something I need to tell you.' She watched as his gaze dropped to the floor.

'I already know, Mum,' he said, raising his eyes to meet hers, and the hurt was there, plain for her to see. 'I know about the baby. I just don't know why you didn't tell me. We tell each other everything, at least I thought we did.'

Along with the relief that flooded through her that she no longer needed to find the right words, Holly felt his pain like an arrow through her own heart. 'I… I…' Holly tried but failed. 'I wanted to tell you, so many times, but I just didn't know what to say,' she finally managed, her eyes never losing contact with his, imploring him to understand.

'What really hurts, Mum, is that you were able to tell someone else but not me.'

'I didn't tell Rosemary, Harry, she guessed because she heard me being sick the night we stayed over with them in Woldingham.'

'I don't mean Rosemary, Mum, that I can sort of understand, but why did you tell Robert before you told me?' There was the slightest hint of petulance in Harry's voice.

'Robert knows? You have to believe me, Harry, I didn't tell Robert,' Holly said quietly, 'and I asked Rosemary not to either.'

'Well, she must have, because he told me yesterday when I was speaking to him on the phone.'

Holly didn't know how to feel. She felt wretched that

she hadn't been brave enough to face Harry sooner and share her news in a more positive way. She was disappointed that Rosemary had betrayed her to Robert, despite saying that she wouldn't and she felt anxious. If Robert had told Harry about the baby maybe, just maybe, he would also tell Philippe.

Once again, as if by telepathy, Harry said, 'Does the Frenchman know? I presume the baby is his?'

Holly shot an indignant look at her son. 'If you're suggesting that I'm in the habit of sleeping around then you can relax, it's definitely Philippe's. Whether he knows or not is another question entirely and rather depends on Robert and who else he has seen fit to share my private life with. I certainly haven't told Philippe and nor do I have any intention of doing so,' she added, her chin jutting forward resolutely.

'Mum, don't be mad at Robert he's been through such a lot over the last couple of years. He would never do anything to hurt you. He absolutely adores you. He didn't so much tell me, it was more an assumption that I already knew, which is fair enough really.'

Holly accepted the rebuke. 'You're right, Harry. I shouldn't blame other people because I've made a mistake but I will have to call him and ask him to keep this to himself.'

'Is the baby a mistake, Mum?'

'Bad choice of words I guess, Harry, more of a happy consequence, really. But if a little bit of you is wondering whether I planned this you couldn't be more wrong. Bringing up a baby single-handed when I was nineteen was tough enough, but now I'm twenty years older I can only imagine how exhausting it is going to be. No, this wasn't planned, but it's happened and I'm going to cherish this new little person just as I have always cherished you,' Holly said, resting her hands protectively on the small rounded bump beneath her ribcage.

'But you're not alone this time, Mum. You've got me. I'll be able to help, particularly when I've finished at uni. That is, assuming you want my help?'

Holly reached her arms out to her son and he moved across the small space to fill them. 'Oh Harry, I can't tell you how relieved I am to hear you say that! I was so worried how you would react. I wasn't sure if you would feel that the new baby threatens our closeness,' she mumbled into his shoulder.

'I can't lie, Mum. I was really shocked and upset when Robert let it slip and I felt a bit jealous that I was going to have to share you with someone else. But then I reasoned that if it had worked out with the Frenchman things within our relationship would have shifted anyway. I was just being selfish.'

'You don't have a selfish bone in your body,' Holly said, hugging him even more fiercely before pushing him away slightly so that she could see his face. 'Things will be different, of course they will, but I will never love you any less than I do right now, I promise.'

'And you've definitely decided that you're not going to tell the Frenchman?'

'Why do you never use his name? And anyway he's only half French.'

'It's less personal, I guess. You won't tell me what he did that made you finish with him but it doesn't really matter. He hurt my mum and for that I can't forgive him.'

'So you think I'm right not to tell him?'

'I don't know. Ultimately, it has to be your decision, but it is hard growing up not knowing who your dad is.' Harry took a deep breath. 'You've never told me anything about my dad.' It was a statement not an accusation.

'You've never asked.'

'Well maybe I'm asking now.'

Holly picked up her mug of tea and took a sip of the hot, comforting liquid with its slightly bitter aftertaste. How appropriate, she thought. 'Harry, I know it's a big ask but you've waited patiently for all these years to find out about your dad, can you wait a bit longer? I'm tired and more than a little emotional right now, and I want this evening to be just the two of us, like it always has been. It's Father's Day tomorrow. I'll tell you everything you want to know about him then, you have my word.'

CHAPTER 8

The sun filtering through the leaves overhead was creating a dappled effect on the hard-baked earth of the path through the woods. Although it was only a few minutes after eight the air was already warm giving the promise of a perfect summer day. I hope it's this nice in Bath, Robert thought, climbing over the quaint old stile and heading towards the road to complete his circuit back to Valley View via the village shop where he planned to pick up the Sunday papers. He didn't usually bother but, as he had been leaving the previous evening, Philippe had suggested that Robert might find something interesting within the pages of a couple of the broadsheets. Clearly it was something to do with his new book, *Tiffany*, and Robert suspected that they may finally be revealing that Veronica Philips was the pen name for his friend. He wondered how Holly would react to the revelation, particularly as his pseudonym had been kept secret from her in Mauritius. Robert had mentioned his misgivings at the lack of honesty to Rosemary but she had explained it away, saying that Philippe wanted someone to love him for himself, not because he was a best-selling author.

There had been no further mention of Holly after Robert had almost given the game away about her having a son and, although he had covered his blunder as best he could, he was now feeling guilty that he had suggested to Philippe that she had moved on to a new boyfriend. Philippe had clearly been shocked as he was obviously still hoping that he and Holly could work things out and Robert had a suspicion that Holly would also like to have given things a second chance. He wished now that he had gone ahead with his original plan to tell Holly about Philippe's stay in hospital but, given time to think things over, he had decided not to meddle. Why does it have to be so complicated? Robert thought, and why does the ball keep landing back in my court to make decisions? Rosemary had always been the decision-maker in their relationship and it made his sense of loss even more acute.

Following his slip of the tongue, Robert hadn't dared have more than one glass of wine over the hastily scrambled together dinner of salmon and new potatoes that they had shared in case he had inadvertently mentioned the baby. Rosemary had always found his trait of opening his mouth and putting his foot in it quite endearing but he wasn't sure that others viewed it with the same degree of affection. He had already planned to drop into the conversation the next time he spoke to Philippe that Holly's fledgling romance was over. Hopefully no harm will have been done, he thought.

The old-fashioned bell clanged as Robert opened the door into the village shop, empty apart from the owner, Fred, who was marking up the papers for delivery.

Fifty years ago Robert had been a paperboy and he could still remember how much they had all dreaded the extra weight of the Sunday papers compared to the rest of the week. These days most of the Sunday papers took the whole week to read with all the magazines and supplements, but he suspected that not as many people had them delivered to their homes, judging by the fairly small pile in front of Fred.

'You're out and about early this morning, Robert,' Fred said out of the opposite corner of his mouth from the marker pen top. 'Run out of milk?'

'No, I'm treating myself to a couple of Sunday papers. My friend is in them today.'

'Not a scandal, I hope?' Fred said.

Robert smiled inwardly. A scandal was exactly what Fred was hoping for. Although a really good sort, nobody told Fred anything unless they wanted it spread around the village like wild fire. 'What sort of friends do you think I have?' said Robert, neatly side-stepping the question.

'Rich ones,' laughed Fred.

'You need to be rich to afford these,' Robert said, looking down at the fifty pence piece in his hand which was the only change from the five-pound note he had handed over, just as the bell tinkled to announce the arrival of another customer. 'I'd forgotten how dear they are.'

'Worth every penny if you ask me. Much better than reading the news online.'

'I'm with you on that, Fred, but I guess newspapers will become extinct within the next twenty years, not that it will affect either of us.'

'You speak for yourself, I'm aiming for a hundred and

a telegram from the Queen.'

Robert didn't bother pointing out that by the time Fred reached his century the reigning monarch would more than likely be a king. He slipped the coin into his pocket and was turning to leave as the other customer approached the counter carrying a pint of milk and a loaf of bread. Robert didn't recognise him which was unusual in such a tight knit community. 'Morning,' he said, pleasantly.

'Oh, morning,' the man replied, pushing his dark curly hair off his face with his free hand.

'Robert, have you met Nick? He's just moved into Wysteria Cottage. I think you're both in the same line of work.'

'Oh really?' Robert said, paying more attention to the man who was scruffily dressed in tatty jeans and a T shirt, both spattered with paint. 'You're a fellow architect?'

Nick grinned. 'I am, although I look more like a painter and decorator this morning. I'm giving the cottage a lick of paint to freshen it up a bit.'

'I didn't realise Dorothy had sold the place,' Robert said.

'She hasn't,' Fred interjected, 'she's gone into a care home and she's refusing to sell in the hope that she might be able to move back in if her health improves.'

'Her son gave me permission to decorate,' Nick said defensively, 'I hope the old lady won't mind.'

Robert and Fred exchanged glances.

'She probably wouldn't notice even if she was allowed to return home,' Robert said, sadly. 'Dorothy's suffering from Alzheimer's. It's such a shame. Until two years ago she was the head mistress of the village school but now...'

Robert shook his head.

'Well, I won't do anything too radical,' Nick said, 'just in case she wants to move back in. Maybe we could get together sometime, Robert? I don't know anyone around here and at least we'd have something to talk about,' he said, pocketing his change.

'That sounds good to me, I could do with a bit of company myself.'

'Yes, Fred mentioned you'd just lost you wife to cancer. I'm so sorry.'

Robert shot Fred a look but he was oblivious to it as his head was down continuing to mark up the Sunday papers. He really is a terrible gossip, Robert thought. 'Fred can give you directions to my house, Valley View, and my phone number so that you can call me first,' said Robert, as Nick headed towards the door. The irony was lost on Fred.

'Nice chap,' Fred remarked as soon as the door was closed. 'Makes you wonder why he and his wife couldn't make a go of it. He's moved here for a fresh start and to be closer to his twins when they start university in September. He doesn't look old enough to have kids that age does he.'

That's enough gossip for one morning, Robert thought, as he tucked the weighty papers under his arm and headed home, looking forward to his first cup of coffee of the day and excited to read about his friend. It was excitement tinged with sadness though. Both he and Rosemary had been sworn to secrecy about Philippe's identity as the author of his bestselling debut novel, *Maman*, and he knew how much his late wife would finally have enjoyed basking in the reflected glory of Philippe's success.

CHAPTER 9

It had been a gamble to reveal Philippe's identity after the debacle in Mauritius but in the end Jo had little choice. As his editor, it was her responsibility to make the decisions and there were too many rumours flying around the book world that Veronica Phillips was not a woman. Jo reasoned that if they didn't do a big reveal in the papers some young journalist, seeking out a big story to make his or her name, would find out about the assault Philippe had committed and may try to stir things up, which could potentially damage sales of the book. It was a gamble but one she hoped would pay off both for Philippe and Ripped Publishing. She was still amazed that the victim hadn't pressed charges but she was grateful nonetheless.

Everything had settled nicely on that front apart from Phil's obsession with finding 'his' Holly, Jo thought. They had both drawn a complete blank with the Plantation House hotel. The offer of a five-hundred-pound donation to a local charity usually did the trick in cases like these but, in this instance, it had worked in reverse with the reception staff threatening to call the police. They were only after the girl's last name, for goodness' sake, not even an address or phone number. The airline was just as bad, or good, depending on your point of view, refusing point blank to give out any passenger information. Jo suspected that as soon as this girl realised that her former boyfriend was set to become a millionaire, particularly if the film option she was currently negotiating came off, she would reappear at the speed of light.

Not for the first time she wondered exactly what this girl had that all Phil's previous conquests, herself included, had lacked. Maybe if she does turn up after the revelation he'll see her for the money-grabber she undoubtedly is, Jo thought bitterly. Well, he needn't think he can come running back to me. She laughed at herself, knowing that, despite her usual rule of not mixing business with pleasure, she would fall back into his arms, and his bed, given half the chance.

Jo's mobile phone, lying on the kitchen countertop next to the blender that she was filling with various types of fruit and vegetables for her morning smoothie, began to ring. She glanced at the screen. It was her friend, Ellie Richmond, the features editor of *HiYa!* magazine.

Well, that didn't take long, thought Jo, immediately switching into work mode. 'Hi, Ellie, what can I do for you this Sunday morning?'

CHAPTER 10

Harry knocked tentatively on Holly's bedroom door while expertly balancing her breakfast tray in his other hand, a skill he had perfected collecting the empties in the bar he worked in. 'Mum,' he called, 'are you awake yet? It's a beautiful morning and you're missing it.'

'What time is it?' asked his mother's sleepy voice, from the other side of the bedroom door.

'It's nearly ten o'clock. Are you decent?'

'Yes,' she replied, 'Come in.'

Still balancing the tray in one hand, Harry opened the door and crossed to the window to raise the blackout blind, allowing brilliant sunshine to spill into the room. 'Happy Birthday, Mum,' he said.

Holly squinted up at him, her eyes adjusting to the sudden influx of light. 'Thanks. I can't believe I've slept so long. What have you got there?'

'My attempt at making you breakfast in bed,' Harry said, waiting for his mum to manoeuvre herself into a sitting position before placing the tray on the silver-grey duvet cover. 'I was going to try poached eggs but I wasn't sure how long to cook them for. I want everything to be perfect today, so I did toast and marmite instead. Hope that's okay?'

Holly looked down at the glass of freshly squeezed orange juice, the plate of marmite toast and the mug of steaming black coffee, laid out on a rarely used wooden tray with a picture of hydrangeas painted on it. Holly had brought it home from one of her sessions volunteering in the charity shop, thinking it might be useful, but it had spent most of the time tucked into the space between the fridge and the wall. 'It's perfect. You know I love marmite and it's exactly what I fancy,' she said. 'I'm just amazed you found the tray,' she added laughing.

'Don't worry, I wiped the cobwebs off it first,' Harry responded.

'Have you had your breakfast?' Holly asked, biting into a thick doorstep of toasted bread.

'About an hour ago. I've been up since six o' clock and I was starting to feel faint from hunger.'

Holly shook her head. 'You do exaggerate. Why so early?'

Harry thought about it for a moment. He could tell his mum that the single bed he had slept in throughout his childhood was not quite as comfy and supportive as it used to be which, although true, may seem a little ungrateful. Or he could say that the thin fabric of the curtains hadn't kept out the early morning sunshine. Both of these were undeniable facts but neither, he suspected, were the real reason that he had slept so restlessly and awoken so early. He hadn't pressured his mum into talking about his dad the previous evening but now that she had agreed to reveal to him the other half of his parentage he was feeling uncharacteristically impatient and more than a little nervous. He knew that today would also be pretty momentous for his mum so rather than lie, or spoil the moment, he side-stepped the question by joking, 'We youngsters don't need as much sleep as you oldies!' and then ducked out of the door on to the upstairs landing to avoid the inevitable pillow that he knew would be headed his way. It landed with a dull thud and Harry called back over his shoulder, 'Don't trip over that when you're finally ready to come downstairs to open your presents.'

Thirty minutes later, having enjoyed her treat of breakfast in bed, followed by a refreshing shower, Holly deposited her tray on the kitchen table and went through to join Harry in the lounge. There was a large white cardboard box on the coffee table and on it were four envelopes. Holly was intrigued. No one but Harry ever sent her a birthday card. She had kept each and every one of them, from the very first one he had made at the age of four, which had a stick drawing of his mummy on the front, through the cuddly teddies phase and on to the comedy ones of more recent years. They were all safely stashed in an old shoe box in the bottom of her wardrobe.

'What's all this?' she asked. She had wondered if maybe Robert would remember that it was her birthday and send a card, but who were the other two from?

Harry detected a tiny wobble in his mum's voice and immediately wished he hadn't laid them all out for her but had instead handed them to her one at a time. He could kick himself for not realising that she might still be harbouring a faint hope that the Frenchman would try to contact her. 'The best way to find out who they are from is to open them,' he said breezily, pushing three cards in her direction. 'This isn't a card,' he added, 'it's my present to you.'

The top card simply had the word 'Mum' on the envelope in Harry's writing so she tucked that underneath to open last. The second one had her name and address neatly printed in Robert's familiar handwriting. She smiled. 'This one's from Robert, but I expect you know that already,' Holly said with a knowing look. She turned her attention to the final envelope which simply had her first name written on the front in handwriting she didn't recognise. Her heart skipped a beat. Could it be from Philippe? They had only ever communicated via email so she had no idea what his handwriting looked like. Did she even want it to be from him? Of course she did. True, he had a lot of explaining to do and her forgiveness would have to be earned, but she fervently wished that this simple cream envelope would hold the start of a new future for her.

Harry was watching his mum running her fingers over the five letters of her name. Until that moment he hadn't realised just how much she had fallen for the Frenchman. A thoughtful gesture from his friends, Jack and Amy, was about to backfire. He could stand it no longer. 'Open it, Mum,' he encouraged, 'it may not be from who you're hoping.'

There was something in Harry's tone of voice that made Holly realise that it had been wishful thinking on her part that this was a card from Philippe. He obviously knew who it was from. She slipped her finger under the flap of the envelope and tore along the top edge, then pulled at the card within. As she opened it a piece of paper fell to the floor. Puzzled, she reached down to retrieve it and discovered it was a book token to the value of ten pounds. There was a simple message inside the card: 'I know you love books as much as I do but I thought you may prefer to choose your own, Love Amy (and Jack) xxx'. Trying not to let her disappointment show, Holly said, 'That is so sweet of Amy. She really didn't need to do that.'

'She likes you, Mum. You were supposed to be staying at the flat and they wanted to make a fuss of you. You and Amy are always nattering about books so it was the perfect present. You're not too disappointed that it wasn't from "him", are you?'

Holly looked at her son's concerned face. 'I was just being silly for a moment. He probably can't even remember my name. He'll have moved on to his next gullible conquest by now. I'm fine, Harry, really I am.'

Holly opened her other two cards and made a big fuss of lining all three of them up on the shelf above the Victorian fireplace.

'Right,' said Harry, 'now it's time for your present.'

'Don't you mean presents, plural?' Holly asked.

'Well, what's in the box is not really a present. You should open that first.'

Holly undid the pink ribbon that was tied around the box and lifted the lid. A chocolaty aroma filled her nostrils as she looked down at the cake Harry had baked, now covered with chocolate-fudge icing and scattered with vermicelli strands. 'Did Amy make this?' she asked.

'How very sexist of you, Mum. No. I made it. My first ever attempt at cake and, depending on the taste, quite possibly my last.'

Holly was speechless. Her son had baked her a birthday cake. Sons don't normally do that sort of thing.

'Before you start blubbing,' Harry said, seeing that his mum was on the point of tears, 'you'd better open this and get it all out of your system in one go,' he added, handing her the remaining envelope.

Holly's hands were trembling as she ripped open the envelope and examined the sheets of paper within. Immediately her eyes filled with the predicted tears. 'I don't know what I've done to deserve you,' she sobbed, 'you actually are the best son in the world.'

'Do you really like it, Mum? I wasn't sure. I didn't know if you would think it's too much like a busman's holiday. But then I thought that at least it's in Tuscany so if you hate the writing course you can still enjoy the food and wine – well, not the wine now that you're pregnant, but I didn't know that when I booked it, and you can probably change the dates if you need to.'

'I love it. And I love you more than anything in the world. Come here and give me a hug.'

'I'm getting too old for this, Mum,' Harry said, wrapping his arms around her.

'You're never too old to show your mum that you love her.' They both fell silent at the stark reminder of the lack of relationship Holly had with her own mother, 'Always assuming that your mum wants that love,' she added sadly.

Instead of the restaurant lunch that he had planned in Bath, Harry prepared salad and new potatoes for the two of them to enjoy at the white, wrought-iron table on the small decked area in the back garden, under the shade of a parasol as the sun climbed high in the sky. Dessert was the chocolate birthday cake with fresh, double-cream and Holly had to admit that it was every bit as good as the cakes she made. Although they had chatted amicably throughout lunch, they had both fallen silent, knowing that they were edging ever nearer to a subject that had been buried for the past twenty years.

A small movement caught Holly's eye. A tiny curled white feather was caught on the twine tying the less than rampant sweet peas to the row of canes supporting them. Since her father's death, Holly had believed that white feathers were symbols of communication from lost loved ones. I know, Dad, she thought. This is the right thing to do.

Abruptly, Holly started to speak. 'I was eighteen when I met Gareth. I'd been at university for four months but I hadn't been dating anyone, which was nothing new for me. He was in his final year and he was the captain of the rugby team. He was tall, blond and very handsome and our paths probably wouldn't have crossed if I hadn't been working in the Student's Union bar to help pay my way through uni. I'd just come back after the Christmas holidays and things at home were even worse than usual. He bought me a drink to cheer me up and we just got chatting. A week later, he asked if I wanted to go to the cinema with him and from then on we were inseparable. In all honesty, I couldn't believe my luck. He was one of the most popular and desired third-year students, clever as well as sporty, and I was a shy, awkward first year who spent most of her spare time in the library reading. Everyone said he would dump me once he got what he wanted, if you know what I mean,' Holly said blushing. 'Well, he didn't dump me. In fact, he suggested that I moved into the house he was sharing with three of his mates, but I didn't want to, although in truth I was probably at his more than I was in the Halls of Residence. We hadn't told either set of parents that we were an item. He was doing his Finals and didn't want his folks thinking that anything would get in the way of his studies. My dad would have been okay, in fact, he would have been really happy for me, but my mum had always warned me off boys and I wasn't going to give her any ammunition to have yet another fight with me.'

Harry had been watching his mum as she spoke. It was almost as though she was remembering the plot of a favourite film, one she had seen dozens of times. There were so many questions he wanted to ask but he didn't want to interrupt her flow.

'As soon as Gareth finished his last exam,' Holly continued, 'he was flying out to a college in Los Angeles to learn about American football. His master's degree was going to be about the similarities and differences between the two sports. I couldn't go to the airport with him because his parents were seeing him off, so the last time I saw him was in our local pub, the Royal Oak, the night before he flew out. We had everything planned. He was going to be away for eight weeks, and when he got back at the end of August he was going to come to Nottingham to meet my mum and dad. I'd told him my mum wasn't very friendly but he was sure he could win her over. He probably would have too. Then he was going to take me to his parents' home in Wales for a holiday, before we both got ready to start back at uni. He always talked with such passion about the beaches on the Gower peninsula. I've never seen them,' she said wistfully, seeming to run out of steam.

'So what happened, Mum?' Harry urged gently.

'He didn't come back,' she said simply.

'What do you mean? He didn't come back to you, or he didn't come back to England?'

Holly looked flustered. 'I don't know if he came back from America. I never heard a word from him after that night in the Royal Oak.'

Harry looked incredulous. 'Didn't you try to contact him?'

'It wasn't that easy twenty years ago, Harry. There was no Twitter or Facebook, computers were in their infancy and mobile phones were great big brick-like things that only a select few people had to make business calls on. I don't think you could even text on them in those days and anyway, I certainly didn't have one.'

'But what about letters? Surely you could have written to him?'

'I didn't want him to think I was being clingy. We had agreed he was coming home to me but... h–he broke his promise.'

Holly had been expecting Harry's next question.

'Did he know about me? Did he know you were pregnant?'

Holly shook her head. 'I didn't even know I was pregnant until just before he was due home. I'd felt sick and listless but I thought that was just because I was missing him so much. I can still remember with absolute clarity the moment I realised that I might be expecting a baby. I was terrified of what my mum would say. I secretly bought a pregnancy test and when it showed up positive I just wanted to cry. I'm sorry, Harry, I shouldn't have felt that way.'

'So even after you discovered you were pregnant, you still didn't try to contact my dad?' The words were out of Harry's mouth before he could stop them.

'Your d-dad, as you called him, was supposed to come home to me. He chose not to. Maybe he met someone in America. I don't know, but he had obviously changed his mind about his feelings towards me. There was no way I was going to force him to marry me just because I had a baby on the way.'

'But Mum, don't you think you should have told him you were pregnant and given him the opportunity to make up his own mind about what to do?'

'If he really loved me, Harry, he would have come back to me, and you and I wouldn't be having this conversation. There really isn't anything else to say. You wanted to know who your father was and now you do.'

Harry recognised the note of finality in his mum's voice and knew she didn't want to talk about it any more, but there was one more question he needed to ask. Being careful not to refer to him as Dad, Harry said, 'What was Gareth's surname?'

Holly stared at her son. Throughout his life he had never asked a single question about his missing father. Her pregnancy had clearly stirred a need to know within Harry and she wondered how far he was going to take it. Was he going to try and trace his father? What good could possibly come of that?

'Mum,' he said, 'I need to know.'

One single word could change their relationship for

ever but Holly knew she had no right to refuse her son. 'Caswell,' she said flatly, 'his name was Gareth Caswell.'

Amy stirred her instant coffee and took a sip. She screwed her face up. 'This is disgusting with powdered milk,' she complained. 'Whose turn was it to go shopping?'

'Harry's,' chorused Hugo and Jack, blaming the only flatmate who wasn't present to defend himself.

'Hmmm, somehow I doubt that,' Amy retorted. 'Harry does more chores than you two put together. If it wasn't for Harry and me this place would be a total tip. I'm so pleased we've managed to keep it for our final year though,' she added, walking over to the sink and pouring the offending liquid down it. 'Yuk, I can't drink that!'

'You're too picky, Amy,' Jack said.

'Clearly not or I wouldn't be going out with you,' she teased.

Jack put on a hurt face, 'You don't mean that?'

'Only sometimes,' she replied, avoiding his outstretched arms. 'When is Harry back? I was so disappointed that he changed his mind about his mum coming here for her birthday.'

'Me too,' said Hugo, 'I was really looking forward to

trying that chocolate cake he made.'

'That's not what I meant. I really like Holly, she's so cool. She's more of a friend to me than a friend's mum. She feels about twenty years younger than my mum but I think they're about the same age. And she loves books. I hope she liked the card and present I got her.'

'We,' corrected Jack.

'Erm, just remind me what part you played in buying the card, writing it and buying the book token?' Amy said.

Jack thought for a moment. 'Well, you wouldn't have known it was Holly's birthday unless I'd told you.

'That's true,' Amy conceded, 'so you have cost me fourteen quid. If you'd like to hand over your half, I'll pop into the supermarket on my way home from work tonight and buy some bread and milk.'

'You sound like a nagging old wife,' Jack grumbled, digging in his jeans pocket and handing her a crumpled ten-pound note. 'You can keep the change.'

'Was that some kind of weird proposal?' Amy said, taking the money and putting it in her purse.

'Maybe…'

'Well the answer is no. We're too young. See you guys later,' she said, swinging her bag up on to her shoulder and blowing a kiss in Jack's direction.

Amy banged the front door behind her, then leant back on it for a moment breathing deeply. She adored Jack but had come to realise in the eighteen months that they had been an item that her love for him wasn't the all-consuming passion she knew it should be. There had been times when she had thought about finishing things between them, particularly as their sex life had been virtually non-existent of late, but she couldn't bear to hurt him. Their current relationship felt more like brother and sister, compared with when they had first met.

Like most people starting at Bath University she knew no one and Fresher's week was a perfect opportunity to mingle with all the new intake of students before everyone separated out on to their various courses. Amy had been drinking in the Student's Union bar with a group of girls who were living in the same block as her in the Halls of Residence when she had first spotted Jack. To be more accurate, she thought, she had spotted one of the people Jack was with. Harry was tall and broad-shouldered, with dark blond hair and a strong jawline. Amy could still remember the somersault her heart had done when she set eyes on him. He was gorgeous, her perfect man. He was laughing at the antics of the slightly shorter, dark-haired man he was with. Jack had clearly been indulging in drinking games with the rest of his crowd and was quite inebriated. Although Harry was joining in the fun he seemed to be the only one of the crowd who could stand without fear of falling over.

Amy had taken her courage in both hands and left the group she was with to go and introduce herself to the 'Adonis'. People always thought that Amy was supremely confident but it was all a front, an act she put on to hide her insecurity about her appearance. She hadn't been blessed with beauteous good looks, and her figure, while nicely proportioned, was a little on the plump side. Amy had to work much harder than prettier girls to get herself noticed and she did this through her personality and sense of humour.

'Hi, I'm Amy,' she said to Harry. 'I think you might want to move away from this area of the bar as the floor surface must be a little uneven judging by the amount of staggering going on.'

Harry had made eye contact with her and smiled warmly, but there wasn't even a hint of interest in them as he said, 'Hello, Amy, I'm Harry. I couldn't possibly leave my very drunk friend to his own devices but I am desperate for a leak. Would you be an angel and look after him for me for a minute? Hey Jack,' he shouted above the music and the raucous laughter, 'this is Amy and she's an angel.'

Jack turned and in his drunken state said, 'I can see that. She has a halo.' He then draped his arm around her shoulders and said, 'Take me to heaven, Amy.'

Amy hadn't taken Jack to heaven, but she had helped Harry half-carry him back to his room where he passed out on his bed. Harry had then walked Amy back to her room but, despite an invitation to go in for a coffee, he had excused himself saying he needed to be up early.

Over the following few weeks Amy had made a conscious effort to be where Harry and Jack were likely to be so that she could spend time with them. She got on well with them both, but it was Harry she was really interested in getting to know better. It became obvious that her feelings weren't reciprocated when the three of them would arrange to meet but only she and Jack would turn up. The first couple of times were awkward but then she realised that she was genuinely starting to have feelings for Jack and they started leaving Harry out of their plans.

When Jack had first mentioned his intention of asking Harry to be the fourth member of their flat-share, Amy was unsure how she felt about it. She had seen Harry around campus from time to time and, although she hid it well, her heart still skipped a beat when she did. It made her feel disloyal to Jack, even though she knew that nothing would ever happen between herself and Harry because he wasn't interested. In the end, she reasoned that the more she saw of him on an everyday basis, leaving dirty cups and socks around the flat, it might turn her off him. The problem was that Harry didn't do that. In fact, he often tidied up the other boys' stuff that they had left lying around so that Amy wouldn't have to. Throughout the past nine months of their flat-share they had grown much closer, but only as friends, because that was the way Harry wanted it and Amy would rather have that much of him than nothing at all.

Lost in thought, she started her short walk to work. The sun had highlighted her strawberry-blond, waist-length hair which swayed as she walked, as did her hips beneath the lightweight clingy fabric of her skirt. A passing lorry honked his horn, startling her back to the present. What's his problem? she thought angrily, not realising that it was a honk of appreciation. Everybody but Amy could see that a transformation had taken place in the two years she had been at university. The yoga she had taken up for relaxation around exam times had the added benefit of toning and shaping her body, which had now lost all its puppy fat. Being in a relationship with Jack meant that she didn't get chatted up as they were always together on nights out and Jack wasn't the sort to tell his girlfriend how stunning she was, or maybe familiarity had simply stopped him noticing.

The interior of Chapters, the bookshop where Amy worked, was dark and cool as she pushed open the door setting off the buzzer to alert staff to a potential customer.

'I'll be with you in a moment,' said a voice from somewhere in the back of the shop.

'It's only me, Geoff,' Amy called, closing the door behind her.

'Amy, did you see this in the Sunday papers?' Geoff asked, the excitement evident in his voice, as he walked through from the small staffroom at the back of the shop into the main area, where books lined the walls from floor to ceiling and were piled high on every available surface. Amy had fallen in love with the shop the moment she had discovered it and, in a purely platonic way, with its owner, Geoff, who was in his late forties but had once been a student at the university himself. He had become so enamoured with Bath that he couldn't bear to leave once he had finished his degree. He had borrowed money off his parents for a deposit to buy a failing gift shop and transformed it into one of the most highly regarded independent book shops in the area.

Amy was wondering what had made her usually easy-going boss so animated. 'I haven't seen yesterday's paper yet,' she replied, 'they're a bit expensive for a student so I always wait to read your copy on a Monday,' she added with a grin.

'They've been speculating for weeks. Looks like some people had some inside information. They've just confirmed that Veronica Philips isn't a woman at all. His name is Phil Marchant, a former Fleet Street journalist. I'm truly surprised. I could have sworn *Maman* was written by a woman.'

Amy was surprised too. The book had been written with such empathy and understanding of the female point of view in a marriage breakdown. 'Maybe he's gay?' she suggested.

'Far from it, according to this article. Apparently he's a bit of a lady's man. Well, who'd have thought it? I wonder if he's going to do a book signing tour now that his identity is out in the open? Do you think he would come here? It would be good for business if we could have a repeat of Godfrey Bowman's successful signing. Do you remember? They were queuing out of the door and you had no idea who he was! At least you've heard of Veronica Philips. Maybe it would attract some younger people?'

True, Amy had been amazed at the number of people that had driven from miles around to get the signature of their former local MP on a copy of his novel, *The Corridors of Lust'*, but she doubted whether Veronica Phillips would create the same level of interest, particularly if all the students had gone home for the summer holidays. 'You could contact the publishing company and see what they say,' Amy suggested, reaching for the paper from her boss. 'Oh my God, he's gorgeous!' she exclaimed, 'definitely see if he wants to come here.'

'Young people today,' Geoff said, 'you're all the same. It's all about what someone looks like not the fact that he's a bloody good writer. Our copies of *Tiffany* should be in later this week. I wish I'd ordered more now. I think it's going to fly off the shelves on the back of this revelation, particularly as the author is so "gorgeous", he emphasised, a hint of jealousy, tinged with sarcasm, creeping into his voice.

CHAPTER 12

On Monday morning, Harry awoke feeling different. Normally he was quite laid-back about things but he was feeling a sense of urgency to get started with his quest. When he had asked his mum for Gareth's surname the previous afternoon he hadn't been sure what he intended to do with the information. At the time, he had thought he simply wanted to know the family name on the other side of his bloodline from his mother. He knew precious little about his maternal grandmother, but that situation was different. She knew about him. She knew she had a grandson and yet had made no attempt to contact him or her estranged daughter. Harry had no interest in trying to trace her. She didn't want to know him, so why would he want to know her? But it was different with Gareth; he was unaware of Harry's existence.

He was still not sure how he felt about his mother not trying to contact Gareth to tell him she was pregnant with his baby. Although Harry was around the same age his mother had been, he couldn't possibly imagine her emotional state, being alone, disowned by her family, homeless and with an unplanned baby on the way. But surely the other party in a situation like this had the right to know? The other party? he thought. Even in his head, it still felt odd for Harry to use the word 'father' or 'dad', especially after witnessing his mum's reaction to his slip yesterday. She saw herself as the wronged person, and maybe she was, but she had never given Gareth the opportunity to explain his absence or have an opinion about the baby.

Throughout Harry's life, his mum had more than compensated for the lack of a father figure. She had given him enough love for two people, or more, and she had had to forego so much herself. The lack of a personal life, always being so short of money because she wanted to be around to bring him up, rather than farming him out to child-minders, these were huge sacrifices that had contributed to a wonderfully close and caring relationship between them. But now, there was just a tiny, niggling doubt that some of it was done out of guilt. He would always love his mum wholeheartedly, but now that he was aware of the circumstances that had led to her becoming a lone parent, he was viewing things from a slightly changed perspective.

Since learning about his mum's latest pregnancy and that, once again, she had no plans to tell the father of the child, Harry had given serious thought to his own situation. Robert had said, 'Every child should know their father', and Harry had come to the conclusion that he agreed. There might never be a close bond between them, after all it was quite likely that Gareth was married with a family of his own and the last thing Harry wanted to do was cause trouble in their lives, but now he knew the name of his biological father, he was going to find him and at least give him the opportunity to explain his heartless behaviour of twenty years earlier.

With all the modern technology available, Harry thought it should be easy to find Gareth, particularly as Caswell was not a common surname. First of all he tried LinkedIn. Gareth was an educated man so it was fair to assume that he would have a professional profile on their website. It drew a blank. There was only one person listed under that name and they were based in Australia. Of course, Gareth could have moved out there in the past twenty years but this person had been educated at the University of Wollongong, a long way from Bath. That was another surprise that the revelations of the previous day had thrown up. With all the universities in the UK, how weird that Harry should have selected the same one as Gareth and Holly. It was also odd that she had never mentioned being a student there, albeit for only a year, and that she hadn't tried to dissuade him from going there. It must have opened up old wounds, he thought, especially when they went to look around the campus prior to him being allocated a place there. It seems Mum has been keeping quite a few secrets from me, thought Harry.

After LinkedIn failed to reveal any useful information, Harry decided to try social media. There was no Gareth Caswell on Twitter and the only profile that came up on Facebook showed a picture of a much younger man with dark hair, very different from the description his mum had given him. It was a setback, and disappointing, but not insurmountable. There was one very obvious way to find out more about Gareth and that was through university records.

Harry hadn't particularly wanted to go down this route. He didn't want people asking questions about his sudden interest in a former student with seemingly no connection to him, but it would appear that this was going to have to be his next course of action. He was driving back to Bath that evening, after taking his mum for lunch at a favourite pub of theirs on the river in Sonning. The plan was to spend a few days with his friends relaxing now that exams were over, and then pack up the rest of the stuff he would need for the ten-week summer break. It would also give him the opportunity to do a bit of digging around and he knew just the person to help him.

As well as her part-time job at Chapters book shop, Amy also volunteered to help out in the main office of the university when they were understaffed. With a bit of luck, some of the full-time members of staff would be taking summer holiday early so that they would be back in time for overseeing the new admissions in August, he thought. Amy had a heart of gold and he knew that she would do all she could to help. He just needed to think of a plausible reason for his interest in Gareth Caswell.

CHAPTER 13

Lunch at The Hart, on the river in picturesque Sonning, was always a delight regardless of the season. In the winter Holly and Harry would enjoy an occasional treat of traditional Sunday lunch in front of a roaring open fire. Today, however, the sun was blazing and they chose a wooden table in the pub garden, under the shade of a majestic weeping willow tree, whose branches dipped and trailed in the cool, green water of the Thames like long, slender fingers. Harry had initially seemed pre-occupied but they were soon chatting as easily as they always had.

'Did you and Robert discuss work at all when you spoke the other day?' Holly asked, sipping her sparkling mineral water.

'Nothing specific,' Harry replied. 'I didn't have my diary handy, not that there is much in it for most of the summer,' he laughed.

'Did he sound like he's coping okay?'

'As well as anyone would in those circumstances, I guess, but he did mention he's thinking of selling Valley View.'

'Really?' Holly said, the surprise evident in her voice.

'Yes. Now that the Frenchman has left Sunset Cottage and is back in the UK, Robert is thinking of moving out to Mauritius permanently, as he and Rosemary had planned to.'

Holly was aware that her son was scrutinising her, looking for a reaction to the news that Philippe was back in the UK. She kept her expression blank but unfortunately she had no control over the slow blush that was rising up her neck and colouring her face. Ignoring the reference to Philippe she asked, 'Do you think it's a good idea to sell Valley View at the moment? Robert is obviously in a state of shock and the housing market isn't great just now. Maybe he could rent it out for a while to see if he still feels the same way in a year or two.'

'Properties like that aren't really affected too much by the housing market, Mum. That house, in that location, must be worth at least four million, and if you've got that kind of money to spend the small matter of a global financial crisis isn't really going to affect you. It might even be worse for him to rent it out, just prolonging the inevitable. What a shame they didn't have any children and then that gorgeous house could have stayed in the family. Didn't they want kids?'

Holly thought back to the day in Mauritius when she had told Rosemary about her unplanned pregnancy that had resulted in Harry. There had been a flicker of envy in her eyes. 'They tried. They even had IVF treatment, but it was unsuccessful. Such a shame. Rosemary would have made a wonderful mother.'

'Not as good as you, Mum. I still think you are the best mum in the world,' Harry said, reaching to squeeze her hand where it rested on the table.

It was the use of the word 'still' that resonated with Holly. Despite his assurances, she knew that hearing the truth about his father had deeply affected him, and therefore their relationship. She was afraid to ask what he intended to do with his newly acquired information. She suspected that she wouldn't like his answer.

CHAPTER 14

'Harry, you're back!' Amy exclaimed, unable to keep the pleasure from her voice.

'I got in late last night. I think you and Jack had already gone to bed. Where is he?'

'Still asleep,' Amy answered. 'Now that he hasn't got to get up for lectures I doubt that we'll see much of him before lunch most days. Did your mum enjoy her birthday?'

'How was the cake?' chipped in Hugo.

'Yes, Amy, she did. She said to say thank you for the card and book token and she'll let you know what she buys with it. And the cake was awesome, even though I say so myself. Way too much for two people, though, such a shame to have to throw it away.'

Hugo looked horrified. 'You're joking! You didn't really throw it away?'

'Yes.' Harry paused for effect. 'I am joking. Mum sent the rest of it back for you lot. It's in the fridge.'

Hugo was off the sofa like a greyhound out of the traps. 'Super, I haven't had breakfast yet.' He peeled back the tin foil and cut himself a huge slab of the cake. 'Anyone else want any?'

'I ate earlier cos I'm working today. I'll have mine when I get back,' said Amy, 'so don't eat it all, Hugo. I mean it.'

Hugo was sinking his teeth into the sponge for a second bite. 'This is bloody gorgeous, Harry. How come you are just so good at everything you touch? It really is annoying. It's a good job we're mates or I wouldn't like you at all.'

'Are you at the book shop today, Amy?' Harry asked.

'No, I was there yesterday. I'm helping in the office today. Can you believe that Sue, Janet and Denise have all been allowed to take holiday at the same time? Lyndsey was rushed off her feet yesterday so she texted me at the shop to ask if I could go in. Geoff didn't mind. We were really quiet yesterday, although hopefully business will pick up if he can get this Veronica Phillips chap to come and do a book signing.'

'Chap? Isn't Veronica a girl's name?'

'I always forget that it's your mum that's interested in books, not you. She must have seen it in the Sunday papers. Everyone thought that the novelist Veronica Phillips was a woman, but now it turns out she's a man.'

'What, like a sex change?' asked Hugo, wiping the back of his hand across his mouth to collect any stray crumbs before licking it.

'That is disgusting,' said Harry.

'Don't be so judgemental,' said Hugo. 'Loads of people have sex-change operations these days. They were just born the wrong gender.'

'Not the sex-change thing, you idiot!' Harry said. 'You, licking the back of your hand to get the last few crumbs of cake. It's like you've never been fed.'

'Don't fall out, you two,' Amy said, sounding like a mother in charge of toddlers, 'and anyway you've got the wrong end of the stick. Veronica Phillips has always been a man. It's just been revealed he's a former journalist writing under a female pen name.'

'Why bother?' asked Hugo.

'Apparently he didn't want his former colleagues taking the piss out of him. He writes emotional stuff for a female audience, although his new book is a bit raunchy by all accounts. Right, I'll see you two later.'

Harry seized the opportunity. 'I'll bring you a sandwich up at lunch if you like?'

'That is so thoughtful, Harry.'

'Oh God, I think I'm going to be sick,' Hugo said, sticking two fingers in his mouth.

'Serves you right for eating cake for breakfast,' chorused the other two.

When Harry arrived at the main office of Bath University, it was empty apart from Amy, who was on the phone.

'Lyndsey's just gone to grab a bite of lunch,' Amy said, replacing the telephone receiver into its cradle. I wasn't sure what time you were coming and her stomach was grumbling. Are you okay to hang around here until she gets back, then we can take our sandwiches outside and I can get a breath of fresh air? It's really stuffy in here. I'm almost regretting agreeing to come in today. What did you bring me?'

'You have a choice. Cheese ploughman's or egg mayo.'

'Both favourites of mine,' Amy said, 'you know me so

well.'

'I'd hope so, we've been living together for nearly a year. Er, that came out a bit wrong,' he laughed, without a hint of awkwardness.

Amy turned away to avoid making eye contact with Harry. 'We can have half a sandwich of each, if you don't mind sharing?' she said, busying herself with a pile of papers.

'Great idea. Talking of sharing, can I tell you something and it will just be between the two of us?'

Amy turned back to face him and Harry was unsure what flickered across her eyes. Sometimes he got the feeling that she wanted to be more than just friends, but that could never happen, she was Jack's girlfriend. Better get on with this, he thought, before she gets the wrong idea.

'A friend of mine, back in Reading, has just found out he's adopted. He's a couple of years younger than us and it's come as a total shock. He managed to trace his birth mother, because her name was on his original birth certificate, which he applied for after he found out he was adopted, but there was no name in the space where it says father. His birth mother reluctantly gave him his father's name but she doesn't know anything else about him, except that he was a student here in Bath. That's why he's asked for my help. He thought maybe I could find some old records that would help him find his biological dad. It's a long shot, I know, but I wanted to try and help.'

Amy's face was full of sympathy and Harry experienced a pang of guilt that he wasn't being entirely truthful with her. She would probably have willingly helped him find his biological father but he wasn't ready to share his secret with anyone yet.

'How awful for him to find out that he's not who he thought he was,' Amy said. 'I don't understand why adoptive parents don't just come clean when the children are young. If they grow up knowing that they are at the heart of a loving family but that two other people gave them life, they can choose whether or not to seek them out when they are old enough. It must have been devastating for your friend. How did he find out?'

Harry had thought the story through. 'His younger sister was diagnosed with leukaemia and needed a stem cell transplant,' he said. Using the knowledge he had acquired after finding out about his mum's friend, Rosemary, he continued, 'Usually the best match is a sibling so of course he volunteered to be tested. That's when his adoptive parents told him that they had come from different families and that he most likely wouldn't be a match.'

'Oh my God,' said Amy, 'that's dreadful, both for him and his adoptive parents. Is she okay?'

'Is who okay?' Harry asked, confused and wondering if he had over-complicated the story.

'The sister? Did they find a match?' asked Amy anxiously.

'Er, n–no. It turns out that they were able to treat her with some of the latest drugs, so they told my friend about being adopted unnecessarily as it turns out.'

'Well, that depends on your point of view,' said Amy. 'I think I would want to know, wouldn't you?'

'Yes. I would,' agreed Harry.

'I'm so relieved she's okay. So, what's his name then?'

'Who? My friend or his dad?' Harry asked.

'His dad. The sooner we start looking the better. He might not like what he finds but, now that he knows his name, he won't be satisfied until they've met.'

'You're so right, Amy,' Harry said, the vague feeling of excitement that he had been experiencing replaced by a feeling of unease at what he could be about to discover. 'His name is Gareth Caswell and he was a student here about twenty years ago.'

'Gareth Caswell?' said Amy, furrowing her brow, 'I'm sure I know that name.'

CHAPTER 15

Philippe was slumped in one of the low leather chairs in Jo's office, staring moodily out of the window, the bronze-tinted glass giving a muted impression of the brightness of the day. The UK was enjoying a mini heat-wave, with temperatures climbing into the low thirties but, on the fifth floor of Pelham Towers, the atmosphere was decidedly cool, and it wasn't just down to the air conditioning.

Jo paced back and forth behind her desk, attempting to calm herself before speaking. She perched on the edge of her swivel chair, strategically adjusted to be several inches higher than the leather chair opposite to give her a feeling of superiority.

'What the hell is wrong with you, Phil?' she demanded. 'I've got the phone ringing off the hook with people wanting you for chat shows, magazine features and book signings. I haven't got time for all this. If you're not going to play ball, you'll have to get yourself an agent.' She glared at him, waiting for a response but Philippe sat mute, with a sulky expression on his face. 'Look,' she said, trying to keep the irritation she felt out of her voice, 'I'm negotiating six-figure sums for the film rights to *Tiffany* and you're moping around like a love-struck adolescent. It's pathetic. You're pathetic. I've told you, with all this publicity she is bound to recognise you and she'll get in touch, you mark my words.'

Philippe knew he was being unreasonable and, to a degree, irrational. He also knew that Holly was clearly over their brief encounter and already dating someone else, because Robert had told him as much. But maybe that's because she thought I'd been unfaithful to her, Philippe reasoned. Before he had finally left Mauritius to return to England, his housekeeper, Delphine, had told him that his drunken night at the Dolphin Bar had not resulted in any kind of intimacy with the exotic dancer he had woken up alongside the following morning. Perhaps Delphine's brother, Jacques, had been telling the truth when he had denied contacting Holly with the story of his infidelity. If that was the case, what had caused Holly to break off their relationship in such an abrupt way? He had to find her and ask her what had happened to make her change her mind, but also to explain that he hadn't been entirely truthful about who he was. Once she knows the whole story, Philippe thought, she will be able to decide if she prefers this Harry chap to me. At least then I would be able to stop torturing myself with the notion that I didn't try hard enough to win her back.

Jo was waiting for him to respond. Finally, he spoke. 'My picture was in two of the Sundays and it's been in at least one paper every day this week and we haven't heard anything from her.'

'Maybe she doesn't read the newspapers. Perhaps she is more of a magazine type of girl,' Jo said pragmatically.

'Why don't you do this piece for *HiYa!* and maybe she'll see that?'

'I've told you already, I will do a piece for them, but only if they call it "Finding Holly", he replied petulantly.

'But what relevance is that to the book?' Jo asked, throwing her arms up in frustration. '"Finding Tiffany", maybe, but not "Finding Holly". Believe me, no one is interested in your sordid little holiday romance in Mauritius, particularly not adoring female fans who want you for themselves. Look at all this stuff we've had sent in already,' she said, indicating a pile of cards, teddy bears and more than a few items of lingerie. 'You are their dream man and they are your audience, the people who are going to make you very rich.'

Philippe rose to his feet and leaned forward across the desk. His eyes, blazing hot with anger, bore into hers, but his tone was icy. 'You really have no idea, do you Jo, what it's like to fall in love with someone so totally. Just because you're happy being rich and powerful and alone, it doesn't mean that everyone is. Find me Holly and, whatever the outcome, I promise I'll do whatever the hell you want,' he said.

Jo maintained eye contact. 'Can I just remind you that you have a contract,' she responded, in an equally cold tone. 'I suggest you reread it, particularly the clauses relating to publicising your book. Close the door behind you on your way out,' she added, dropping her gaze down to the papers on her desk.

After the office door slammed, Jo leaned forward on her elbows and rested her burning forehead in her hands.

She was shaking, but not from anger. She knew exactly what it was like to fall totally in love with someone and not have that love returned but Philippe was clearly unaware of the way she felt. Jo didn't do tears, but at that moment she was perilously close. 'Bloody arrogant fool,' she said to the empty room, a description which could have applied to either of them, 'why did you have to come back into my life?'

She could remember the flutter of excitement she had felt when he had contacted her with the manuscript of his first book. It was good, very good, but the excitement she felt was at meeting up with him again. Because of her feelings for him, she had given him a chance, saving him from the ignominy of the slush pile, where thousands of manuscripts from unknown authors ended up every year.

It had been a very different Phil that had come to her office needing her help. He had been charming and humble, and had happily agreed to accompany her to dinner at The Ivy so that they could continue their contract discussions. She had gone the extra mile for him and it had paid off with a best-selling debut. *Tiffany* promised even greater things, which would earn her a generous bonus but, as Phil had so pointedly highlighted, she had no one to share her success with.

Maybe that's all this obsession with Holly is, Jo thought, the need to have a significant other in his life. Well, I can't make her materialise out of thin air and in the meantime I've got a very awkward author on my hands, refusing to cooperate with the publicity drive. The usual 'kid gloves' approach she normally adopted when dealing with her authors, to get the best out of them, simply wasn't working with Philippe. He needs a reality check, she thought, a slow smile spreading across her face. Forget all the glamorous stuff. A provincial tour of dusty old book shops, with half a dozen people wanting his signature, might just bring him down to earth with a bang.

She pressed the intercom button to speak to her PA.

'Alice, have we had any book tour requests from small, out-of-town independents?'

CHAPTER 16

Harry headed back towards the M23 motorway, this time heading north, having dropped his mum at Gatwick airport. Soleil Resorts had readily agreed to her suggestion of making more frequent trips until she was too pregnant to fly. Her Liberty Sands blog was growing in popularity and the benefit to their business was becoming more and more evident with an increase in both positive traveller reviews and repeat bookings. For Holly, it meant only two weeks at home between assignments instead of three, but it was a relief to be able to earn the extra money before she would once again be relying on freelance copy-editing work, which was erratic at the best of times.

Harry had arrived home from Bath the previous Monday, his car stuffed full of his belongings, to find his mum busy working on a manuscript, so they hadn't spent much time together apart from mealtimes. If Holly wanted to know what Harry had done with the information she had given him about his biological father she didn't say. Harry was relieved. He wanted to talk over his findings with Robert and ask his advice on what to do next without having to explain things to his mum.

When Amy had exclaimed that she knew the name Gareth Caswell, Harry had been surprised. Thousands of students had passed through Bath University in the past twenty years, so why would she be familiar with that one? She had been secretive, making him wait until Lyndsey had come back from her lunch break, then dragging him along corridors to the main hall where photographs of former high-flying individuals and teams lined the walls. Harry had never paid much attention to them but, clearly, Amy had. She stopped in front of a photograph of the rugby first team from 1993. Underneath the picture were all the names of the team members, and there, in black and white, it said Gareth Caswell (captain). Even though his mum had told him that Gareth had captained the rugby team, Harry had been unable to suppress the surge of pride he had felt seeing it written down. His eyes rapidly scanned the photo to locate the person seated fourth from the left on the front row. Amy must have found him at the same time because they both gasped.

Amy had spoken first. 'How weird is that? Your friend's dad could be your brother. It's not just the hair and the build, you've got the same high cheekbones and strong jawline.'

There was no point in denying his and Gareth's striking resemblance so instead he had said, 'Crikey you're right. Mind you, look at that bloke on the back row, and that one, they could all be related couldn't they?' he bluffed.

Amy had seemed to accept his observation without question. 'Well, that should make tracing him easier,' she said, 'now that we know he was captain of the rugby team. There will definitely be stuff about him in the uni magazine, and they keep all the back issues in the library. Do you want me to bunk off work this afternoon and help you look?'

'No, I can take it from here,' he had assured her, part of him wishing that he had thought of checking old copies of the magazine before asking Amy to help with his search. He had thought they would need to look at official university papers but, with a bit of luck, he might find what he needed without involving Amy further and arousing her suspicions. 'Thanks for giving me this starting point. What an incredible stroke of luck that you had remembered his name from that photo. Shall I test you with another name?' he teased.

'You could, but I would probably fail. I only remembered his name because we used to go on camping holidays to a place in Wales called Caswell Bay when I was little. Maybe he comes from there?'

'You could be right. If I don't get any joy with the magazine I could follow up on that idea.'

Forty minutes after dropping off his mum at Gatwick, Harry was pulling into the driveway of Valley View. There had been little point staying at home in Reading if his mum wasn't going to be around, so when Robert had asked if he would like to go to Woldingham for a few days, he had jumped at the chance. Robert was lonely, so could do with the companionship, and Harry needed advice following his findings in the library.

There had been no room in the boot of his Vauxhall Corsa, affectionately known as Toby, for his sports bag once he had put his mum's suitcase in there, so he was just reaching for it on the back seat of the car when the front door of Valley View opened and Robert hurried out to greet him.

'Harry, you're a sight for sore eyes.'

There was a degree of accuracy in the statement, Harry noted, observing that Robert was obviously still grieving his recent loss.

'Did your mum get off all right? I was hoping she might have squeezed in a visit with me after her birthday but I expect she has been too busy with, well, things,' Robert added vaguely.

Harry couldn't remember if his mum had told Robert about her copy-editing job so he avoided the subject. 'She's already started nesting, Robert. She didn't keep any of my baby things so she is having to buy everything all over again. Yesterday we took delivery of a flat-packed cot, which apparently I'm going to help her construct. Not yet though, we don't want to tempt fate and besides there's not much room at our house.'

'You know, I did wonder if I'd put my foot in it mentioning the baby to you. I presumed she had told you but when I hung up the phone the other day I had a nagging doubt that I had spoken out of turn. Rosie was always telling me off for not engaging my brain before my mouth. Are you going to be able to stay for the whole week that Holly is away? Come on in. Where is she off to this time?'

Relieved not to have to lie about Robert's slip on the phone, Harry followed him into the house. 'She's on her way to Porto Santo. It's a little island near Madeira. Soleil bought a six-star hotel there in January but, according to Mum, they've had all sorts of problems since they opened in May, so they've sent her out there on a spying mission. I can't tell you any more, Robert, or I would have to shoot you,' he joked.

Robert held his hands up in a mock gesture of surrender. 'Make yourself comfy, Harry, and I'll get us a drink. Tea or coffee?'

'Tea would be great, thanks.'

The sound of Robert clattering around in the kitchen was heart-warming. Although Harry had his own reasons for the visit, he was acutely aware that what Robert needed in his life, more than anything else at that moment, was a sense of purpose. Harry was relishing the idea of working alongside him, learning from the master, but he hoped that, just by being there, he could ease the older man's feelings of loneliness.

'Here we go,' Robert said, pushing the door open with his foot, 'I've brought us biscuits as well. Shall we have it in here or do you want to go straight into the office?'

Harry laughed. 'I've only just got here and you want to set me to work straightaway. Is it okay if we have a chat first? I need to ask your advice about something.'

'Of course, of course,' Robert said, setting the tray on the coffee table, 'I'm not a slave driver you know. I hope I'll be able to help. Rosie was always better than me at dishing out advice.'

'I'll get straight to the point, Robert. In a way you're responsible for stirring up a bit of a hornets' nest,' he said, without accusation in his voice.

Robert raised his eyebrows, 'How so?'

'When we were talking on the phone and you said every child should know their father, it set me thinking that maybe it was time to find out about mine. I've never really wanted to know before and, besides, I didn't want to upset Mum. Maybe it's because of the new baby on the way or perhaps it's simply the right time, either way, I confronted Mum and asked her to tell me about my dad. As you can imagine, she wasn't that keen to start with but I did get a sense that, once it was all out in the open, it was a relief to have told me.'

'Are we going where I think we are with this, Harry?' Robert asked, a look of concern on his face.

'Probably,' admitted Harry. 'I found out that Mum was deserted by my dad just after she discovered she was pregnant but, crucially, he didn't know she was pregnant. He broke his promise to come back to the UK to her but would things have been different if he'd known about me?'

'When you say, "come back to the UK", what do you mean? Was he a foreigner? Was it a holiday romance?'

'No, nothing like that. They were at university together. They had been going out for six months or so. He went to America to do some studying during the summer holidays and never came back. Coincidentally, they were both students at Bath too so, once I knew his name, I was able to do a bit of digging with the help of a friend of mine. Mum was never really sure whether Gareth had come back to the UK and simply not bothered to contact her, but I've found out that although he was meant to return to start a master's degree in September 1993, he didn't take up his place. I want to know why he didn't come back.'

'Are you absolutely sure you want to stir all this up, Harry?'

'Yes,' Harry replied. 'I've thought about nothing else

for the past two weeks. I don't want anything from him, not even to get to know him if he doesn't want to, but I have to know what was so special in America that caused him to stay there and in doing so break my mum's heart.'

'Does Holly know that you're looking for him?'

Harry shook his head. 'Once she told me his name, neither of us has spoken about it again.'

'So, what advice do you want from me? It seems you've already made your mind up.'

'The advice I'm after is more practical, really. I know he went to Los Angeles to do some research on American football, at UCLA, but I'm not sure how to go about getting any information out of them.'

Robert thought for a moment. LA, aka tinsel town, where everything revolved around the media. 'How about you pretend to be a researcher from one of those television shows that traces long-lost relatives?'

'That's not a bad idea,' said Harry thoughtfully, 'and not that far from the truth, but surely if I email them from my private email they'll be suspicious that it's not from a television company?'

'Hmmm, true. It would be better to ring them and set up a meeting in person. You're a handsome, polite young man, Harry, I would imagine you could charm information out of most people.'

'One slight problem with that plan, Robert. I don't have the money to fly halfway round the world.'

'Hold on a minute,' Robert said, disappearing into his office and emerging twenty seconds later with some papers in his hand. 'This was in my rejection pile but it might just provide us with a solution. This hotel, near the Santa Monica Pier, are looking to do a refurbishment.

It's not a huge job and I wasn't going to bother with it but I could send you out as my assistant to do some preliminary sketches and they would pick up the tab for the flights and put you up in the hotel.'

Harry was starting to see possibilities in this plan, particularly if the hotel liked his sketches. It might even start his career as an architect before he'd graduated. 'There's still the problem with ID though. Everyone is so hot on it these days.'

'Not if we get you some business cards printed up with this phone number and my email on them. If they were to contact me to check your identity, I would simply confirm it.'

'You know, it might just work,' said Harry. 'What could we call this imaginary television show?'

'How about… *Building Bridges?*'

CHAPTER 17

A my unzipped the front flap of her tent and peered out at the dismal morning. Her sister Lucy, two years her junior, was snuggled up in her sleeping bag blissfully unaware of the disappointment another damp day in the Lake District was going to bring. Amy's parents had been coming to this area, or the Gower peninsula in south Wales, on their annual summer camping holidays since before the girls were born and, despite protestations from them both when plans were made back in April, they were expected to holiday with their parents until each had a family of their own. It wasn't that Amy didn't enjoy the company of her family within four brick walls where there was space to remove herself to if discussions got heated or she simply wanted a bit of time alone to read, but sharing a small tent with a sister who snored was no longer Amy's idea of a holiday. She wanted sunshine, sandy beaches and sangria or ouzo, not the pebbly shore of Lake Windermere and a hot cup of tea to warm her chilled bones. She was also upset at the reaction from her parents when she had suggested bringing Jack, which from her point of view might have made this years' experience slightly more pleasurable.

'When he's put a ring on your finger and you are his wife, he'll be welcomed with open arms,' her mum had said, 'but until that point he's just a boyfriend, and as such not a member of the family.' There had been no point arguing with her mum who was very set in her ways, and Jack hadn't exactly been devastated by the news that he wouldn't have to give up two weeks of his precious summer break to pretend he was enjoying himself living in a field. 'How come it's okay to live in a squalid tent at rock festivals for a few days?' she had demanded, to which he had replied, 'I think you've answered your own question there, Ames.'

Amy reached back inside the tent for her washbag and towel, pulled her cagoule over her head to protect her pyjamas from the heavy drizzle and slipped her feet into trainers that were still damp from the hill walk they had gone on the previous day before heading towards the shower block at the far end of the field. Her parents always pitched their tents as far as possible from the toilets because of the smell. It was a good idea in some respects but not if you were dying for the loo or when it was raining, as it was now. Why bother with a shower? Amy thought. By the time I've walked back across the field the backs of my legs will be spattered in mud. She shook her head in resignation, thankful that she only had to survive this purgatory for another two days. No matter what, she thought, I am not coming camping next year, and if I ever have children of my own, I vow I will not put them through this hell.

Fortunately only one of the showers was in use. Amy walked to the far end of the narrow tiled room and bolted the shower stall door behind her, draping her towel and pyjamas over it to keep dry, before turning on the water which was gratifyingly hot. As she lathered up her hair she heard her mobile phone ring from the safety of the waterproof washbag. There was no way she could answer it mid-shower but hopefully whoever it was would leave a message. That was another annoyance, she thought, covering her body with the creamy foam, with the only decent mobile phone signal being in the toilet block, it doesn't exactly make for romantic exchanges with Jack. She giggled as she remembered their conversation from two nights previously, with her sitting on a toilet and someone singing 'My Heart Will Go On' at the top of their voice, which wasn't exactly up to Celine Dion's high standards, from one of the shower cubicles.

After showering and brushing her teeth, Amy reached for her phone. There was a message but not from Jack, it was from Geoff at the book shop.

'Amy, you will never believe it but I've just had a call from Ripped Publishing and guess what? They want to do a book signing at Chapters. How amazing is that! Only one small problem, they want to do it soon, in the next fortnight preferably. I said it didn't give me much time for publicity and also mentioned that it might be better to wait until the new university term starts in September but they were keen to do it as soon as possible. Two questions. When are you back from your holiday? And will you be able to come down to Bath to help me? The copies I ordered in have already sold out so this should be really good for business. Call me back when you get the message.'

Amy rang straight back.

'Chapters book shop. How can I help?'

'Geoff, it's me. I just got your message. Are we talking about doing a book signing with Veronica Phillips, aka Philippe Marchant?' she asked excitedly.

'The very same,' replied Geoff.

'That's great news!'

'I know, but I'm starting to panic a bit. I wish you were here to organise things. When are you back from holiday? Are you having a nice time by the way?'

'Yes, yes, fine,' Amy said vaguely, 'apart from the weather, which has done its absolute worst. One dry day out of eleven so far which is grim when you're camping. Only two more days of it though and then back to civilisation. I used to love camping as a kid but I've grown to absolutely hate it and this is definitely the last time I'm holidaying with my folks. I love them dearly, but one more game of travel monopoly or scrabble and I don't think I could be held responsible for my actions.'

'Er… right. But the weather is not their fault.'

'Oh, it's not just the weather. They treat me like a baby. I'm twenty for goodness sake, not ten! Anyway it doesn't matter, I'll survive and of course I'll come down to Bath for the book signing. Did you really think I'd pass up on the chance to meet the gorgeous Phil Marchant? Give me a couple of days back at home to thaw out and then I'll come down to Bath to help you set things up.'

'Brilliant. Thanks, Amy.'

'My pleasure,' Amy said, disconnecting the call. It *would* be her pleasure to meet the handsome writer. He's old enough to be my dad but there all similarity ends, she thought.

CHAPTER 18

The clock on the wall of the doctor's waiting room was showing 10.30. Holly sighed. Her appointment had been at 9.45 and she was certain some of the people who had arrived after her had already been seen. She was not usually one to grumble but Holly needed to wee and she wasn't sure if the doctor needed a sample, so she was starting to feel quite uncomfortable. Her baby bump had grown considerably over the past four weeks since she had told Harry or, more accurately, he had told her that he knew. It was almost as though his knowledge of her condition had given her body permission to expand around the middle – and it had certainly taken advantage of the permission. Not only had she been buying things for the baby, she had also had to invest in some elasticated waistband trousers for herself rather than her usual snug-fitting jeans. Most of her tops had stretch in the fabric so for the moment she was managing with what she had. She couldn't afford to start throwing money around when soon she would be losing one of her sources of income.

Holly had hoped that Harry would have been able to come with her for this appointment, after all it was him that had been pressuring her to see the doctor. 'Aren't you supposed to have scans and stuff to make sure the baby is all right?' he had asked on more than one occasion. Eventually she had organised this appointment, between her Liberty Sands assignments, to appease Harry, but he had gone on a trip to America for Robert. It was all very exciting for him so she would never have asked him to cancel, but the timing could have been better.

'Mrs Wilson to Doctor Padgett,' the receptionist announced.

Holly gathered her bag and umbrella and headed in the direction indicated. She tapped on the door displaying Dr Padgett's name.

'Come in,' said a stressed-sounding female voice.

Holly did as instructed and stood self-consciously looking at the top of the doctor's head, noticing that another appointment was overdue as the doctor's grey roots were showing, until she indicated for her to sit down saying, 'I'll be with you in a minute, Mrs Wilson.'

'It's Miss,' said Holly, finally gaining the doctor's attention, 'Miss Wilson.'

'Right. Sorry, it does say Miss on your records. What can I do for you today?'

'I'm pregnant,' said Holly.

Doctor Padgett's eyes rested on her stomach, 'Well it certainly looks that way. Have we confirmed it or did you do your own test at home?'

'Just a home test.'

'When was the date of your last period?'

'I don't know I'm afraid. My periods have been pretty erratic over the last year or so, but I do know that I'm eighteen weeks.'

The doctor raised her eyebrows. 'How can you be so sure?' she asked.

Holly could feel the colour rising in her cheeks. 'Let's just say that there was only a small window of opportunity,' she replied.

'I see. You know you really should have contacted us before now, particularly as you're an older mum. We like to do a scan at twelve weeks to see if we can detect any problems early. It's less traumatic then if a termination is recommended.'

Holly smiled but her voice was firm, 'Then there is no need to reprimand me because I wouldn't have a termination anyway.'

'Let's have a look at you. Jump up on the bed and pull your trousers down to the top of your legs so that I can feel your tummy.'

Holly did as instructed. The doctor's bedside manner left a little to be desired but she seemed to know what she was doing. 'Well, the proportions seem about right for twenty weeks. We measure from the date of your last period normally and it is usual to fall pregnant around mid-cycle. It feels like you have quite a full bladder. I can get the nurse to do a scan now if you've got a few minutes?'

It was clear to Holly that Dr Padgett was worried that she may not come back for a scan if she arranged it for a different day. 'Yes, that's fine, as long as I won't have to wait long.'

Dr Padgett spoke to the nurse briefly on the phone and then said, 'She's just getting ready for you. I'll do your blood pressure and a blood sample and we can take a urine sample after the scan.'

Holly had forgotten all the monitoring procedures that took place during pregnancy. Who said it was the most natural thing in the world? she thought. Not in the Western world.

Ten minutes later Holly was lying on a different bed with paper tucked into the top of her knickers and the bottom of her bra.

'This might be a little cold,' the nurse said kindly, spreading a generous amount of conductive gel across her abdomen.

She wasn't joking, thought Holly, flinching slightly.

'You've got a lovely colour. Have you been away on holiday?'

Holly thought back to her recent trip to Porto Santo. It certainly hadn't been a holiday. She had really liked the island itself with the seven-kilometre beach stretching along its southern coast, backed by dunes and with no high-rise buildings spoiling the view. Even the small town was quaint in its own way with cafes and bars spilling out on to cobbled pavements, but the hotel was something else. It had reminded Holly of the hotel that featured in the Bond film *Quantum of Solace*, which she had also been less than enamoured with. It was only two storeys in height, like all the newer buildings, but instead of being built in a traditional Madeiran way it was boxy and prison-like from the outside. As she had driven up in the taxi from the airport she had realised that this first impression was going to be very difficult for holidaymakers to overcome regardless of the no-expense spared interior. Robert would never design anything like this, Holly had thought, and neither would Harry.

It very quickly became apparent to Holly that Soleil resorts had a job on their hands with this resort. She had started posting her blogs from Porto Santo earlier in the week and there had already been lots of negative comments left. Hopefully the hotel manager would do his best to resolve some of the issues or he would be out of a job, Holly thought.

'Yes… a holiday,' Holly replied, somewhat belatedly.

'Last one before the baby's born, eh? Is it your first?'

'No, I have a son,' Holly said, hoping the nurse wouldn't ask his age.

'So you're used to this then. Here's baby's head. And can you see the hands up near its face. I always think it looks like baby is sucking its thumb. Do you want to know the sex if I can tell?'

'No,' said Holly, 'I just want to know that everything looks okay.'

'Oh yes. Judging by the size and your dates you may just have yourself a little Christmas baby here.'

Holly was oblivious to the gooey gel covering her stomach as she placed her hands on it, a tear trickling from the corner of her eye. Just at that moment the baby kicked out.

'Did you feel that, Holly?' the nurse said, 'oh, and again. I think you've got a little ballerina here, or a footballer, of course. I'll just take the photo and then you can go and pee.'

Was that a hint? Holly wondered, wiping the gel off her tummy and rearranging her clothes. Holly dearly wanted this baby to be a girl so that she could name it Rosie in honour of her friend, but the most important thing was that the baby was healthy and she wasn't averse to calling it Ross if it was a boy.

CHAPTER 19

The initial excitement of arriving at LAX airport, being picked up in a chauffeur-driven car and dropped off at a plush five-star hotel, where Harry had been booked into a junior suite with a view of the Pacific Ocean and a bathroom bigger than his bedroom back in Reading, had only slightly dissipated. He had been given a day to get over his jet lag before his meeting with the hotel management team for talks about remodelling the interior of the hotel and he had taken full advantage of it.

It had felt vaguely surreal to walk on the very beach where they had filmed *Baywatch*, one of his favourite television shows as a youngster. There were no lithesome lifeguards in skimpy red swimming costumes and no David Hasselhoff but that didn't lessen the thrill. He had strolled along the pier, stopping from time to time to watch the entertainers, and then sat for a while drinking in the view down the Californian coastline, imagining what it would be like to live in one of the multi-million dollar houses perched on top of the cliffs. It was only the second time Harry had travelled abroad and he was loving it, despite his feelings of trepidation over the real reason for being there. No wonder his mum loved being Liberty Sands, he thought, it had opened up a whole new world to a girl from a council estate in Nottingham.

Holly had been surprised to learn of Harry's imminent trip to America when she had arrived back from Porto Santo the week before, but he had noticed the gleam of pride in her eyes when he told her that Robert was trusting him with a design project. He felt bad that this was only partly the truth but there was no point involving her in his search for Gareth at this stage. He had no idea what he was going to uncover and he wanted to be able to choose whether or not to tell his mum about his findings. She hadn't mentioned Gareth's name since her birthday and Harry got the distinct impression that she wouldn't, unless he raised the subject.

The meeting with the hotel management team had gone really well. Harry didn't want to change the Art Deco character of the Philmore Hotel but it was obvious to all that it needed updating. Harry wanted to open the reception area up to give it an airier feel and make the current restaurant into a coffee shop with a soft seating area. He proposed moving the restaurant to the first floor, which had raised a few eyebrows as it meant losing some bedrooms, but Harry had pointed out that the restaurant would have a view of the ocean and might become a destination in its own right. Unlike its famous neighbour Shutters, which was right on the beach, the Philmore was across the main road and the elevation would give a wonderful view of the beach and the pier. His final suggestion was to open a cocktail bar on the top floor. The pitched roof space could be developed and again the addition of the ocean view would give people a reason to visit. Harry struggled to comprehend why they hadn't really taken advantage of the amazing view for public areas previously. Maybe they're just blasé about it because they live with it all the time, he thought. He had told them that he needed to stay a few days to take measurements and do calculations, and had promised them some preliminary sketches before his return to the UK.

The following morning Harry had made sure he was seen around the lobby area with his notebook and electronic measuring device, before slipping out for his rendezvous with the admissions secretary at UCLA. Harry had no idea how huge and sprawling LA was so he was very relieved that he had Robert's credit card to pay the large taxi fare from Santa Monica to the university campus. He decided he would try and get back to the hotel by bus, if it was feasible, rather than take advantage of Robert's generosity.

Robert had been right about him being able to charm information out of the secretary. Most Americans loved an English accent but when the words were being spoken by a very handsome and earnest twenty-year-old it had double the impact. Surprisingly, they hadn't done any identity checks on Harry prior to his arrival but he did have to show his newly acquired business card at the security gate for the guard to check it against the list of appointments for the day.

Harry was met in the reception area by Cheryl di Angelo, the admissions secretary he had spoken to on the phone, and taken to an unremarkable office with sparse furniture and blinds at the window. After explaining a little bit about the programme and how it reconnected estranged family members, for which Harry drew on his knowledge of the TV show, *Surprise Surprise,* he got to the point of his visit.

'So the last information we can find on Gareth Caswell was when he left the UK to come here and learn about American football,' Harry said.

'Well, I wasn't here at the time,' said Cheryl, 'but I've done a bit of digging and it would seem that Mr Caswell arrived here in June 1993. He had been communicating with Ricky Domes who was the assistant head coach of football here at the time. According to the paperwork I have found, Mr Caswell was to spend six weeks here observing our coaching staff working on the summer training camps. '

A prickle of excitement started in the pit of Harry's stomach. This Ricky Domes might know the reason that Gareth hadn't returned home.

He started to write the name down, but Cheryl stopped him. 'Unfortunately, Ricky Domes passed away eight years ago so you won't be able to speak to him and I'm afraid I have some more bad news.'

Harry could feel the blood drain from his face. What bad news? In all the scenarios he had imagined, he had never considered that Gareth may no longer be alive.

'It seems there was an accident,' Cheryl continued.

'Accident?'

'Yes, at one of the training sessions. I don't have much information but it would appear to have been quite serious. I discovered a lot of receipts for medical bills, running into tens of thousands of dollars, all paid for by the university's insurance, so they must have accepted responsibility.'

Harry was gripping the edge of the table to stop his hands from shaking. He had to rein his emotions in. A researcher would be disappointed not devastated upon hearing this news.

'Do you know if Gareth Caswell survived the accident?' Harry asked, trying to keep the tremor from his voice.

'It would appear so. There is a final discharge bill from the hospital but more bills after that for physiotherapy.'

Inwardly, Harry breathed a sigh of relief. 'May I see the bills please?'

'I'm afraid not,' Cheryl said, looking at him intently, 'and I'm not really sure of their relevance in trying to locate Mr Caswell for your TV show.'

Harry could sense that Cheryl was beginning to get suspicious about his real motive for tracing Gareth Caswell. Maybe she thinks I'm some kind of lawyer, here to try and screw compensation out of the university for the accident, he thought.

'No, of course, I understand. I just wondered if there was a last known address for Mr Caswell after he was discharged from the hospital?'

Cheryl's body language relaxed slightly. 'Well, we are talking twenty years ago, so there are no guarantees that he is still there, but I do have an address and phone number for you. He was released into the care of Jim Caswell, who I assume must be his father.'

And my grandfather, thought Harry.

'Thank you, you've been most helpful. I'll let you know if we manage to trace him and reunite him with his family,' Harry said, reaching for the piece of paper Cheryl was offering.

Robert was the closest thing to a grandparent that Harry had experienced and it was to him that he turned when he arrived back at his hotel in Santa Monica, armed with the contact details Cheryl di Angelo had given him.

'What do I do now, Robert?' Harry asked, after he had related what had happened at the university.

'Well first you need to find out if they still live at that address. It's highly unlikely, Harry. They probably went over to be close to Gareth after the accident so it was more than likely a rented property. You could ring the number and ask to speak to Jim Caswell but you need to be prepared with a reason for your call just in case they do still live there. Maybe you could stick with your researcher story for the *Building Bridges* programme? At least you've got the business card for identification but you'll need a story about a distant cousin or someone who moved abroad and is back in the UK trying to reconnect with his or her family.'

'Thanks, Robert. I'm so grateful to have someone to talk to about all this.'

'Are you still not ready to tell Holly, now that we know it was the accident that prevented Gareth from coming home to her?' Robert asked.

'No, not yet. I need to find out why he didn't try to contact her. He could have written to her once he was out of the hospital.'

'You must handle it your way, Harry,' Robert said. 'By the way, I had an email from the manager of the Philmore. Seems you've made something of an impression with your ideas. Maybe I'll have to reconsider the project if they're willing to come up with the finances. Well done,

Harry, this could open up a great new contact with this hotel chain. I'm going to have to talk to you about a salary when you get back.'

Harry's delight at the prospect of doing some real, paid-for architectural work was tempered by the nerves he was experiencing regarding the phone call he was about to make. Robert's suggestion was a good one. Keeping close to the cover story he had told the university would mean he was less likely to fumble or make mistakes. Nevertheless he was terribly nervous as he picked up the telephone receiver and dialled the number he had been given.

'Hello,' said a female voice.

Harry noticed, with a pang of disappointment, that the voice had an American accent. 'Er, hello. May I speak to Jim please?'

'Sure. Who's calling?'

Keep it simple, Harry reminded himself, his hopes soaring like an eagle. 'It's Harry.'

'Just a moment,' the woman said into the receiver and then Harry heard her shout, 'Jim, it's someone called Harry for you.'

It might not be the same Jim, Harry thought, trying to calm himself. Jim is a common name. It could just be a coincidence. Harry could hear the rustle as the phone was passed from one person to the other.

'Jim Caswell. Who am I speaking to?'

There was an American accent but only slight, as though it had been acquired over a number of years rather than someone who had been born in the States. The tone of voice was wary and slightly abrupt.

'My name's Harry Wilson. I'm a researcher on a

television show called *Building Bridges*.'

'Never heard of it.'

Harry was afraid Jim might hang up. 'It's a new British show, a bit like *Surprise Surprise*,' he said quickly.

'So what do you want from me?'

Harry was deliberately vague. 'A cousin of yours went to live abroad and is now back in the UK trying to trace long-lost relatives.'

There was a pause on the other end of the phone. 'Are you talking about Sally? Crikey, that's a blast from the past.'

Harry hadn't expected that there would be a long-lost cousin. What a stroke of good fortune. 'That's right. She's moved back to the UK and asked our help to put her back in touch with her family. I've got a photograph of her from when she was little,' Harry improvised. 'Would we be able to meet up so that you can confirm it's her?'

'Well, I guess so,' Jim said. 'When?'

'I'm going back to the UK on Wednesday morning so would tomorrow be any good for you?'

'I'm sure we can squeeze you into our hectic schedule,' Jim said, a hint of humour creeping into his voice. 'Where are you staying? LA's a big town.'

'I'm in Santa Monica, near the pier.'

'Can your television company stretch to lunch at Shutters?'

'Great idea,' Harry responded, once again thankful that he had Robert's credit card.

'You book a table for three and we'll meet you there at 12.30.'

The next morning Harry sat sipping a cup of coffee on his balcony and sketching his ideas for the transformation of the Philmore while watching the sun glint off the Ferris wheel on Santa Monica pier. The hotel receptionist had informed him that the wheel was solar-powered and it did make sense, thought Harry. Considering the amount of sunshine they get here in California it would be a crime to waste it.

He glanced at his watch, the one his mum had bought him for his eighteenth birthday. It was just past 11 a.m. In little over an hour he was meeting with Jim Caswell and his wife. He was certain they were Gareth's parents – and his grandparents. He could stop this now. Jim didn't know which hotel he was staying at, and the television programme he had said he was working on didn't exist. It wasn't too late to change his mind. He could leave things alone and not cause the inevitable upheaval in others' lives. No, he thought, it's not an option. I've come this far, I need to know the rest of the story.

CHAPTER 20

'Hugo, how lovely to hear your voice,' Amy said. 'Where are you calling from? You sound miles away.'

'I'm in Barbados at my parents' house. How was your holiday?'

Amy suppressed a giggle. There was Hugo lounging around in his parents' luxury holiday home on the prestigious west coast of Barbados, and she had spent the last two weeks cooped up in a damp tent in the Lake District. 'Well, as holidays go, I've had better,' she answered. 'It's as bad here in Bath. I may have to start taking a vitamin D supplement if the weather doesn't improve, it's been lashing down all day.'

'What are you doing in Bath? I thought you were staying up north with your folks for the whole summer break.'

'I was supposed to be but I had a phone call from Geoff a few days ago in a right old state. You know the author we were discussing, the one you thought was transgender? Well, apparently his publishers have persuaded him to do a book tour and his first stop is Chapters. Geoff's panicking because they didn't give him much notice so he hasn't been able to get much publicity about it. I think it's in the local paper tomorrow though. How's things with you?'

Amy could hear the loud sigh quite clearly down the phone line.

'God, it's awful. Mother and Father are constantly at each other's throats. This was supposed to be a sort of reconciliation attempt but it's just not working. Father's had enough. He's flying back to England tomorrow. Actually that's why I'm ringing.'

Amy was puzzled. Why would Hugo's dad flying back to England have anything to do with her? 'You're not expecting me to pick him up from the airport in my little VW Polo are you,' she laughed.

'Of course not,' said Hugo, without sounding in the least bit condescending. 'No, it's altogether something nicer. Mother is moping around because she isn't allowed to invite her tennis coach out here. As if? They've been having an affair for goodness' sake. Surely she can see that Father would never allow him to stay under this roof. She is making it so miserable that I was thinking of flying back with Father, but he suggested I invite some friends out to join me instead. What do you think?'

'What do you mean, what do I think?' asked Amy, excitement creeping into her voice. 'Are you actually asking me to come out to Barbados for a holiday?'

'Well that's if you can get away now that you've got this book signing thing to organise. I've already spoken to Jack and he's up for it. He probably told you he's hating his summer job at Sports 4 You, so he's going to give them a week's notice today and hopefully fly out the next day. He was going to ring you,' Hugo added quickly, 'but I thought the invitation should come from me. When is your book signing do?'

'It's next Tuesday lunchtime. Bit of an odd choice if you ask me. The publishers usually like evening events or Saturdays. They must be really confident that Veronica Phillips will be able to draw the crowds. Maybe they thought it would just be too busy at a more convenient time. Whatever. It does mean that I could come out with Jack next week but there is one slight problem.'

Amy could imagine Hugo wafting his hand in a dismissive way as he said, 'Don't worry about the flights, Pops said he would pay for everybody. It's the least he can do, considering he and Mother have totally cocked up my holiday so far. So you'll come then?'

'I'd love to,' said Amy. She was normally very proud of her working-class roots and liked to pay her way, but there was no way she could afford the flights and this was too good an opportunity to miss. Besides, she reasoned, they would be helping their friend out. 'Is Harry coming too?'

'I haven't been able to get hold of him yet, but of course he's invited. You'd better ring Jack and sort out which airport you're going to fly from and what day. Harry can make his own arrangements if he's able to come. I've got to go, Pops and I have a round of golf booked at Sandy Lane and they get a bit arsy if you're late. I'm really pleased you said yes, Amy, I can't wait to show you around.'

'I am beyond excited. Thanks so much, Hugo.'

Amy disconnected the call and immediately dialled Jack's number. It went to voicemail as it seemed to quite often lately. It didn't dampen Amy's good mood though. 'Hi Jack, I've just been speaking to Hugo. I can't be believe we're going to Barbados. Ring me back when you get the message so we can organise the flights.'

For the rest of the afternoon Amy had the song 'Oh, I'm going to Barbados' running through her head on repeat, a song that she didn't even know she knew!

CHAPTER 21

Harry arrived at Shutters ten minutes before the arranged time and was shown to a small table towards the rear of the restaurant, away from the windows with their view directly on to Santa Monica beach. He didn't mind. He regarded himself lucky to have got booked in at all at such short notice. His friendly attitude towards the reception staff at the Philmore Hotel had certainly paid off.

The restaurant had a great ambience and he could imagine how cosy it would be in the winter months when the huge log fire was lit. Not that it ever got really cold in Los Angeles, Harry thought, remembering the information he had read in the travel guide he had bought at Heathrow airport.

'Can I get you something to drink,' asked the smartly dressed waiter, 'or would you prefer to wait for your friends?'

Harry smiled. Friends? he thought. He wondered just how friendly the Caswells would be towards him once they discovered that he had set up the meeting under false pretences. His palms were starting to feel quite clammy as the enormity of what he was about to share with these two unsuspecting people dawned on him. He had been able to prepare himself for meeting his grandparents but they had absolutely no idea of what was about to transpire. Perhaps somewhere more private for this meeting would have been more appropriate, he thought, hoping that neither of them had any kind of heart condition.

'I'll just have some water, please.'

'No problem, sir. Shall I bring you the menu?'

'Yes, please,' replied Harry, thinking it would at least keep him occupied until his guests arrived.

While he was waiting for the waiter to return with his water and menu, Harry cast his eyes around the room. Most of the tables were occupied, their diners deep in conversation with each other. However, an elderly couple, sat at one of the tables next to the windows, were quite obviously staring at him and instinctively Harry knew that they were the Caswells. Smart, he thought. They must have made their own reservation so that they could arrive early and check me out. The woman in particular seemed to be transfixed by him. Harry pushed his chair back from the table and made his way across the crowded restaurant.

'Excuse me, are you Jim Caswell?' he asked, extending his hand towards the man. 'I'm sorry, I must have misunderstood. I thought I was making the lunch reservation.'

'You must be Harry Wilson,' Jim said evenly, holding Harry's gaze. 'Your call caught me by surprise yesterday evening and when I'd hung up the phone I couldn't recall who was making the booking. This place gets very busy so I thought it was better to have two reservations rather than none at all. This is my wife Bethan.'

Harry smiled in the woman's direction and once again held out his hand in greeting but she didn't take it, she simply continued to stare at him in an intense and unnerving way. She was probably in her mid-sixties, Harry thought, but she looked older and not as a result of the Californian sunshine. Her skin was pale and there was a gauntness about her, with worry lines creasing her forehead.

'Who are you?' she whispered.

'Come on now, Beth,' Jim said, 'let's not forget our manners. Take a seat, Harry. I'm assuming that is your real name? The Internet is a wonderful research tool, don't you think? I very quickly discovered that there is no British television show called *Building Bridges* so we're wondering exactly what is it you want with us.'

Harry glanced back in the direction of his table. The waiter was hovering with a menu and a bottle of water, unsure whether to pour or not. Harry motioned him over as he pulled out the chair to sit down. 'I'm terribly sorry,' he said to the waiter, 'it appears we have double-booked.'

'No problem, sir,' said the waiter, totally unperturbed, 'these things happen. Shall I bring some more menus and maybe the wine list?'

'Just the menus, thank you,' said Jim, somewhat abruptly. 'Right, so let's get to the point shall we. Who are you really, Harry Wilson?' Jim asked.

'It's funny you should phrase it like that,' Harry said, 'because, in a way, that's what I'm here to find out.'

Two pairs of eyes stared at him questioningly.

'But please bear with me for a few moments as I have

to ask you a couple of questions, to make sure that you are who I think you are,' said Harry. 'Am I right in thinking that you have a son called Gareth?'

Bethan's hand flew up to her mouth and her eyes opened wide with fear as she gasped, 'What's happened to him?'

Harry immediately regretted his choice of words, realising that from the Caswell's point of view he might be there to deliver bad news. 'Please don't worry,' he said reassuringly, reaching his hand out to touch Bethan's arm. She recoiled, as though she had been scalded. 'It's nothing like that. I just need to know that I have found the right people. You're right, I don't work for a programme called *Building Bridges* but my reason for meeting with you is to do with reuniting family members.'

'What are you getting at?' Jim asked.

The waiter had returned with the other two menus. 'Would you like me to talk you through the chef's specials?' he asked uncertainly.

'No, we'll just order off the menu,' Jim said. 'Perhaps you can give us a few minutes before you come back to take our order?'

'Of course, sir. Just let me know when you are ready,' the waiter responded, backing away from the table.

'Where were we?' Jim asked.

Harry took a deep breath. 'Did your son ever talk to you about a girlfriend he had while he was studying at university?'

'Gareth had lots of girlfriends at university,' Bethan replied. 'He was the captain of the rugby team and he was very handsome, so there were always girls hanging around after him. He didn't get serious with any of them, though. He was working hard to get his degree and he had all his rugby commitments too. He simply didn't have time.'

'So he never mentioned anyone called Holly?' Harry asked, fearing that maybe his mother hadn't been quite as important to Gareth as he had been to her.

'Like Beth said, there were lots of girls. We even met a few of them in his first couple of years at Bath. But in his final year he just kept his head down and did some work. I don't recall him mentioning anyone by name in his final six months before he came out here and the accident happened. Then of course he couldn't remember anyone or anything. Not his friends, not us, and thankfully not that dreadful accident,' said Jim grimacing.

Harry's heart was starting to thump in his chest. Gareth's accident had caused him to lose his memory. Not only had he been unable to return to Holly in England because he had been injured in an accident, he hadn't been able to ask anyone to let Holly know what had happened to him. Gareth's parents had clearly been unaware of Holly's existence, so she had been left to reach her own conclusions as to why he hadn't come home. Poor Mum, Harry thought, what a terrible chain of events. 'Do you mind me asking what happened? Of course you don't have to tell me if it's too painful for you,' Harry added.

'It's all a long time ago,' said Jim. 'Why is it of interest to you?'

Harry knew that he had reached the point of no return. He could not sidestep the issue any longer; this was why he had come halfway round the world, after all. He took another deep breath. 'By the way the two of you have been looking at me, you must already suspect that I

133

may have a family connection with you. There is no easy way to tell you this. Until a few weeks ago, I had no idea who my father was. I was brought up by my mum and she never spoke to me about my father. I never asked because I didn't want to spoil the incredibly close relationship we have by making her think that having only a mum wasn't enough for me. But something has happened to change the dynamic of our relationship and I felt I needed to know who my father was.' Harry paused. He couldn't read the expression on Jim's face but Bethan was like an open book. She was gripping her husband's hand very tightly and her eyes showed a glimmer of hope. 'My mum told me his name. I think you know whose name it was.'

'That doesn't mean a thing,' Jim said. 'I'm assuming your mother is this Holly person? She may well have known of our son, even fancied him from afar, and just given you his name to satisfy your curiosity. She might not even know who your father is.'

Harry bristled. He didn't like Jim's suggestion that his mum had slept around. Of course he only had her side of the story, and maybe over the years she had rewritten elements of it in her head, but he was pretty sure that his mum was telling the truth about Gareth being his father.

'That's cruel and unkind of you, Jim,' Bethan said, reaching out a hand to rest on Harry's forearm. 'I think we both knew from the moment Harry walked into the restaurant that he had to be related to Gareth. He is the image of him at a similar age. How old are you, Harry?'

'I turned twenty in March,' he answered, exhaling deeply.

'I see. So your mother must have fallen pregnant with you just before Gareth came out to America and because of his accident he forgot all about your existence.'

'He never knew about me in the first place,' Harry corrected. 'My mum only discovered she was carrying me after your son had flown out here. She was expecting him to come home to her in the August, but he never contacted her again.'

'Let's not get carried away here, Beth, just because you want this lad to be the grandson we never had. There are a lot of unanswered questions. Why didn't your mother try to get in touch with us for one?'

'I think it may have been misplaced pride. She had no idea that Gareth had been unable not unwilling to return to her in England. She told me that she didn't want to pressure him into marriage or anything because of me. When he didn't come back to her and her own parents had disowned her, she cut off all ties with her friends at university. I guess she became something of a recluse.'

'Poor girl,' Bethan said. 'I wish we had known about her. We could have flown her out here after the accident. It might have helped Gareth's recovery. It may have prevented some of the damage,' she said, the anguish evident in her voice. She was still gripping Harry's arm and he placed his other hand on hers.

'Please tell me what happened,' Harry said.

Bethan shook her head. 'I'm sorry, I can't talk about it.'

Harry turned to Jim. 'Jim?'

'It was a ridiculous freak accident. Gareth had been playing rugby since he was eight years old. He loved the game and he could have gone on to be a professional after university if he'd wanted. Several clubs had offered him trials, but he wanted to get his studies out of the way first. He'd had a few injuries over the years, the odd broken finger, a dislocated shoulder, cuts and bruises, but nothing major, not even a broken nose to spoil his good looks. He had come out here to study American football and was on the sidelines watching a practice session, asking questions and making notes. As Gareth was only observing, not playing, he had no protective gear on. He didn't see the line-back heading in his direction to make a catch until it was too late. Twenty stone of beefcake knocked him to the floor and landed on him, crushing him and breaking numerous bones, but the worst damage occurred as his head crashed against the ground, knocking him unconscious and causing him to swallow his tongue. If it hadn't been for the quick actions of the university medical team before the paramedics arrived he would probably have died.'

Jim shuddered and Bethan's grip on Harry's arm tightened. It was clear that hearing the retelling of the story was having a distressing effect on her.

'The first we knew about it was a long-distance phone call in the early hours of the morning,' Jim continued. 'Gareth was in an induced coma in hospital. The doctors thought that would give him the best chance of a full recovery. We were flown out on the first available flight and there started six months of hell.'

Harry could feel their pain with every word that Jim spoke. They were talking about his dad. The father he had been deprived of. There was no way of knowing for sure whether Gareth would have married his mum once he had found out about the baby, but Harry sensed, simply from speaking to his parents for a few minutes, that his father would have done the right thing and been supportive both financially and in terms of being involved in his upbringing. He might even have had brothers or sisters. There was no point dwelling on past history but Harry couldn't help feeling that fate had cheated him.

'I want to know more about my dad but I think perhaps we should order some lunch before we get thrown out.'

'You're right, lad,' Jim said, gesturing for the waiter to come over to their table, 'and I think perhaps we should have a bottle of something. I know I could do with a drink and, in a way, we're celebrating. It's not every day that you find out you are grandparents.'

CHAPTER 22

The leaden skies were threatening rain as Amy briskly walked along pavements still damp from the previous heavy rain shower. She was heading towards Chapters book shop, and this morning had paid special attention to her hair and make-up but noticed with annoyance that the damp conditions were causing the tendrils of hair around her face to curl, despite her best efforts with the hair straighteners. Why am I making such a fuss over my appearance? she thought. This Philippe Marchant probably won't even notice me among the throng of adoring female fans. And why would I want him to notice me anyway? she thought. He's old enough to be my dad, and I have a boyfriend. She had finally managed to speak to Jack on Sunday evening and they had agreed that a flight from Manchester to Barbados on Thursday morning would be their best option. That gave Amy a full day to go shopping for some suitable clothes to pack and take on their holiday. She still couldn't believe they were actually going and flying Business Class as well. She was really looking forward to seeing how the other half lived.

As she approached Chapters, she was a little surprised

to note that there wasn't yet a crowd gathering. She glanced at her watch. It's only 11 a.m., she thought, and he's not due here until midday, so there's plenty of time. She pushed open the front door of the shop and was met by a near life-size cardboard cut-out of the author that had been provided by his publishing company. He bore a passing resemblance to Harry, she thought, apart from his nose, which was much more slender. What is wrong with me? Why am I imagining that everyone looks like Harry, even his friend's dad in that old university picture? I really do need this holiday in the sun.

Laughter from the small room at the back of the shop broke into her thoughts. It was quite out of place in Chapters. Geoff didn't have much of a sense of humour and besides Amy could swear it was a female voice laughing.

Not wanting to disturb anything she called out, 'Hello. It's me, Geoff. Are you in?'

'We're in the back, Amy, just making the final preparations for the book signing.'

Amy was wondering what final preparations needed to be made as she crossed the short distance to the back of the shop. She had stayed until nine the previous evening helping Geoff set up a table and chair for Philippe to sit at and sign books. They had decided that if it was too near the front people would be spilling out on to the pavement and getting wet in the inclement weather. She had instructed Geoff to put the books in piles of six so that Philippe could still be clearly seen for anyone wanting photos, while she had popped to the local florist and bought hydrangeas in white, purple and pink to match with the colours used on the cover. The only things missing were the author and his fans.

The door to the back room opened just as she reached for the handle, startling her. Standing there was a tall slim woman aged around forty wearing a Stella McCartney suit and Jimmy Choo's. Her copper hair was cut into an angular jaw-length bob that filled her slightly too thin face out and her smile was full of over-whitened teeth. Geoff peered over the woman's shoulder. 'Amy, meet Jo.'

'Hi,' Amy said.

She shook Jo's hand, and couldn't help but notice its perfectly manicured gel nails and a huge ring sporting what looked like an emerald. Amy noticed immediately that there were no rings on her other hand as her eyes rested on the latest Prada handbag nestled in the crook of her arm. This woman was everything Amy was not. Sophisticated, stylish, confident and fake.

'I've heard a lot about you, Amy. It seems I owe you a debt of gratitude. Geoff tells me that but for you this little event today might not have been able to go ahead, particularly at such short notice. He also said you've been all over social media for the last few days advertising it. Thanks so much.'

Amy thought she detected a hint of annoyance in Jo's voice but accepted the thanks modestly. 'Oh it was nothing really. We've organised signings before but they've usually been at the weekend or in the evening so we've just had to work a bit harder to spread the word. It would be awful if no one turns up.'

'Yes, it would,' said Jo, her voice lacking sincerity. 'Geoff says you're at the university here. What are you studying?'

'English. I love books. I'd like to be a writer myself one

day.'

'No time like the present. We have quite a few very young authors who write for the older teenage and young adult audience. They have some brilliant ideas but most of them can't spell and their grammar is appalling. Thank goodness for copy editors, I say. If you do ever put pen to paper, drop me a line,' said Jo, dipping into her handbag for a business card.

Amy took the card and slipped it into the pocket of her skinny jeans. People often talked about good fortune and chance meetings when they'd become an overnight success. Perhaps it really does happen, Amy thought, acutely aware of all the local authors who had come into the book shop over the past two years, asking them to stock two or three copies of their self-published work, which usually had to be returned to them after the three-month trial period. Sometimes, if the work was really good, Geoff would lie and say that the books had been sold and hand over money from the till, before giving the books to libraries. He just couldn't bear the thought of discouraging talented unknowns.

The bell over the door tinkled into life as a man in a beige trench coat backed into the shop, folding up his wet umbrella. 'Bloody English weather,' he swore, unaware that he had company.

'Nice to see you too, Phil,' Jo said, before he could make a disparaging remark about the town or the shop. 'Did you walk from the station or have you driven down?'

'As if you're interested, Jo. I'm here, like you ordered, that's the main thing isn't it?'

'Try to lighten up a bit, Phil. For all you knew the shop could already have been full of adoring fans.'

Philippe regarded her disdainfully. 'On a rainy Tuesday lunchtime. Highly likely scenario.'

The tension between the two of them was evident, and Amy sensed that Geoff had taken an instant dislike to this big-time author from London. 'Here, let me take your wet things. Can I get you a cup of tea?' she asked.

Philippe seemed to notice Amy for the first time. 'I don't suppose you've got any whisky – just to warm me up you understand, I'm chilled to the bone.'

'I don't keep alcohol in the shop,' Geoff said frostily, 'but the pub up the street opened at eleven. You've got time to nip out for a quick drink if you need one and if you want to brave the rain again.'

Philippe changed his tone of voice. 'No, a hot drink will be just fine, although I prefer coffee to tea if you've got it. And is there somewhere I can sit in comfort out of the shop before people start arriving?'

'Yes, of course,' said Amy, 'come through to the back room. There's a comfy sofa in there and I'll make you a coffee.'

Philippe glared at Jo before following Amy through the shop.

'Arrogant prick,' Geoff muttered under his breath.

Four hours later, the final Veronica Phillips fan was ushered from the shop and Geoff flipped the sign on the door to read closed. Jo was amazed by the turnout. She had deliberately planned this book signing midweek and midday and yet still people had turned out in their droves. Jo had only arranged for three hundred copies of the book to be delivered to Chapters and had imagined that at least two hundred and fifty books would be unsold. She couldn't have been more wrong. All the copies had gone by 1.30 so, not wanting to send away disappointed customers, Amy had come up with the idea of making a list of names and addresses for Philippe to sign back in London and the publishers to mail out. She had also suggested that Geoff still got his 30 per cent cut as it was his customers who had bought the books. Clever girl, Jo conceded, particularly as she had managed to keep Philippe in a buoyant mood all afternoon.

'I don't know about writing a book, Amy, maybe you should put your talent into marketing or event organising. You were absolutely brilliant, particularly when we had long queues.' Jo's praise was heartfelt.

'I really enjoyed it. I'm not normally one for big crowds but everyone was really nice. I even picked up a couple of phone numbers. I wouldn't have thought there would have been any guys here but they insisted they were getting a signed copy for their mum.' She shot a look at Geoff. 'Don't you dare tell Jack, I'm obviously not going to call any of them.'

'What's it worth? Jack could do with a kick up the backside. I don't think he's got any idea just how special you are,' said Geoff.

'Who's Jack?' Philippe asked.

'He's my boyfriend. Geoff doesn't think he's good enough for me which is ridiculous as he's taking me to Barbados on holiday on Thursday,' said Amy.

'Not actually accurate, Amy. True you are going to Barbados together but he's not technically taking you is he?' persisted Geoff.

'Let's not split hairs, Geoff. I'm shattered. You know

that drink you were after earlier, Philippe, well I could murder one now. Anyone else fancy it?'

Geoff didn't really drink but he didn't want Amy going off on her own with the smarmy Frenchman. 'I'm game,' he said.

'Me too,' said Jo. She had noticed how Philippe had been looking at Amy admiringly for most of the day and didn't want him drunkenly taking advantage of her. That sort of publicity she didn't need, but it was also amazing how his darling Holly had seemingly slipped his mind.

CHAPTER 23

Delicious as the food in Shutters was, none of the trio had much of an appetite. Harry had kept the conversation fairly general as they had all toyed with their food, but once the waiter had cleared their plates away he was anxious to return to the topic of his father. Over coffee, Jim filled him in on the six months Gareth had spent in hospital. The broken bones had mended and the bruises faded while he was in the induced coma, but it wasn't until he was gradually brought out of the coma that the doctors were able to assess the extent of the damage caused to Gareth's brain by the impact of the fall.

'It was very soon apparent that Gareth was suffering post-traumatic amnesia,' Jim said. 'He couldn't remember anything at all, not even his own name. It was heart-breaking for Beth and me, sitting at his bedside every day, to not even be rewarded with a flicker of recognition as we talked to him and showed him pictures of the three of us on seaside holidays to try and trigger his memory.'

Harry noticed that Bethan had her eyes closed. Even after twenty years the memories were still raw and painful.

'Very gradually he began to recall random things.

His speech was a bit slurred but he kept asking for his dog Ozzie, who had been his best friend throughout his childhood. Ozzie had been put to sleep, following a stroke, when Gareth was fifteen. He got very upset, and quite violent, even raising his hand to me, when we tried to explain that it wouldn't be possible to bring Ozzie to the hospital. Eventually, after months of psychiatric assessments, plus the physiotherapy sessions to help his broken body, the day arrived that I honestly thought we might never see. He was discharged from hospital into our care, even though he still had no recollection of anything that had happened in the previous twelve months. It was sad. We had his first class honours degree framed for him, because we were so proud of him, but he didn't connect with it at all and it certainly didn't spark any recollection of all the hard work he had put in to achieve that result.'

'It must have been an enormous relief for you to have him home though,' Harry said, 'although presumably he still had to go back to the hospital as an out-patient,' he added, remembering the physiotherapy bills that Cheryl di Angelo had told him about.

'Yes. It was a shame, as we would have liked to return to the UK, but the insurance company would only agree to pay for treatment that he had in America so we had to stay here. Fortunately for me, the bank that I work for have offices in LA, so I was able to get a transfer out here and they helped me get my green card, otherwise I would have had to go back and leave Bethan here with Gareth.'

Harry had been wondering why his grandparents had stayed in America rather than returning home. He was also itching to ask after Gareth's current whereabouts and whether or not he would be able to meet up with him before returning to the UK tomorrow, but he felt he needed to let Jim talk. It seemed that telling Gareth's tragic story to someone who had a vested interest was cathartic for Jim.

'As the months went on, Gareth settled into a routine of treatment sessions at home and at the hospital. He was determined to learn to walk again.'

Harry's head shot upright. 'What did you just say?'

Jim looked flustered for a moment, unsure what he had said that had prompted Harry's question.

'You forgot to mention that Gareth left hospital in a wheelchair,' Bethan said reproachfully to her husband. 'You see, Harry, to us the physical injuries weren't as important as the psychological ones. Gareth broke his back in the accident and for a long time nobody thought he would ever walk again.'

Harry was shocked. He tried to process the information he had just been given. As Jim was speaking, Harry had been visualising an older version of the man he had seen in the rugby team photo. Broad-shouldered, muscly, upright. The idea of what it must have felt like for this athlete to be confined to a wheelchair was almost impossible for Harry to comprehend. 'Is... is he still in a wheelchair?'

'Most of the time,' Jim said. 'Apparently he can get around on his crutches in the house, but only for short periods of time.'

'It's okay, Harry,' Bethan said, reaching for her grandson's hand. 'Gareth's accepted it and so have we. It's not what any of us would have planned his life to be but he makes the most of it. We're very proud of the way he has coped with everything, particularly after Kate died.'

Harry looked from one to the other. 'Who's Kate?' he asked.

'Beth, you're confusing the boy,' Jim reprimanded. 'Kate was Gareth's physiotherapist. She was assigned to him when he left the hospital. In the early days she visited every other day and Gareth used to look forward to seeing her, even though the sessions often left him frustrated and sometimes in pain. She was wonderful with him, so patient and kind, and he grew to absolutely adore her. She was the one person he never lost his temper with. After a year or so they started to make plans for their wedding. Gareth was determined he was going to walk down the aisle on his crutches. He worked so hard, physically exhausting himself. In the April, Kate went home to Oklahoma to see her mother and sister, Janie, who was going to be the chief bridesmaid, to plan their outfits.' Jim paused. 'There was a bomb attack on the federal building where Janie worked. The girls were both killed instantly. It totally devastated Gareth. He didn't speak for weeks, and when he did it was to say that he wanted to go home to Wales.'

Harry didn't know what to say. He didn't know this Kate and in some way she had taken Gareth away from his mother, but it wasn't her fault: she knew nothing about Holly, and his dad had obviously loved her. He saw Bethan reach into her handbag for a tissue to wipe the tears away from her eyes.

'Kate was a lovely girl,' Bethan said. 'She didn't have a bad bone in her body. Kate's mum said it would be less expensive to have the dresses made in Oklahoma. Poor woman. She never recovered. At least they're all together again now.'

Harry was beginning to understand why Bethan looked so defeated. Since Gareth had set foot in America her life had turned upside down. 'Did Gareth go back to Wales?'

'Yes, he did. Eighteen years ago and he's never been back here since.'

'So why did you stay?' Harry asked, puzzled.

'He didn't want us around him,' she said sadly. 'He said it brought back too many unhappy memories. After Kate died he completely withdrew into himself, but I sometimes got the feeling that odd flashes of his life in the year before the accident were coming back to him. Maybe he remembered that it was me who had encouraged him to come out to America in the first place. I thought it would be a wonderful experience for him. He never said as much but I think maybe he blamed us, well, me anyway, for what happened. W-we stayed away because he didn't want us. It nearly broke my heart,' she sobbed.

Harry put his arms around Bethan and hugged her to him. He barely knew her but the pain she had suffered was etched on her face for all to see. She clung to him as though her life depended on it.

'I couldn't believe it when I saw you at the restaurant entrance today,' she murmured, 'it was like the last twenty years of my life had been wiped away. You look just like him, you know.'

'I'm so sorry to have upset you like this. I didn't mean to. I just wanted to find my dad. Please forgive me.'

Bethan pushed him away so that she could look into his eyes. 'There's nothing to forgive. Believe me when I tell you that this is one of the happiest days of my life. I hope you'll let us be part of your life now that we know about you, Harry.'

'Nothing would make me happier. Because my mum's family disowned her before I was born, I've never had any grandparents. I need to find out what I've been missing out on,' he said, forcing a smile. 'I have to go back to the UK tomorrow but I promise I will find a way to come back and see you, you have my word. And you must come and visit us in the UK.'

'Us?' Bethan questioned.

'Yes,' said Harry. 'Mum and me. I think you would have liked my mum, if you'd known her. She truly loved Gareth, you know. She's never married nor even had boyfriends until very recently because she still had the faintest hope that he would come back to her.'

'What are you planning to do now that you know that Gareth is living in Wales? Are you going to go and see him?' asked Jim.

'Will you give me his address?'

'Of course, but be warned, he won't have any recollection of your mother and he knows nothing about you. He's wary of strangers, so tread gently,' Jim said, patting Harry on the shoulder in an unexpected show of affection.

'Don't worry, Jim. I will.'

CHAPTER 24

Come on, Amy,' Jack said, 'they've called our flight. You'll be able to buy suntan lotion in Barbados, and anyway Hugo will have plenty.'

'They might not have the one I want,' she replied, 'besides, I'm nearly at the front of the queue now. It's all right for you. You just have to look at the sun and you get a tan. It's different for redheads. It's less suntan lotion, more sun protection. I need factor 50 plus or I'll be stuck indoors or in the shade the whole time.'

'Okay, but if we miss the flight it'll be your fault,' Jack replied grumpily. 'I told you we should have arranged the cab for earlier.'

'What is up with you? How was I supposed to know that the traffic would be that bad? We're off on holiday to Barbados, flying Business Class which, I might remind you, someone else is paying for, and you're as miserable as sin. You'd better lighten up. We're supposed to be going out there to salvage Hugo's holiday, the last thing he wants is us arguing.'

'Cashier number five please,' said the automated announcement, preventing further comment from Jack.

Amy handed over her purchase and her boarding card, paid with cash, to make the transaction quicker, and hurried out of the chemist to catch up with Jack who was already heading for the boarding gate.

'Have I done something wrong? Would you rather I wasn't going on this holiday with you? I can always go home and you can make some excuse to Hugo.'

Jack stopped mid-stride and turned to face her. 'Don't be daft, Amy. Look, I'm sorry. It's me, not you. I've just got a lot on my plate at the moment. Of course we're both going. We're both Hugo's friends, right? We're going to have a great time.'

Amy leaned towards Jack to kiss him but he turned away. 'No time for that stuff now,' he said, hurrying ahead of her, 'we've got a plane to catch.'

Amy followed, her new Accessorize carry-on bag, bought with the money Geoff had given her for helping with the book signing and now heavy with books, water and sun lotion, banging into her legs as she almost had to run to keep up. 'There never seems to be any time for that stuff these days,' she muttered.

'This is lush,' said Jack, relaxing into his Upper Class Virgin Atlantic seat and stretching his legs out into the ample foot well while unzipping the complimentary wash bag that he had almost sat on. 'There's socks, a blindfold thing, washing stuff, even a toothbrush and toothpaste. Blimey, they've thought of everything.'

'A blindfold thing? Do you mean the eye mask?' Amy asked, giggling.

'Whatever,' said Jack, back to his normal good humour,

'and look there's even a menu to choose our meals from. Talk about posh. I could get used to this.'

'Maybe we should start playing the lottery, cos that's the only way the likes of you and me would ever be able to afford this. It's very generous of Hugo's dad to pay for the flights but I'd rather it hadn't been out of guilt,' Amy sighed. 'I feel really bad for Hugo. I think his parents have behaved so selfishly, don't you?'

'It's a tricky one, Ames. None of us really knows what goes on in other people's lives. Maybe his mum and dad just fell out of love with each other.'

'Or maybe they never loved each other in the first place? I think his mum is way younger than his dad. Perhaps she was the trophy wife and he was her meal ticket.'

'We probably shouldn't speculate on things we know nothing about.'

'You're right, Jack,' Amy agreed, 'but it does make me appreciate my mum and dad more. They might be boring, and have an unhealthy penchant for camping holidays, but at least they still love each other as much as they ever did.'

'You're in a minority, Amy.'

'What do you mean?'

'I can't think of many of my friends whose parents are even speaking, let alone still married, mine included. Maybe there's just too much choice available these days, what with Internet dating and the like. It's a different world from when our parents were young,' he said, reaching for another glass of buck's fizz from the tray the stewardess was offering.

Amy shot a sidelong glance at Jack. What was he

getting at? she wondered.

The flight was long but imminently more comfortable than if they had travelled Economy class. Amy had been hoping for some in-depth conversation with Jack but, following their meal, where he had consumed several glasses of wine and barely spoken because he was watching *The Wolf of Wall Street* on his seat back television, he'd fallen asleep. Amy had dozed off too from time to time, in between movies, and games of *Who Wants to be a Millionaire* and *Tetris*, but she had made sure she was awake whenever the crew passed through the cabin with water.

Unlike Jack, Amy hadn't had a drink with her meal. She had only been on one previous foreign holiday, to Malia with her friends from the sixth form after they had finished their A levels. They had all got quite drunk. Most of her friends just got a bit loud and lairey but Amy was sick in the confined space of the smelly aircraft toilet. She had vowed then never to drink during a flight again. She couldn't break a vow so soon after making it, despite all the free alcohol on offer.

At one point Amy did wonder if Jack was actually asleep or just pretending because he didn't want to talk to her. She realised it wasn't an act when the stewardess had to gently shake his shoulder to ask him to put his seat in the upright position for landing. It was a relief to get off the plane and have something to do, other than trying to strike up a conversation with someone who was clearly not feeling very communicative. After passport control, Jack went in search of a luggage trolley while Amy minded the carry-on bags and kept an eye on the conveyor belt for their cases. Amazingly, they were among the first off. A perk of travelling Business Class I guess, thought Amy.

The moment they were through the exit doors Hugo bounded over to them like an over-excited St Bernard puppy. 'Am I glad to see you guys!' he said, hugging Amy and giving Jack a friendly punch on the arm. 'This place might be paradise but the last two weeks with mater and pater have been hell. Now the fun can start.' He took control of the trolley and steered it in the direction of a black limousine, which was illegally waiting in a no-parking zone. 'Hop in, while I sling these in the boot. It's okay, Rodney,' he shouted to the driver who was starting to get out of the car to help, 'I've got it. Help yourself to water, guys, we'll save the cocktails for when we get home.'

It must be nice to call somewhere on the paradise island of Barbados home, thought Amy, climbing into the back seat alongside Jack.

'Did you manage to get hold of Harry in the end?' Amy asked as Hugo slid into the front seat and Rodney steered the car through the chaos of people and luggage.

'Eventually. He's been in Los Angeles but he should be home in Reading now.'

'Los Angeles?' said Jack, clearly surprised, 'he didn't mention anything about going on holiday there. Did he go with his mum? Maybe it was another one of her spying missions.'

'No, his mum didn't go. He said he was doing some work for that elderly friend of his mum's.'

'I'm sure Robert would be delighted to hear himself described as elderly,' said Amy. 'He's only sixty you know, not ninety!'

'True. Pops is only two years off sixty and there's plenty of life in that old dog, if you get my drift!'

Unfortunately Amy did get his drift, so she changed the subject before Hugo could dwell on the disaster that was his parents' marriage. 'It looks quite a lot like England really,' she said, looking out of the car window, 'not what I was expecting at all, apart from all the sugar cane of course.'

'They've cut a lot of it down in recent years to make way for building more houses. I guess there isn't such a call for it now that people are more health conscious. It makes great rum, though. What do you want to try first? Rum punch, banana daiquiri?'

'Piña colada for me,' said Amy, leaning against Jack's shoulder, already imagining how good it would taste with real pineapple juice and real coconut. 'How about you, Jack?'

'Rum punch, and lots of it. I fancy getting totally slaughtered!'

CHAPTER 25

Harry had the house to himself. He had arrived back from Los Angeles on Thursday morning around the same time that his mum was making her way to Gatwick airport for her flight to Barbados. They had missed each other by a couple of hours and, although Harry would like to have seen his mum, at least it meant he didn't have to answer awkward questions about his trip to LA, nor tell any lies. He had also avoided mentioning that his university friends were in Barbados on holiday and that there was a distinct possibility that he might fly out to join them after the weekend, but he hadn't wanted to get her hopes up. It was a fabulous opportunity that Hugo had offered them all and he didn't want to miss out on it, plus it would be a lovely surprise for his mum if he could make it, but he had no idea how the next few days in the UK were going to go. It was best to stay vague with both his mum and his friends, he had decided.

The moment he had got home to their little house in Reading, Harry had ignored his mum's advice about trying to stay awake for the whole day to combat jet-lag, and had gone to bed for a nap. He was feeling physically and emotionally exhausted, and his last waking thought was total admiration for his mum, who did these long-haul flights on a very regular basis and coped with the different time zones much better than him, despite being twenty years his senior and almost five months pregnant.

Predictably, he had woken up on Thursday evening just as he should have been going to bed. He knew there was no way he was going to be able to get back to sleep so, after watching late-night television for a while, tucking into a plate of buttered toast and half-emptying the biscuit tin with his cup of coffee, Harry decided to set off on his journey to Wales. At least I'll avoid the holiday traffic, he thought, climbing into his little car well before dawn.

Although Harry was familiar with the section of the M4 motorway between Reading and the exit for Bath, he had never ventured along it further west, towards Bristol and then on into Wales. It had only taken him a little over an hour and a half to reach the toll booths on the border and the time had flown by, so deep in thought was he about the significant moment that lay ahead.

The verdant Welsh countryside was speeding by almost invisibly in the pre-dawn, the sky stained an inky blue with tinges of magenta before the sun would make its presence felt, creeping over the horizon in shades of orange. Since arriving back from LA, Harry had stressed over and looked forward to the meeting with Gareth in equal measure. Finding out that it hadn't been his father's choice to stay away from his mum had made all the difference to his perception of Gareth. Harry had no idea what to expect when he revealed his identity, but he had promised Jim and Bethan that he would do it with as much sensitivity as possible.

The last few miles of the journey were on smaller roads, heading out onto the picturesque Gower peninsula towards the tiny village of Oxwich, where Gareth now called home. When he had returned to Wales after the accident he hadn't wanted to live close to the people he had spent his youth with. Bethan had said that Gareth couldn't bear to see pity in people's eyes. He had instead moved into a small farmhouse in a sparsely populated area and, according to his grandparents, led a fairly solitary existence, although they couldn't be sure as they had such little contact with him.

'You have reached your destination,' announced the satellite navigation system.

Harry pulled over to the side of the road, next to a five-bar gate. Beyond it, he could just make out the outline of a house. He glanced at the clock on his dashboard. It wasn't even 6 a.m. Clearly there was no way he could make himself known to the occupant of the house at this early hour. Slowly he eased Toby back onto the road and continued along until it eventually split, one direction heading further out onto the Gower peninsula, the other signposted for the beach. Harry hesitated. He didn't want to have come all this way and risk Gareth going out for the day but it would be a couple of hours before he could go knocking on the door. Maybe I'll be able to find a beach café open in an hour or so, he decided, making a left turn towards the beach, the tyres of his car almost immediately crunching on the gravel of a car park. Unsurprisingly, his was the only car, although there were several camper vans parked at one end, close to what looked like a toilet block.

Harry got out of the car and stretched his long limbs before reaching into the back seat for his hoodie. He was glad he had brought it as there was a distinct chill in the air, despite it being August, and a dampness caused by a fine sea mist. He pulled the hood up and stuck his hands in the pockets then headed across the pebbles at the top of the beach on to the fine sand, continued onto the firmer sand, recently washed by the outgoing tide, and stopped just short of the reach of the waves. He turned his back on the outline of a large building, which he guessed might be a hotel, and began to walk in the opposite direction. To his right the waves broke onto the shore, rushing up towards him and then fell back with a sucking sound. Ahead he could just make out the shape of cliffs rising up to greet the sunrise and to his left the car park and café buildings were receding to be replaced by soft dunes and patches of marram grass.

He breathed in deeply, filling his lungs with the fresh salty air until his chest felt it would burst open and then slowly exhaled. Until now, Harry hadn't allowed himself to think too clearly about what exactly he was going to say to Gareth. How was he going to break the news to this man that he had a son?

CHAPTER 26

'I'm not stupid you know. I know why you did it,' Philippe said, pausing between signing books, gel pen in hand. 'You did it to stop me acting like Billy Big Bollocks. Well your little plan backfired, although it did make me realise that I've been a bit of an idiot.'

'Apology accepted,' said Jo from the comfort of the red leather Chesterfield sofa in the corner of her office. 'Sorry I had to drag you in so early but these needed signing and you have to be at the television studio for 9 a.m.' Philippe was using her desk to sign all the books that needed sending out to the customers from Chapters. Once signed, he placed the slip of paper with the name and address on it back into each book before closing it and handing to Alice to stack on a trolley. 'I'm pretty sure it would have flopped if Miss "I'm going to make a success of this" hadn't stuck her nose in.'

'Ah yes, the lovely Amy. If only I was twenty years younger,' Philippe sighed, 'and not totally in love with another woman.'

'I must admit I was pretty convinced you were going to hit on her. That was my second surprise of the day.'

'Even if I'd wanted to, I don't think I'd have got very far with her chaperone hanging around.'

'Do you mean Geoff? I thought it was rather sweet the way he was looking out for her.' That had been Jo's third and fourth surprises of the day. She had actually felt quite attracted to Geoff and he was definitely not her type. It would appear that he felt the same way as he had pressed a Chapters bookshop business card into her hand as they all dispersed outside the pub. It had his private mobile number on it and the words 'call me'.

'You did give Amy a signed book didn't you, to thank her for all her help?'

'Of course. I'm not totally evil, you know, and anyway she bought another one. I think she added the person's name to the list.'

Philippe closed the book he had just signed and reached for the last one. 'Phew, last one. My wrist is aching and that's after only a couple of hundred. Imagine what it will be like when you put me into a proper venue,' he teased.

'Erm, I thought you said you'd learned your lesson?' Jo said, but Philippe wasn't listening. He was looking down at the name on the last piece of paper. Holly Wilson. And the address was in Reading. Philippe had the weirdest feeling that, for once, fate was on his side.

'This one doesn't have a slip of paper in it,' he said, quickly snapping the book closed. 'Do you mind if I keep it? I haven't had any writer's copies for friends and family yet.'

'I didn't think there was any rush getting them to you. I know you don't get on with your family and I didn't think you'd got any friends left,' she teased. 'Be my guest.'

What neither of them had noticed was the white feather spiralling to the floor as Philippe had opened the last book.

CHAPTER 27

Harry had walked the length of the beach and arrived back just as the café was opening at 8 a.m. He was tempted to stop for a cup of tea but didn't want to risk missing Gareth. He drove back up the hill and parked across the gate, beyond which he was now able to see a tarmac driveway leading to a whitewashed house nestled into the protection of the hillside. The door and window frames were painted in Wedgewood blue and, although there were no roses around the door, the front garden looked well tended with hydrangea and lavender bushes and the overall impression was welcoming.

Harry sat for a moment, his hands resting loosely on the steering wheel. From this vantage point the view of the countryside was panoramic, hillsides dotted with sheep and the sand dunes and white-capped waves beyond. He could understand why someone wanting privacy would choose a spot like this.

'You're stalling,' he said out loud, 'come on, Harry, man up.'

With that he got out of the car, let himself in through the gate and strode purposefully towards the front door.

Even before the cast-iron knocker had connected with the base plate a voice from inside called out, 'Come in, it's not locked.'

Harry's hand trembled as he lifted the latch and entered. It took a few moments for his eyes to adjust to the dim interior after coming in from the bright August morning but when they did the inside of the house was not what he had expected. Rather than a more traditional layout of small rooms, the whole of the downstairs was completely open plan, although some of the character had been retained with oak beams and an inglenook fireplace. The floor was polished wood with no rugs breaking up the expanse and the furniture was modern and quite sparse. To one side was a generous kitchen, again done in a very modern style, separated from the dining area by a sweeping wooden breakfast bar, sat at which was a man clearly in the middle of his breakfast. Harry instantly recognised him from the rugby team photo, despite the passing of twenty years.

'Oh, sorry, I thought it was Megan from the village with my groceries. I don't get many visitors. Are you after directions?'

For a moment Harry couldn't reply. Hearing his father's voice for the first time in his life totally overwhelmed him. He wanted to rush over to him and fling his arms around him, but he knew he had to exercise restraint. 'I, er, no, I'm not lost. I came to see you.'

Gareth raised his eyebrows. 'Really? Look if you're trying to get on the team, you have to be recommended by a scout. Who do you play for?'

'No, I'm not trying to get on the team,' Harry said, unsure which team Gareth was referring to. 'I've just come back from America. I've been speaking with your mum and dad.'

A cloud passed across Gareth's amiable face. 'Right. And they sent you to check up on me.'

'Not exactly. I–I met them because I was looking for you.'

'Why would you be looking for me?' Gareth asked, his eyes narrowing. 'Who are you?'

'Um, well, it's a bit of a long story.'

'Well then, we'd better sit down.'

To Harry's surprise, Gareth got up from his wheelchair in which he'd been sitting behind the low breakfast bar and carefully walked round it to the dining table. Harry joined him.

'You weren't expecting that, were you? Mum and Dad obviously told you about the wheelchair because it didn't faze you but they don't know how well I've been doing with my walking. Ben's been a great help, forcing me to go out for a walk every day, whatever the weather.'

'Ben?' Harry questioned.

'My golden retriever. He fetches his lead off the hook and puts it at my feet when he's ready to go. Very intelligent dog he is. So let's have it then. What do you want with me?'

This is it, thought Harry. This is what I've come here for.

'I think you may know my mum,' Harry said tentatively, 'but I'm not sure if you remember her because of your accident. You were at university together in Bath.'

Gareth's forehead puckered slightly.

'I don't have the best memory of my university days, particularly the last year, but I'll try. What was her name?'

'Holly Wilson.'

Gareth gripped the table, a puzzled look on his face. He thought the lad had said Holly was his mum but he must have mis-heard.

'I do remember Holly. She was one of the first people I remembered after the shock of the bombing. It was like a door opened in my brain and I could see her as clear as day. Those beautiful green eyes and her dark curly hair. She was a stunner. I came back to find her but I was too late, she'd already gone.'

'Yes. She left Bath when you didn't come back from America. She didn't know about the accident and thought you'd abandoned her.'

'I would never have done that. Holly should have known that. But I don't understand why she left university. She was really clever and always had her nose in a book. Why would she throw away her education?'

'She discovered she was pregnant.'

'Pregnant?' Gareth's face contorted. 'Do you mean I got her pregnant?'

'Yes. She didn't find out until after you had left for America and then when you didn't come back, she thought maybe you'd found a new girlfriend over there and she couldn't bear the thought of you feeling that you were duty bound to marry her. She didn't want you to feel trapped.'

'I loved her. She was different from all the other girls who hung around me because I was the rugby team captain. I don't think that impressed her at all. I would have married her if she would have let me. Her mother never told me she was pregnant.'

It was Harry's turn to grip the table.

'You met Holly's mother?' he asked, his voice strangled in his throat.

'Just the once. I didn't like her much but I felt so sorry for her. I got her address from the university records when I came home to the UK. I may have scared her a bit, being in the wheelchair and all, but she was a very odd character, even when she told me about the accident. Did the baby die too? She never mentioned anything about the baby. Maybe she was too upset.'

'No, the baby didn't die in the accident.' Harry was surprised that Gareth hadn't made the connection yet that he was that baby, but maybe that was part of the damage to his brain. 'It was just her dad.'

'And Holly, of course,' he said, his face a mask of misery. 'My beautiful Holly.'

An awful realisation started to dawn on Harry. His heart began to thump in his chest and his throat tightened. He had been wondering why Gareth hadn't continued his search for Holly even if her mother hadn't been able to give him an address.

'No,' he said, gently, 'it was just her dad who died. Holly wasn't in the car with him and neither was the baby.'

'What are you saying? Her mother wouldn't lie to me about a thing like that. She said Holly died the day of the accident.'

Metaphorically maybe, Harry thought, finding it difficult to comprehend how his grandmother could be so cruel. 'Mum always said that her mother blamed her for the accident.'

'You said it again. You called Holly "Mum".'

'She is my mum and… and you're my dad.'

Gareth stared at Harry. He rubbed his temples as

though he couldn't quite understand what he was being told.

'I'm the baby she was pregnant with when you left for America,' Harry said.

'You're my son?'

'I'm your son.'

Neither of them spoke for quite some time. Gareth kept looking at Harry as though at any moment he expected him to disappear in a puff of smoke.

Eventually he said, 'So where is she then? You haven't got her in the car have you?'

Harry was relieved by the attempt at humour. At least he presumed it was meant in jest. Surely he didn't really think he would leave his mum waiting in the car?

'Right at this minute she's working in Barbados, but we live in Reading. Well I say "we" but I've been away at university for the past two years. I'm at Bath too.'

Gareth raised his eyebrows. 'Did your mum want you to go there?' he asked.

'No. She didn't try and influence my choice. I went there because they have a good reputation for architecture and it was quite close to home if Mum needed me in a hurry.'

'I'm glad you're not studying sport. Look what happened to me.'

'Your mum and dad told me about the accident. You were just incredibly unlucky.'

'I used to think that but now I realise I've actually been very fortunate. The rugby club have been brilliant. Not only did they offer me a coaching role they gave me access to the latest medical advances and physiotherapy. I left America believing I would never walk unaided again and as you've seen, I can. Not fast and not far but I get stronger every day. Anyway, enough about me. You said, "we" live in Reading. Have you got brothers and sisters then?'

It was obvious to Harry what Gareth really wanted to know. 'No. Mum didn't have any more children and she's never been married. How about you?'

'Who'd want to marry a wreck like me?' Gareth asked.

'You've never asked me,' said a voice from behind a box piled high with groceries. 'I hope I'm not interrupting anything. The door was open. I'll just take these things through to the kitchen, shall I?'

'Harry this is Megan. Megan, this is… well, actually, this is my son.'

Fortunately the box of supplies was already on the counter top otherwise Megan may well have dropped it, judging by her facial expression.

'Well, I wasn't expecting that,' she admitted.

'It's come as a bit of a shock to me,' said Gareth. 'Perhaps you could make us a cup of tea? That's supposed to be good for shock, isn't it?' he said, his eyes twinkling.

'You've always got some excuse or other to have me make you tea. He's a cheeky one is Gareth.'

Gareth and Megan clearly had a great friendship but Harry couldn't help wondering if she would have liked more.

Once Megan had left, Gareth and Harry continued where they had left off, each wanting to know as much as possible about the other. Gareth explained the pioneering surgery that had given him back the ability to walk. The club knew of a surgeon who had performed the same operation on one of their players who had broken his neck during a game. There were no guarantees of success and months of painful physiotherapy to endure but the surgeon had felt confident of a successful outcome, although even he hadn't expected the near miracle that had Gareth walking completely unaided. He said it was a combination of hard work and will power, but Gareth maintained it was the genius of Professor Williams. The two had remained great friends.

Gareth asked about Harry's early life and about his studies at Bath but he seemed to be skirting around asking direct questions about Holly. He insisted that Harry stayed for lunch and, after they had loaded the dishes into the dishwasher, Ben appeared with his lead, ready to go for his daily walk. Gareth drove them all to Port Eynon beach, in his specially adapted Land Rover and wheeled his chair down the ramp to the sand.

'I'm a bit wobbly on the soft sand,' he said, unclamping his feet and reaching underneath his wheelchair for a cane, which he unfolded and used to help him stand. 'I'm all right once it's firmer under foot though,' he said, unclipping Ben's lead, and ruffling the fur on his neck. The dog bounded off down the beach for a few seconds and then galloped back to Gareth. 'He never leaves my side for more than a few minutes. He's like my version of a guide dog.'

Father and son walked at a slowish pace, pausing from time to time for Gareth to rest on his stick.

'So why now, Harry?' Gareth asked, finally voicing the question he most wanted an answer to. 'Why did you come looking for me now, after all these years?'

'Mum never talked to me about you. Of course there were times when I would like to have known who my dad was, but Mum never mentioned you and I didn't want to upset our relationship by asking. We're really close. She never bothered with boyfriends. It was always just the two of us until fairly recently. She went on one of her work trips to Mauritius and she… she met someone. It all happened very quickly.'

Harry glanced at Gareth, trying to gauge his reaction, but his face remained impassive apart from the twitch of a muscle at the side of his mouth.

'She came home from Mauritius all loved up but then something happened, she won't tell me what, and she broke it off with him.'

Gareth looked puzzled. 'So, that was when she decided to tell you about me?'

'Not exactly,' Harry replied. 'She didn't know when she split with this man that she was pregnant.'

'So, they are back together because of the baby and it prompted you to find out about your own dad.'

'No. They're not back together. She hasn't told him.'

'And you think she should?'

'I suppose I do. Don't get me wrong. I adore Mum and fully appreciate everything she has sacrificed to give me the best upbringing she could. She's amazing but, given the chance, I think I would rather have had a father around. Does that make me sound ungrateful?'

'No, Harry, just human. So, it was the pregnancy that prompted you to ask her about me?'

'Exactly. She was a bit reluctant at first but, eventually, she told me the story and I started my search. I'm really glad I did,' Harry said, the wobble in his voice betraying the emotion he felt.

'Come here, son,' Gareth said, pulling him into a hug, tears welling in his eyes. 'I'm really glad you did too.'

CHAPTER 28

Amy's eyelids fluttered in the few seconds preceding total consciousness, her mind whirring to try to place where she was in the instant before she opened her eyes. Pale gold walls, decorated with paintings of exotic plants and beautiful beaches overhung by palm trees, welcomed her to a new day in paradise. She stretched her arms above her head and reached out to Jack's side of the bed. It was empty and felt cold, suggesting that he had long since departed. Amy bit her lip, supressing a feeling of disappointment.

True to his word, Jack had got very drunk the previous evening and had fallen asleep almost before his head had hit the pillow. Although it was a setback in Amy's plan to get reacquainted physically, she had comforted herself with the thought that they could start their holiday in Barbados with a bit of intimacy the following morning, or at the very least she could lie, her head on his naked chest, and talk about what was troubling him. Clearly neither was going to be an option, she thought, reaching for her watch to check the time. It was 7 a.m. Barbados time, equating to midday in the UK. This surprised Amy as Jack normally wasn't up until noon even when he hadn't been drinking. For a moment she wondered if he was feeling unwell, after all he and Hugo had demolished a bottle of rum between them last evening. Perhaps he was slumped over the toilet in the sumptuous en suite bathroom.

'Jack,' she called, 'are you in there?' There was no reply.

Although early, there was no point lingering in bed, however comfortable, now that she was fully awake. She reached for her thin cotton nightshirt, with a picture of a cow sleeping in a human bed and the words 'dozy moo' on it, a present from Jack last Christmas, and slipped it over her head before padding to the bathroom in her bare feet. Amy had a long hard look at herself in the bathroom mirror as she brushed her teeth. This just isn't right. Jack has made no attempt to have any kind of physical contact with me for months, not even a proper kiss. If he really loved me, she thought, he should want to talk to me about whatever is troubling him.

Amy had first noticed Jack distancing himself from her after he had been back at his dad's house for the Easter holidays. At first she had put it down to nerves and lack of time with the end-of-term exams approaching, and anyway she had been equally as busy, particularly with her part-time jobs in the bookshop and helping out in the university office. But exams had come and gone and things were still the same. We have to talk about the situation, she decided, twisting her long hair into an elastic band and slipping her feet into flip-flops, and the sooner the better.

The photographs of Hugo's parents Barbadian home didn't do it justice, Amy thought, crossing the vast living room with its vaulted ceiling to the door that led to the kitchen. Although anxious to explore, she was hungry and could smell delicious aromas of cooking wafting through the air. As she was about to open the door, Rodney's wife, Jenneen, who was the housekeeper, came bustling out carrying a tray laden with scrambled eggs, streaky bacon and pancakes with syrup.

'Good morning, Miss Amy, I hope you slept well? Are you going to join the young gentlemen on the terrace for your breakfast?'

'Sounds like a good idea,' said Amy, following Jenneen towards the doors that led out on to the terrace. 'Something smells good. I can't believe how hungry I am and it's still so early,' she said holding the door open for the housekeeper.

'Amy, come and join us for breakfast. Did you sleep okay?' Hugo asked.

'Like a log. That bed is sooo comfy,' she replied, following Jenneen across the paved terrace.

'Morning, sleepyhead,' said Jack, pulling out a chair for Amy to sit on and planting a kiss on her cheek.

'It's only just after seven, you know. I couldn't believe it when I woke up and you weren't there. What time did you get up?' she asked, shuffling her chair into the shade being cast by the canopy of the generous stone-coloured parasol, to avoid the bright sunshine which already felt hot on her pale skin.

'Probably about an hour ago. I've been exploring Hugo's private beach,' he said, lifting one sand-covered foot and showering Amy with the gritty powder that reminded her of golden caster sugar.

'Well, it's not really private,' Hugo said. 'Anyone can use it if they have a boat. It's just that Pops owns the land around the beach and the rocks stop people beach-hopping from the next bay.'

'Don't be embarrassed by it, Hugo,' Amy said, piling eggs, bacon and pancakes on to her plate. 'It's unbelievably kind of you to invite us out here to share your parents' place for a few days. Next year you are welcome to share my tent in the Lake District.'

'I thought you said you were never going camping again,' Jack interjected, shovelling a forkful of perfectly cooked eggs into his mouth, 'and I'm not sure I can allow you two to share a tent.'

Amy examined Jack's expression. Perhaps I've been imagining the distance between us, she thought, if he is still thinking of us as an item so far into the future. Amy wasn't sure how she felt about that. Unless things changed drastically between them on an intimate level, there was no way she could see them still being together as a couple.

'You're not jealous are you, Jack?' Amy teased. 'The offer was there for you this year but you declined.'

'Of course I'm not jealous,' Jack retorted, 'it's just I wouldn't want you two...' his voice tailed off. 'Never mind. Forget I said anything.'

Amy and Hugo looked at Jack, who was concentrating on eating his breakfast, and then at each other. Amy raised her eyebrows and Hugo shrugged his shoulders.

'It was only a joke, Jack,' Amy said light-heartedly, trying to defuse the tension in the air.

'Yeah, and I was only joking too, so there's no need to

make a big deal out of it, right?' he answered brusquely.

Amy was acutely aware of Hugo tensing up on the other side of the table. She really wanted to have things out with Jack once and for all, but this was not the time or the place.

'What have you got planned for us today?' she asked Hugo brightly.

'Well, this morning I thought maybe we could go out and see the turtles,' he said. 'Rodney keeps a glass-bottom boat at Mullins Bay. On Tuesdays and Saturdays he takes the tourists out, but the rest of the time he works for us. I'm sure he won't mind bringing the boat and we can go for a ride down the coast to look at all the posh houses and hotels, and then head to the place where the turtles congregate. They're probably the best-fed turtles in the world,' he added, 'the amount of bait the boatmen throw out to attract them for the tourists. While we're out, Jenneen can get one of the gardeners to light the barbecue down on the beach and she'll make us our lunch, if you fancy it?'

'Sounds great to me,' Amy said enthusiastically. Jack just grunted. 'Will there be shade on the beach though? I don't want to be in the sun too long on my first day.'

'Loads. Mother is paranoid about staying out of the midday sun.'

'Will she be joining us for lunch, Hugo?' Amy had only ever seen pictures of Hugo's mum and those had been quite intimidating. The woman looked like a super-model despite her forty-something years.

'Maybe,' Hugo answered uncertainly, 'she doesn't really do food.'

Hence the super-model figure, Amy thought. 'Well, I

think it all sounds brilliant. I can't wait to see the turtles. Are we allowed to swim with them?'

'Of course. Rodney will make you wear a life vest though. Force of habit, I guess. What time shall I ask him to bring the boat? Ten?'

'Perfect,' said Amy, thinking she could make a start on reading her book, while lounging around the pool before their little excursion. 'Is that okay with you, Jack?'

'I'm happy with whatever suits everyone else,' he answered sheepishly.

The motion of the boat bobbing around on the water was starting to make Amy feel a little sea-sick. She had been absolutely fine when *Betsy*, the small wooden vessel that was Rodney's pride and joy, was making its way to its destination, but since they had stopped to see the turtles she was enjoying the trip less and less.

After Rodney had picked them up from the cove beneath Hugo's house, he had steered the boat down the west coast of Barbados, pointing out the stunning holiday retreats of the super-rich, until they had reached Sandy Lane. The hotel looked magnificent from the ocean, hiding behind palm trees and fronting onto a white sand beach that was dotted with luxurious looking sun-loungers, their cushions a vivid blue.

'Looks like paradise, doesn't it?' Hugo said, 'a place where you can come to get away from it all. But look over there,' he said, pointing to one side of the beach.

Amy and Jack had followed the line of his outstretched arm and could see half a dozen bodies, lying prone and fully clothed on the sand, in front of a row of changing huts, heads covered with beach towels from which protruded giant zoom lenses.

'Are they what I think they are?' Amy asked, aghast.

Hugo nodded. 'The paparazzi, the scourge of the famous. Even the wannabe celebrities and reality TV stars soon tire of the paps prying into their every move.'

'I guess it's a case of be careful what you wish for,' Jack said.

'Well, there's no denying that some actors and musicians court publicity, but surely they're entitled to a private life out of the public glare?'

'The trouble is, Amy,' Hugo said, 'when people are starting out, they need to be seen going to parties and awards ceremonies, so they want to be photographed. Then, when they're famous, they don't want the intrusion. It's a bit like selling your soul to the devil. Once you've sold it you can't retrieve it.'

'I don't think I'd like to be famous,' Amy concluded.

'Me neither,' confirmed Jack.

From Sandy Lane, Rodney steered *Betsy* out into slightly deeper water to go in search of turtles. The water changed colour from turquoise to royal as the depth of it increased but it was still clear enough to see the sandy bottom and the coral formations. Rodney avoided the clusters of tourist boats, all vying to attract the turtles, and headed back up the coast, periodically tossing fish heads over the side of the boat. Suddenly, he cut the engines, and started to fold back the wooden flooring of the boat to reveal a glass panel, with an underwater view. It had an inch of water sloshing around on it,

'Is that normal?' Amy whispered to Hugo. 'We're not sinking are we?'

Rodney had obviously overheard her concerns. 'Don't you worry miss, *Betsy* here is as seaworthy as they come. You just keep your eyes on the glass, the turtles are coming.'

And come they had. Half a dozen or more, swimming back and forth beneath the boat, putting on quite a performance. The three of them donned their life jackets and slid over the side of the boat to join them in the water. Amy stayed in for fifteen minutes or so, but got nervous after she thought she saw a shark's fin. The boys insisted she had imagined it.

Her breakfast was perilously close to making a reappearance when the boys finally clambered up the small steps at the back of the boat and Rodney headed her back towards the shore.

As Hugo's house came into view, Amy couldn't help thinking that there was a certain familiarity about it. None of the photos Hugo had shown her were taken from the ocean so she hadn't seen it from this angle before, perched on the top of small cliffs above a perfect horseshoe-shaped bay.

'Can you guys keep a secret?' Hugo asked.

'Of course,' Jack and Amy chorused together.

'Does this house look familiar to either of you?'

Jack shook his head but Amy said, 'I was just thinking that. Why do you ask?'

'This is one of the judge's houses on the *X Factor*,' Hugo said, looking smug.

'So don't your parents own it then? Do they just rent it for holidays?' Jack asked, somewhat confused.

'No, it is ours, but we rent it out to film and television companies when we're not here. It's not like Pops needs the money but I think he just likes to show it off.'

'Yes, of course,' Amy said. 'Now I realise where I've seen it before. Doesn't that judge own a home here then?'

'He does, but it's further up the coast and I don't think it's big enough to house all the contestants on the show. That's the difference between old money and new money, I suppose. Pops bought this nearly forty years ago when he received his inheritance on turning twenty-one. It's probably worth twenty times what he paid for it.'

'Shrewd move,' said Jack. 'Will you get an inheritance at twenty-one?'

'Yes,' said Hugo, 'but it won't go very far in today's world. Not that I'm complaining of course,' he added quickly.

'I'll know where to come for a loan then,' Jack said good-naturedly.

'We're friends, mate. If you needed help, of course I would be there for you. That goes for both of you and Harry too,' he added, turning to include Amy.

'You're a truly lovely person, Hugo,' Amy said, giving her friend a big hug. 'Have you heard yet whether Harry's going to be able to come out and join us?'

'Not yet, but he sounded quite hopeful in his last text message. I hope he can make it,' Hugo said.

'Me too,' said Amy.

'And me,' added Jack, turning away from his two friends and adding under his breath, 'at least that might soften the blow.'

CHAPTER 29

Harry had arrived back from Wales very late on Friday night and had fallen into bed physically and emotionally exhausted. He was only just getting up at midday on Saturday when there was a knock on the front door. Harry pulled his jeans on over his sleep shorts and grabbed a clean T shirt, then hurtled down the stairs calling out, 'I'm coming.'

Philippe had arrived in Reading just after lunch on Friday afternoon. He had parked his car virtually opposite the address he had found in the last copy of *Tiffany* that he was supposed to have signed in Jo's office. He had waited in his car patiently for several hours hoping that someone would either arrive or leave home, but not a soul crossed the threshold. At dusk, no lights were turned on inside the house, so Philippe concluded that there was probably no one home and headed off to the Holiday Inn, where he had booked himself a room for the night.

The parking space Philippe had occupied for seven hours the previous day was taken when he arrived back on

Town Street at 8 a.m. on Saturday morning to continue his vigil. He parked further along the street but had a decent view of the front door, painted pillar-box red, from his vantage point. After a further four hours of waiting and watching with nothing to show for it, Philippe realised that he couldn't stay there for ever. He was only acting on a hunch. This Holly, who coincidentally happened to live in Reading, may not be 'his' Holly. It still didn't look as though there was anyone home but, just to satisfy his curiosity, Philippe decided to take his courage in both hands and knock on the front door. What's the worst that can happen? he reasoned. Most likely there is no one home, but if there is, and it's not her, I can make an excuse that I'm on the wrong street, he thought.

Philippe lifted the door-knocker and rapped sharply three times. There was no response. He was just about to head back to his car when he heard a muffled voice call out, 'I'm coming.' The voice was male. That was a situation Philippe hadn't considered. What if this is 'my' Holly's house? he thought. What if the voice belongs to her new boyfriend? Before he could even contemplate a course of action, the key turned in the lock and the door was flung open. Standing there was a tall blond man that Philippe judged to be no more than twenty, and who had the ruffled look of someone who had just got out of bed. I must be at the wrong house, he thought, there is no way that this could be Holly's new boyfriend.

'Can I help you?'

'Erm, I was looking for Holly,' Philippe said.

'I'm sorry, she's not here. Is there anything I can help with?' Harry asked.

'Not really. Will she be back soon?'

'Not until next Saturday, I'm afraid but, if it's anything urgent, I can get a message to her,' Harry offered.

Philippe had a sinking feeling. He had been so certain, when he had seen the address written on the slip of paper the day before, that this was going to be 'his' Holly. He'd primed himself with what he was going to say when she opened the front door to stop her slamming it in his face before he'd had time to explain things. He was beyond disappointed to have his hopes dashed.

'So, do you want me to give Mum a message?' Harry pressed. 'Who shall I say called?'

Philippe was now sure that he had made a mistake. His Holly didn't have any children. He might as well leave his name, after all it wouldn't mean anything to the wrong Holly and he didn't want this young man thinking that he was a burglar casing the joint and reporting him to the police, particularly if he was alert enough to make a note of his number plate as he drove off.

'Just say Philippe called, would you?' he said, turning to leave.

'Philippe?' Harry said, shock evident in his voice. 'But you're not French.'

The older man stopped in his tracks and turned back to face Harry. 'What did you say?' he questioned, looking into Harry's eyes which had now turned positively hostile.

'I said, you're not French,' replied Harry.

'French mother, English father, hence the name but the lack of accent. Why are you glaring at me?'

'I think you had better come inside,' said Harry.

Philippe could feel the animosity directed towards him but he couldn't understand why. Who was this angry young man and who does he think I am? wondered

Philippe. He hesitated. 'Well if I'm being invited into your house, I should at least know your name.'

'I'm Harry. Holly is my mum,' Harry responded, his eyes still dark with anger, 'and you hurt her.'

'I think there has been some kind of misunderstanding,' Philippe said, his face a portrait of confusion. 'I am looking for someone called Holly, but she doesn't have any children, although weirdly I think she has a new boyfriend called Harry, at least that's what Robert told me.'

'Robert who?' questioned Harry.

'My friend, Robert Forrester.'

'You really do need to come inside so that we can sort this out,' Harry said. 'Don't worry, I'm not going to kill you, although believe me I have considered it, metaphorically speaking, several times over the past few months. You've got a lot of explaining to do, and one hell of a nerve coming here.'

Philippe was still not sure what was going on but, reluctantly, he followed Harry into the house.

Harry pushed open the door to the small living room, where he had left Philippe a few minutes earlier, his hands carrying two mugs of black coffee, which he set down on the coffee table in front of the wary-looking man. In the time it had taken the kettle to boil, Harry had tried to assess the situation. Knowing Robert's remarkable inability to keep a secret, Harry suspected that there had been a slip of the tongue that Robert had try to cover up, which had resulted in the ridiculous misinformation that Holly was seeing someone called Harry. But why on earth would he give Philippe our address? Harry thought.

For a few moments neither man spoke, then Philippe asked the inevitable question, 'So I take it you know Robert Forrester?'

'Yes. He's a friend of Mum's, and mine too now. She met him and his wife, Rosemary when she visited Mauritius a few months ago, which is where you met her I believe?'

'That's right. Rosemary and Robert introduced us and we— we fell in love,' replied Philippe. 'But I didn't know she had a grown-up son. Why would she keep something like that from me?' he asked, a hurt expression clouding his light green eyes.

'She was in Mauritius working and she needed to keep her real identity secret, which meant telling a few lies. Does it make a difference now that you know about me?'

'Well, it's all a bit irrelevant at the moment really. She broke things off with me because she thought I was unfaithful to her.'

'And were you?' asked Harry, clenching his fists in preparation for the answer.

'Apparently not, although I'm not proud to admit that I was so drunk that even I thought I had betrayed Holly's trust.'

'So why didn't you just tell her the truth?'

'Because she wouldn't allow me to contact her. I only had her email address and she blocked me. I didn't even know her surname, only that she lived in Reading.'

'What I don't understand is why Robert gave you this address after telling you she was seeing someone else.'

'He didn't,' Philippe said.

'Then how did you find us? Surely it must be virtually impossible to trace someone when all you have to go on is a first name and a city?

'It was all a bit of a fluke. You see, I'm a writer and I'd done a book signing in Bath. We ran out of books on the day, so the girl in the shop suggested we made a list of people who had missed out and send them signed books in the post. The last book was requested for someone called Holly, who lives in Reading, but I think it may have been requested by the girl in the shop because I would have remembered meeting someone called Holly.'

'Was the shop called Chapters, by any chance?'

'Yes it was,' said Philippe, 'do you know it?'

'I do, and I'm also guessing the girl who helped you out was called Amy.'

'That's right. A really pretty girl and bright as a button.'

'This just gets weirder and weirder. Amy is one of my best friends. We're both students at Bath University.' Harry was racking his brains to try and remember if his mum had told him what sort of books Philippe wrote. He had an idea it was something to do with travelling, but those sort of books wouldn't normally have a huge demand. 'What's your last name,' Harry asked, 'maybe I've read something you've written?'

'I doubt it. My audience is predominantly female, and anyway I write under the pseudonym of Veronica Phillips.'

The name rang a bell with Harry. Wasn't that the author Amy had been talking about the day she had helped him with his search for Gareth? He remembered her commenting that his book was quite raunchy. What sort of a man had his mum fallen in love with? he wondered. And what was Amy thinking of buying his mum a book like that? Unless... What if his mum had confided in

Amy about her holiday romance and this was her way of trying to get them back together? Lovely as she was, Amy did have a habit of meddling in other people's business, always in search of a happy ending like in the books she read. He would have to speak to her about it in Barbados.

'So, now I know how you found my mum but, what I really want to know is, why were you looking for her?' Harry said, narrowing his eyes. 'Don't you think you've hurt her enough already?'

'That was never my intention, Harry. True, I have a bit of a bad-boy reputation with women but that was before I met your mum. I knew the minute I set eyes on her that this was someone I could spend the rest of my life with. I genuinely don't know the real reason she broke up with me. Do you?'

Harry was observing Philippe closely. The anguished expression on his face could have been put on for Harry's benefit, but what would be the point? He's gone to the trouble of tracking Mum down and risked a bloody nose from me, now that I know who he is, he thought. Harry wasn't prepared to reveal that he had no clue as to what lay behind his mum's actions, but he did know that Holly had been devastated about something Philippe had done. Or had she only thought he had done something, and over-reacted?

'That's not for me to say,' Harry replied, 'but I do think that maybe you two should at least meet up to try and sort things out.' He paused. 'You see, there's more than just you two to consider.'

'You're right, Harry. This has obviously had quite an impact on you.'

More than you could ever imagine, Harry thought.

'I'm not talking about me,' he said. 'Mum is pregnant with your baby.'

CHAPTER 30

Philippe unlocked the door to his rented house in Battersea, dropped the keys on the table in the hallway and hung his battered old leather jacket on the coat hook. When he had arrived back from Mauritius two months previously he hadn't the heart to evict his mate Jason from his Pimlico flat, but he didn't want to share with him either.

Jo had come to the rescue – again. A friend of hers had recently married but didn't want to give up her house in case things didn't work out. It had suited Philippe. He was getting the house for half the market value rent, on the understanding that he would vacate at a moment's notice. Jo had been pleased too. It was less than half a mile from her riverside apartment in Chelsea and she had joked that she would be able to keep an eye on him and make sure he didn't get into any more scrapes.

As he crossed the living room, the heels of his leather shoes loud and echoey on the polished oak floorboards, he noticed the light on his answer machine was blinking. He hit the play button, then continued on his way to the drinks cupboard. He needed a drink. It had been a hell of a day.

Jo's voice filled the room.

'Why is your mobile off, Phil? I've been trying to call you all day. Please don't tell me you've gone AWOL again. Ring me back as soon as you get this message – I've got some exciting news.'

You've got some exciting news, thought Philippe. For once I'll bet you can't top mine, he thought, knocking back his first scotch and immediately pouring another before slumping into the unforgiving, hessian-covered sofa and reaching for the phone. Jo picked up on the second ring.

'Where have you been, Phil?' she demanded. 'I've been trying to reach you since yesterday evening. You're not drinking are you?'

'Drinking yes, drunk no,' replied Philippe. 'What's this exciting news?'

'Tell me where you've been first.'

'Not that there is any reason I should tell you, because you're not my keeper, but I've been in Reading.'

'Reading? Why Reading? Hang on a minute. Isn't that where your Holly lives? Don't tell me you've found her?'

'Actually I have, although I've yet to meet up with her again. You'll never believe it, Jo,' Philippe said, unable to stop himself, 'she's pregnant. I'm going to be a dad.'

There was silence on the other end of the line.

'Jo,' Philippe said. 'Are you still there?'

'Yes. I'm still here. I hate to ask, but are you sure it's yours?'

'Yes, I'm sure,' Philippe said, a prickle of irritation creeping into his voice. 'Why do you have to bloody spoil everything?'

'I'm just looking out for you, Phil. Now that you're going to be filthy rich I don't want some woman fleecing you for maintenance. Did she tell you on the phone? You said you haven't met up with her yet. Why not? Maybe she's not pregnant at all and she's going to claim she lost the baby after you've paid up.'

'Oh my God, Jo! Listen to yourself. You are such a cynic. I wanted to share the happiest news of my life with someone and I mistakenly chose you. Why can't you just be happy for me? You know how hard I've fallen for Holly and now maybe, just maybe, she'll give me a second chance because of the baby.'

'I'm sorry, Phil,' Jo said, rapidly trying to backtrack, 'I'm only—'

'Save it, Jo. I can't bear to hear another word out of your vicious mouth tonight.' He pressed the end call button. He finished the whisky in his crystal tumbler and then threw it against the cast-iron back plate of the fireplace, where it shattered into a thousand tiny splinters. 'And she can bloody pay for that,' he fumed.

CHAPTER 31

I've really done it this time, thought Jo, looking at the disconnected handset. What is wrong with me? Why couldn't I just be pleased for him? Not only has he found the love of his life, she's going to make him a dad. A tear squeezed out of the corner of Jo's eye, then another, and another. Before it could turn into a downpour, she took a tissue from the box and blew her nose. Any residual hope that she and Philippe could ever be happy together had been extinguished once and for all.

She reached over to the clear Perspex occasional table to place the phone back in its cradle and her attention was caught by the business card from Chapters bookshop that was lying abandoned next to it. She had been toying with the idea of giving Geoff a call. She punched in his number and was about to give up on the tenth ring when Geoff finally answered.

'Hello,' he said sleepily.

Jo checked the time. It was only 10 p.m. on a Saturday night. Clearly Geoff had a very active social life.

'Hi Geoff, it's Jo, from Ripped Publishing. I wondered if you'd like to take me to lunch tomorrow?'

Ten minutes later, with her date arranged for the next day, Jo contemplated trying to ring Philippe back to tell him that he was number 1 in the fiction charts. She decided it could wait until Monday.

CHAPTER 32

After the excitement of the previous evening, Holly had overslept, only just managing to get to the restaurant in time for breakfast. Like most of the other guests, she was bleary-eyed as a result of the disrupted sleep they had all had. At 3 a.m., the hotel fire alarm had sounded and everyone had left the comfort of their respective, air-conditioned bedrooms to congregate in the Cane Hill hotel's small reception area which, even in the early hours of the morning, was oppressively warm. Some of the guests were expressing concern that the temperature was as a result of the hotel being on fire but Holly was not alarmed. Before leaving her room, she had looked out of her window to the hillside across the gulley and could see a bright orange glow illuminating the sky, with an occasional shower of sparks that reminded her of fireworks on Bonfire Night back home. She was pretty sure they had been summoned to the reception area as a precaution, in case they needed to be evacuated in a hurry, if the wind picked up and blew the fire in their direction. Just to be on the safe side, and contrary to the instructions on the card stuck on the back of her door, which said to leave all possessions in your room if the fire alarm sounded, Holly had quickly grabbed her phone, laptop, passport and keys. If everything else was burnt to a crisp she would at least be able to let Harry know she was safe, write her Liberty Sands blog and be allowed back into the UK.

It had been an uncomfortable couple of hours with too few seats for the number of guests that were crammed into a comparatively small space. Holly was thankful that her pregnancy was now quite obvious so she was offered a seat without needing to ask. The hotel staff were very attentive, providing drinks from the bar at no charge but, as always, there were still some people moaning about not being allowed back to their rooms earlier. The funny thing is, thought Holly, they would be the first to complain if the hotel hadn't taken the action of bringing all the guests together for a safe evacuation. What a shame, she thought, if last night's experience put some of the guests off from returning to this idyllic spot.

The Cane Hill was a boutique hotel located at the top of a hill half a mile inland from Speightstown on the north-west coast of Barbados. Although the area wasn't as popular as St James, where a lot of the prestigious hotels were located, Holly liked the less pretentious surroundings. So far, she only had one complaint, the distance from the airport, and there was obviously nothing the hotel could do about that.

She had arrived at Cane Hill three days earlier after a tedious journey in the hotel's mini-bus from Grantley Adams International airport in the south-east of the island. Her flight had landed in the middle of the afternoon so, by the time she and the six other guests who were booked at the same hotel had retrieved their luggage, they hit some of the rush-hour traffic. It had taken two hours to complete their journey and some of the roads left a bit to be desired, with pot-holes a foot across and almost as deep. The check-in had been very efficient though, which meant she had time for a refreshing shower before enjoying the sunset from the privacy of her balcony. Holly's room was described in Soleil's brochure as having a partial sea view, but the actuality exceeded her expectations, with a perfect V shape between the trees acting as a frame for the remnants of the sun as it dipped over the horizon.

Dinner on Holly's first evening had been booked for her at 7 p.m., which was usual for guests arriving from the UK. It was presumed they would be tired after a long flight and also took into consideration the five-hour time difference. The hotel could accommodate sixty guests, but the restaurant was small so dinner had to be served in two sittings, 7 p.m. and 8.30 p.m. Holly decided it was a good trade off to maintain the intimacy of the dining experience. Her table was near the front of the balcony with a view over the pool area where, according to the itinerary she had read while relaxing on her balcony, the staff would set up a Caribbean-style barbecue on two evenings during her week-long stay. Holly was keen to try some of the local dishes she had read about, but on her first evening she stuck with macaroni pie, similar to the macaroni cheese she had often made for herself and Harry when money was really tight, served with steamed locally grown vegetables tossed in garlic butter.

Breakfast in the restaurant wasn't organised into two sittings. Guests could come and go at a time to suit them and so far Holly hadn't noticed it causing an issue with queues, although latecomers were less likely to get the tables near the front. On her first morning, Holly had woken early and been treated to the spectacle of the famed green monkeys playing in the trees and jumping on to the roofs of the bungalows situated in the extensive gardens away from the main hotel building, which were apparently very popular with honeymooners.

The first two days of her stay Holly hadn't ventured out of the hotel. She sat by the pool, or in the shade of the palm trees in the gardens, and chatted to guests to try and ascertain their satisfaction levels but on her third day, the morning after the fire, she had planned to go to Bridgetown for a look around. One of the couples she had arrived with, Rachel and Jacob Kramer, who had visited the island on many previous occasions, had told her that it was a really easy journey on the bus and only cost two Barbados dollars. If only I wasn't feeling so shattered, thought Holly, draining her glass of pineapple juice and checking her watch. The complimentary mini-bus service down to Speightstown, from where she would get the bus into Bridgetown, was leaving in ten minutes. Decision time. Shall I go or shall I stay? she thought.

Holly was pleased that she had summoned up the energy to leave the confines of the hotel. Although it was undoubtedly luxurious and catered for her every need, she felt it helped to add colour to her Liberty Sands blogs when she ventured out into the local community and could give recommendations on what and what not to do. The following day she was booked to go on a glass-bottom boat trip in the morning, then Tuesday and Wednesday she had booked a hire car and was planning to visit the dramatic Atlantic coast, apparently very different from the more developed, tranquil west coast. Holly wasn't always confident driving in foreign countries but at least in Barbados they drove on the same side of the road as the UK, so that was one less thing to worry about on unfamiliar roads.

Speightstown was small and quite basic as a shopping centre, with just a few shops selling food, clothing and inexpensive souvenirs. Holly had been dropped off opposite the bus station to wait for a bus to take her to the island's capital city. The Kramers had told her there were two different types of bus she could choose from. The big blue single decker buses were operated by the government and were just like regular buses back home. You paid the driver on entry and they gave no change so you needed to have the correct money. The yellow buses were independently operated and were much smaller, but had both a driver and a fare collector. Rachel had told Holly that the latter were also known locally as 'boogie' buses because the drivers had reggae music playing loudly throughout the journey, but she had also warned her that some of the drivers were a little reckless. Despite the warning, Holly decided she would experience both by trying a different one in each direction and that she would get on whichever came first, which just happened to be a 'boogie' bus. She climbed aboard and settled herself in a seat next to an open window, hoping to benefit from a cooling breeze once the bus set off.

This is definitely not one of the reckless drivers, Holly thought, as the bus meandered along the road at a snail's pace, with the conductor, dressed in a T-shirt and jeans, standing on the step of the open doorway. Every few hundred yards the bus stopped and the conductor would hustle the people at the bus stops to ride with them. The bus, which had left Speightstown with only a handful of people on it, was beginning to get quite crowded and, as the bus filled up, the level of noise increased with people trying to talk over the volume of the music. Everyone seems so happy, Holly thought. When she occasionally travelled on buses or tube trains in London people seemed wrapped up in their own little world. They didn't speak to their fellow passengers, usually because they had earphones in their ears to listen to music or merely to isolate themselves from having to strike up a conversation, and most looked stressed and tired. Here everyone seemed so vibrant and full of energy.

The slow pace of the bus had given Holly the opportunity to really examine her surroundings. A lot of the houses that lined the main road were made from weatherboard and painted various shades of pastel and bright colours but, every now and then, the bus passed developments of new houses built in concrete in a pseudo-colonial style. Holly wondered if these developments were aimed at locals or overseas investors looking for holiday homes. How fabulous to be able to afford to come somewhere like this on a regular basis, she thought.

The bus was picking up speed and the conductor was no longer standing on the step but was now inside collecting fares. He squeezed himself between the people who were forced to stand due to lack of seats, stuffing notes into the back pocket of his jeans and sourcing change from the bum bag he had loosely fastened around his waist.

Clearly, once the bus was at capacity, it was in the best interest of the driver to get his vehicle to Bridgetown in the shortest time possible so that they could make their return journey. Although the bus was now hurtling along at an alarming speed, Holly comforted herself with the thought that the locals wouldn't travel this way if it was truly dangerous.

The bus stopped several times en route to Bridgetown to allow people to get off, particularly around the swish shopping area in St James, where Holly could see shops advertising Prada, Gucci and Armani. The bus also passed the Chattel House Village. It was a collection of shops that had been set up in modernised traditional chattel houses to cater for tourists. Holly was tempted to get off the bus for a look around. It was just the sort of thing that may appeal to holidaymakers, and her blog readers, however she stuck to her original decision to visit Bridgetown.

Two hours later, Holly climbed aboard a blue bus for her return journey and once again found herself a seat next to an open window. She had thought about staying in Bridgetown for lunch but as she was all inclusive at the Cane Hill hotel it seemed like an extravagance she could ill afford. She had enjoyed having a look around Bridgetown but it was hot and with the extra weight she was now carrying, Holly's ankles were beginning to swell. As more people piled on to the bus, Holly moved her bag from the seat at her side on to her lap and reached inside to put her purse back in the zip compartment, to keep it safe.

'Is this seat free?' a female voice asked.

'Yes, help yourself,' Holly said, looking up. She gasped with surprise. 'What on earth are you doing here?'

Amy, who was about to take her place at Holly's side, looked equally astonished. 'I could ask you the same thing. Where's Harry?' she asked, looking around. 'He didn't say he was bringing you too. In fact he didn't actually confirm that he was coming. What a lovely surprise. Have you just got here?'

Holly was puzzled. What was Harry's friend, Amy, doing on a bus in Barbados and why did she seem to think Harry was there with her? 'No, I arrived three days ago, and I'm on my own. Why would you think Harry was with me?'

It was Amy's turn to look confused. 'Hugo invited all us flatmates to come out and stay at his parents' house with him but Harry was out in LA so he wasn't sure he could make it. Jack and I arrived on Thursday too, it's amazing we didn't bump into each other at the airport. Where did you fly from?'

'Gatwick. Heathrow is actually easier for me but this was a last-minute work trip so I had to take what I could,' said Holly, feeling disappointed that Harry hadn't mentioned anything to her.

'Oh yes, your secret missions,' Amy said smiling. 'Don't worry, Harry hasn't spilled the beans. None of us are any the wiser about your second job, despite Jack and Hugo constantly prying. I just think it's brilliant that you get to go globetrotting every few weeks. I know Harry has kept your secret but I'm amazed he didn't tell you we were all going to be out here. He did know you would be here at the same time, didn't he?'

A lot of Harry's actions had been quite out of character

lately, Holly thought. Ever since he had found out about her pregnancy, her usually reliable son had been behaving strangely. Wanting to know about his biological father had been quite a predictable reaction, but swanning off to LA on a project for Robert, when he had more or less promised to accompany Holly to her first doctor's appointment, was not the sort of thoughtless behaviour she expected from her son.

'Perhaps he has committed to something else for Robert and didn't want to disappoint me by telling me he could have been out here,' she said, trying to sound convincing.

Amy looked dubious. 'Well he could have told you I was going to be here,' she said. 'He knows we get on really well and, to be honest, I could have done with some company. Hugo and Jack keep organising boys' things to do and leaving me on my own at the house. Not that I'm complaining,' she added, 'the house is absolutely amazing. It's right on the beach and the swimming pool has a fountain at one end and a Jacuzzi at the other. I know,' she said, 'why don't you stop and have lunch with me? They're playing golf today, not that Jack has ever played anything other than pitch and putt before, so Sandy Lane is going to be totally wasted on him. They won't be back until late afternoon and although Hugo's mum is really pleasant, we don't have much in common so conversation is kind of non-existent. Please say you will, Holly. The housekeeper makes really delicious food,' she added persuasively.

Holly looked at Amy's pleading face. She didn't want to refuse and it would be amazing to have a look inside one of the extravagant beachfront properties, but she was pretty sure Harry wouldn't have told his friends about the baby. That must be why he didn't tell her that we would be in Barbados at the same time, she thought. He's probably embarrassed that his mum is pregnant and boyfriendless.

'I'd love to Amy—'

Before Holly could finish, Amy quickly said, 'Thank you, Holly. It will be so good to have someone I can really talk to.'

There was no way Holly could back out now, not that she really wanted to, but she wondered how she was going to explain her baby bump which so far had been hidden beneath the bag on her lap.

Amy had clearly not had much conversation in the past few days. She chattered non-stop, pointing out interesting landmarks as the bus trundled along.

'Up there is The Cliff restaurant,' she said, as the bus approached Payne's Bay, 'and that is the Cubana Monument,' she said indicating a tall narrow pyramid. 'It's a memorial to all the people who died in the plane crash off the coast in 1976. It was a terrorist attack, I think, and some of those who died were children.'

As if to acknowledge the tragedy, Holly's baby gave a little kick.

'It's made of coral, just like the island itself. Did you know that this is one of the only Caribbean islands where you can drink water from the tap? The water gets filtered through the coral so it's really pure. Apparently, all the visiting cruise ships fill up their water reserves here.'

'Did Hugo's mum tell you all this?' Holly asked.

'You're joking. All she wants to talk about is designer shoes, handbags and the latest fad diet. How Hugo has turned out to be such a kind and considerate person when you look at his mum and dad is beyond me. Unlike Harry. I know why he is so lovely, it's because he has you for a mum.'

Holly blushed. 'Well, I've made a few mistakes along the way but I've done my best to give him a happy upbringing.'

'He's very lucky to have you for a mum and rest assured he knows it. Come on,' Amy said, grabbing Holly's arm, 'that was Pamela. We're off at Mandy.'

'What?' asked Holly.

'The bus stops. Hadn't you noticed? They all have girls' names.'

CHAPTER 33

Harry yawned. Motorway driving was always tiring but the Sunday morning sunshine on the M25 was creating mirages, making it appear as though Toby was about to splash into a river. It didn't help that the old Vauxhall Corsa had no air conditioning and, even with the window open, Harry was struggling to keep his eyes open. The warning signs, periodically placed at the side of the motorway, saying, 'Tiredness kills, take a break' were spot on, but Harry was almost at junction 6 and he had told Robert 12.30 for lunch. The problem is my body clock is still not back to normal, he thought, and it's about to be disrupted again with the flight to Barbados tomorrow. After the events of the past week there was a fair bit of explaining to do.

It had been a conscious decision to tell Philippe about the baby, in part to gauge his reaction but also because Harry truly believed that he had a right to know. Having met his own father just a few hours previously, Harry was in a fairly emotional state when Philippe had arrived on the doorstep in Reading. To his twenty-year-old mind there was no reason not to tell Philippe that his mother was pregnant. He wanted his sibling to at least have a chance of a normal upbringing, even if things didn't work out in the end.

Harry had expected the shock that Philippe initially exhibited but what had been more surprising and, he had to admit, pleasing, was the subsequent reaction of joy and excitement. He had even slapped Harry on the shoulder, proclaiming, 'I'm going to be a dad!' Once he had come down off cloud nine though, he asked the obvious question. 'Why didn't she tell me? Was she ever going to tell me?'

Harry had no answer. He knew his mum was going to be furious with him for telling Philippe about the baby, but he hadn't deliberately sought out the Frenchman to impart the news. It was clear that Philippe was still very much in love with Holly and had gone to great lengths to find her. He genuinely doesn't seem to know what has caused the break-up between them, thought Harry, but seems prepared to accept most, if not all the responsibility for it.

Harry had wanted to dislike the man who had broken his mum's heart, but had found himself empathising with him. Their situations were totally different, but Holly had kept secrets from both of them, and now those secrets were out in the open and had to be faced. Harry knew that his mum must have her reasons for the decisions she made, but he couldn't help feeling that they were sometimes coloured by the isolation she had experienced as a child, growing up with an unloving, alcoholic mother. He had always known that his grandmother had wanted nothing to do with them, but he had been shocked to the core when Gareth had revealed that she had lied to him, telling him that Holly had died in the crash with her father. And there had been absolutely no mention of her having a baby.

Harry feared that there was too much water under the bridge for his mum and real dad to get back together, although he had promised Gareth that he would take Holly to Wales to be reacquainted, but he wanted things to work out for his mum and Philippe. He wanted her to have a loving partner and a father for the new baby. She deserves to know what it feels like to be part of a happy, normal family, if such a thing exists, Harry concluded.

As usual, Robert had been at the front door before Harry had even turned off his engine. Over a proper roast lunch, with pale pink beef and fluffy Yorkshire puddings, Robert listened as Harry recounted his activities of the previous week. At times Robert interjected with a question, but mostly he just listened. He was delighted to hear that, although not a total recovery, Gareth could now walk again unaided for small distances.

'I would like to meet your dad, Harry. It is okay to call him that?'

Harry nodded, smiling, pouring some more rich brown gravy over his remaining roast potatoes, and mashing them together with the back of his fork before scooping the mush into his mouth. It was the first proper meal he had eaten since his last evening in LA. You couldn't really count aircraft meals.

'You know, I never thought I would be able to accept the person who abandoned us so easily but it wasn't his fault and he did try to find Mum once his memory had started to return. He's really nice, Robert. When I get back from Barbados I'm going to spend a week in Wales if that's okay with you?'

'Of course it is, although you will have to do a bit of work on the drawings for the Philmore while you're there. I was going to wait to tell you until you'd finished all your news but, they've green-lighted the renovation with a couple of amendments. I've been working on a costing for them.'

'Really?' said Harry, dropping his fork on to his empty plate. 'That is so cool. I really can't believe how quickly my life has changed in the space of seven days and I haven't even told you about Philippe yet.'

'What about Philippe?' asked Robert, concern flashing across his face.

'He showed up at our house in Reading yesterday.'

'What? I didn't tell him your address, I swear.'

'I know, I know. Don't panic, I wasn't about to accuse you of it.'

'Then how did he find you?'

'Pure chance. He'd been made to do a book signing at my friend Amy's bookshop in Bath, would you believe. She knows Mum liked his first book so she arranged for a signed copy of the new book to be sent to her. Philippe saw the name and the town and just turned up in the hope that it might be his Holly. Maybe it's fate; perhaps the two of them are meant to be together.'

'How do you feel about that?'

'I just want Mum to be happy and if they can iron out their problems, I really think they have a chance. He told me about your blunder, by the way.'

Robert looked embarrassed. 'I'm a terrible liar,' he said.

'Your name just slipped out so I had to try and explain you, somehow.'

'I'm glad you are a terrible liar, Robert,' Harry said laughing, 'at least I'll know if you don't like any of my designs.'

'Honesty is always the best policy, I think. Which brings me to the crunch question: did you tell Philippe about the baby?'

'Actually, Robert, I did, and it's because of something you said. You said that every child should know its father, and I believe you're right.'

'So what happens next, Harry?'

'Well, I spoke to my friend Hugo and asked if it was okay for me to bring a friend with me to Barbados tomorrow. He said yes, because he thinks it's a girlfriend. He and Jack are always nagging me to get a girlfriend.'

'Do you think that's a good idea, Harry?'

'Honestly? I don't know. But I'm hoping that when Mum sees Philippe in an exotic location, not dissimilar to Mauritius, it might just rekindle their romance.'

While they had been enjoying their lunch, there had been a sudden downpour of rain but it had stopped and the sunshine was out again forming a vivid rainbow.

Under his breath Robert said, 'I hope you're right, Rosie, I hope you're right.'

CHAPTER 34

The loose-fitting kaftan was doing a good job of disguising Holly's baby bump but nevertheless she held her bag in the crook of her arm to provide a bit more coverage, rather than hoisting it on to her shoulder in the normal way, as she followed Amy down a narrow path between two stone walls.

'I prefer coming in this way,' Amy said, stopping in front of an arched wooden gate and pressing the code into a keypad. 'The front entrance is very grand and spectacular but you have to wait for Rodney or one of the gardeners to open the gates from the inside. I don't like to drag them away from whatever work they are doing just to let me in.'

What a considerate girl she is, thought Holly, as Amy pushed open the gate. She had always had a soft spot for Amy, particularly as they shared a passion for books. Holly caught her breath, 'Oh my God, this is incredible!'

The gate had opened on to a short sandy path between palm trees but now they were at the end of it, the magnificence of the property was apparent. The house, built in a colonial style, stood to the left of them and the gardens, similar in size to the park where Holly had taken Harry to the swings as a young child, surrounded it. Looking back towards the road she could see the sweeping drive and the gates that required opening from inside. There was even a small gate-house. But it was the view spread out in front of them that really took Holly's breath away. The path they were on split, one direction leading to the main entrance of the house and the other snaking down between raised flower beds, filled with exotic bird of paradise flowers and anthuriums in vibrant shades of orange and red, leading eventually to the pool area. Beyond that, Holly could just catch a glimpse of the sandy cove being gently washed by the Caribbean Sea. Her job had taken Holly to some stunning hotels but it was difficult to comprehend that this was someone's home.

'I'll just go and let Jenneen know that there is an extra guest for lunch and then, while she is preparing it, I'll show you around. I'll meet you down by the pool,' Amy said, disappearing in the direction of the house.

Holly strolled down the gentle incline of the path, pausing occasionally to truly appreciate the beauty surrounding her, the intense heat tempered by the breeze from the ocean. The area around the pool was empty apart from the sun-loungers, each equipped with a yellow-and-stone-coloured cushion, the thickness of a mattress, and its own sunshade for the face. She perched on the closest one moments before Amy appeared at the French doors with a curvy lady in her early fifties wearing an apron, who Holly guessed was Jenneen. The woman bustled towards her.

'Nice to meet you my dear, and so pleased you are

going to be company for Amy here. I think she is getting bored with my stories about the island.'

'I'm sure that's not the case,' Holly said, reaching her hand out to shake the one extended to her. 'Amy was most informative on our bus journey from Bridgetown.'

Jenneen chuckled. 'I'll bet she was, she's a fast learner that one. I'm just checking that you are not a fussy eater and are happy with what I have planned for lunch today. There is plenty of fruit and salad, fresh crab and lobster, and also cheese. Maybe you should stay away from the soft cheese though. It's made with unpasteurised milk and not recommended during pregnancy.'

Over Jenneen's shoulder, Holly could see Amy's jaw drop.

'Absolutely. Thanks for the advice and everything else sounds delicious and more than enough for a light lunch.' Holly waited until Jenneen had gone back into the house before speaking, 'So I guess Harry hasn't mentioned that I'm pregnant.'

The moment the words were out of Jenneen's mouth Amy took a proper look at Holly. She was surprised she hadn't noticed her thickened waistline earlier. Maybe I did notice it, she thought, but just assumed she had put on a few pounds because I wouldn't have entertained the idea of her being pregnant. Harry never even mentioned she had a boyfriend, let alone that they were starting a family together. This was totally unexpected.

'No,' Amy said, trying to sound casual, 'he didn't. When is the baby due?'

'Just before Christmas.'

'If it's a girl you could call it Ivy. Do you get it? Holly and Ivy...' Amy's sentence trailed away, 'or maybe Carol?'

Holly shivered, despite the heat of the day. Carol was her estranged mother's name. 'I'm sorry if this is awkward for you, Amy. I'm sure Harry would have told you eventually but this was a bit of a shock for him too, and for me come to that. Shall we walk and talk?'

'Yes,' Amy said, walking over to Holly and linking arms. 'You don't have to tell me anything you don't want to. It's not really any of my business.'

'To be honest, it's nice to have a female friend to share this with. I've never really given priority to building friendships, I've always concentrated on the relationship between Harry and me. I suppose I could have made more of an effort though, to be fair. It's all pretty straightforward. I let my guard down and fell head over heels in love with someone I met on one of my work trips and he didn't feel the same way about me. Well,' she paused, 'he said he did at the time, but I suspect that was just so that I would... you know. I must have got carried away with the romantic setting. I should have been more careful.'

It was clear to Amy that Holly had been totally besotted with the man, and the thought that he had pretended to reciprocate the feeling, just to have sex with her, made Amy's blood boil. Harry had once told her that his mum hadn't had boyfriends while he was growing up so that there wouldn't be a string of men that he would have to call uncle. That selflessness was one of the things that had drawn her to Holly in the first place, that and a shared desire to make Harry happy.

'You can't just blame yourself for this, Holly. There

was someone else involved. What has he had to say for himself?'

Holly looked sheepish. 'He doesn't actually know about the baby.'

Yet. Amy was waiting for Holly to say 'yet', but she didn't. 'You are going to tell him, right?'

Holly shook her head. 'I can't. I found something out, which I don't want to talk about, that removed any possibility of us ever being together, so there is no point telling him about a baby that he is never going to see.'

'Is the bastard married? Oops, sorry, I didn't mean to swear.'

'No, nothing like that. Or should I say not as far as I know. I really didn't know him that well to be sure he was telling me the truth about it, and he was certainly lying about other things. Who knows? It's all irrelevant now. I feel a fool for not taking precautions and getting myself into this predicament, but this baby will have plenty of love, rest assured.'

'Well I'm happy to be Aunty Amy if you'll let me, Holly. And I'll bet Harry is looking forward to having a brother or sister.'

'You know, I thought he was, but now I'm not so sure. Obviously he was a bit shocked at first, which is to be expected, but after promising to be there for us he disappeared on the trip to LA for Robert. If I'm honest, Amy,' Holly said, stopping and looking her in the eyes, 'I get the distinct impression that he feels I've let him down... and maybe he's right.'

'Harry loves you. Even if it takes him a while to get to grips with the situation, he will be there for you. I know it, and I think you do too.'

'I hope you're right, Amy. The last thing I ever wanted to do was drive a wedge between us.'

Lunch had been simple but delicious, after which the girls had retired to the sun-loungers, despite Holly's protestations that she needed to get back to the hotel. Although she had done her best to stay awake, the heat of the day, the comfort of the sun-lounger cushion and the filling lunch exacted a toll on Holly and she was asleep within a few minutes. She woke up with a start thirty minutes later.

'Was I snoring, Amy?' she asked, looking across to where Amy was reclining, deeply engrossed in her book.

'Only ever so slightly,' Amy giggled, 'nothing that would register more than six on the Richter scale!'

'I hope you're teasing me,' Holly said, a blush rising up her cheeks. 'What are you reading?'

'It's the new book from Veronica Phillips. It's called *Tiffany* and mine's a signed copy.' Holly could feel her throat tightening as Amy continued, 'Did you know that Veronica Phillips is actually a man?' Holly could only nod, grateful that the deep blush she was currently enduring could be interpreted by Amy as the embarrassment about snoring. 'He came to the bookshop I work in for a book signing.'

'Philippe was at Chapters?' Holly blurted out, unable to stop herself.

Amy dropped the book down on to her lap and observed Holly. 'Oh, Philippe, is it? You make it sound as though you know him. I take it you saw the reveal in the Sunday papers then?'

'No. I mean yes. Yes, that's it. I saw his name in the Sunday papers. Philippe ... erm, I can't quite remember what his last name is. How did the signing go?' Holly asked, hoping beyond hope that nobody had turned up.

'Unbelievably well. I got the distinct impression that his publisher was hoping it was going to be a flop, but I wasn't having that. Not on my patch. I got on to the local radio station and the papers, tweeted and put a picture of him on Facebook. That must have done it, the picture I mean. He's ever so handsome don't you think?' Amy asked, holding up the book which had a photograph of him on the back cover.

'I can't really see from here, so I'll take your word for it. Actually, Amy, I should be getting back. I'm not sure what time the last courtesy bus leaves Speightstown to go up to the hotel but I don't want to miss it.'

'Okay,' said Amy reluctantly, 'but it's a shame you'll miss the boys, they'll be back soon. I'd offer to lend you my copy of *Tiffany* but then it would spoil the surprise.'

'Surprise?'

'Well, I've kind of spoilt it now so I might as well tell you,' Amy said. 'We ran out of books on the day of the signing, so I suggested making a list of people's names and addresses who had come to the shop so that Philippe could sign them and the publisher could send them out in the post. And guess what?'

Holly was flushing furiously again and her head felt slightly dizzy. Knowing how kind and thoughtful Amy was, she was pretty sure that her name had been slipped on to the list. Don't panic, she thought. He will have been signing books in a hurry and probably didn't even register your name, let alone the fact that the address was in Reading.

'I'm guessing you popped my name on the list,' said Holly, forcing a smile.

'Spot on. It should be waiting for you when you get home,' Amy said, looking pleased with herself. 'You'll be able to take it with you on your next trip abroad, although won't you have to stop doing that pretty soon until after the baby is born?'

'Oh, I've got a couple of months yet,' Holly replied. 'Thank you for thinking of me, Amy, that was such a kind thing to do,' she said, lifting her bag on to her shoulder.

'Do you think we could meet up again tomorrow? I know you're working, but perhaps just for a couple of hours?' Amy said.

'Well, I've booked to go on a glass-bottom boat ride in the morning, but we could meet after that maybe. Won't you be spending some time with Jack?'

'To be honest, I'm not sure what those two will have planned for tomorrow. Where are you taking the trip from and what time are you back? If I'm on my own I'll come and meet you.'

'It leaves Heywoods Beach at 10.30 and drops us at Mullins Bay at noon or thereabouts. If you're there I'll treat you to lunch.'

'Deal,' said Amy, 'although if I'm not waiting for you, don't worry. Maybe Jack will have remembered that he and I are supposed to be on holiday together.'

Holly said goodbye to Amy at the side gate and walked back up the path towards the bus stop, her mind racing. What if Philippe had noticed her name and Reading address? What if he turns up on my doorstep? What if he already had? I need to speak to Harry urgently, she thought. I'll FaceTime him when I get back to the hotel.

But Holly wasn't able to FaceTime Harry. The hotel courtesy bus had a puncture and by the time the driver had changed the wheel and got his frustrated guests back to the Cane Hill hotel it was past 6 p.m., meaning it was gone 11 p.m. in the UK. Even knowing the late hour, Holly tried to reach her son, but he didn't pick up.

CHAPTER 35

The candle sputtered for a final time before extinguishing. Amy glanced at her watch. It was 11 p.m. She had sat through dinner with only Natalia, Hugo's mum, for company, but she had long since retired to her room, leaving Amy to go from worry to anger and back to worry again. Where were Jack and Hugo? Although Amy and Jack had agreed not to use their mobile phones in Barbados unless it was an emergency, due to the cost, she had tried Jack's number repeatedly since around 6 p.m. when she had gone in from the pool to get showered and dressed for dinner. None of her calls had connected. Amy wasn't sure but she thought she could sense something strange in Jenneen's manner as she served dinner, as though she knew something but had been sworn to secrecy. When asked a direct question she merely shrugged her shoulders and confirmed that Rodney was also not home, suggesting that he was chauffeuring the boys.

Dinner had been wasted on Amy and Natalia. They had both pushed the beautifully prepared food around their plates for different reasons. Amy hoped that the remainder of the spread would be given to the staff rather than going to waste. She rose heavily from the wicker chair where she had spent the past four hours and made her way to the luxurious bedroom. A tear rolled down her cheek as she observed the inviting bed, turned down by the maid, and the subtle, almost sensual lighting. There had been a different excuse from Jack each night for not getting intimate, despite Amy's best efforts, wearing her sexiest lingerie and lying provocatively across the bed. Enough was enough, and tonight Amy was determined to confront him and find out once and for all what his issue was. She brushed her teeth, turned out the lights and lay down on the bed, waiting.

At 2 a.m., Amy finally heard the click of the bedroom door opening. A shaft of light from the landing illuminated the room before Jack closed it as silently as he could.

'No need to be quiet, Jack,' Amy said, 'I'm awake. Where the hell have you been? I've been worried to death.'

Jack padded softly across the room and perched on the edge of the bed. 'I'm sorry, Amy, I'm so sorry. We need to talk.'

Amy was fully alert now. Every nerve ending stood to attention. She had expected some lame excuse about being too drunk to talk so Jack had caught her off guard. She reached for the light switch but Jack pulled her arm back. 'Leave it, Amy, I won't be brave enough to say what I need to in the light.'

She could feel her heart thumping against her rib cage. This was serious. 'What is it Jack?'

'Firstly you need to know that I love you,' he said

softly. 'There has never been another girl that has made me feel the way you do. I love every hair on your head, your beautiful blue eyes, the paleness of your skin and softness of your touch. You are the perfect woman, Amy, and I don't deserve you,' Jack's voice cracked as he struggled with his emotions. 'I honestly thought that we would get married, have kids and spend the rest of our lives together.'

Amy's breath was coming in short, shallow gasps. She didn't understand what was happening. He was confessing his undying love for her and yet she knew there was a huge but coming. She waited. Jack seemed to have lost the ability to talk.

'Talk to me, Jack. What are you trying to say?'

'I've been hiding something. I thought if I just shut it away then I could live a happy normal life with you but... I realise now, that's not fair. When I went home at Easter, something happened. I met someone. But it's not what you think.'

'What the hell? You've just told me how much you love me and then you reveal you've been cheating on me with another girl.'

'I didn't say that, Amy. Please listen to me,' Jack said, trying to put his arms around her.

She pushed him away roughly. 'Don't touch me. And I don't want to listen to you either, Jack,' she said, tears welling in her eyes. 'I thought something was wrong, the way you've been avoiding having sex with me for months, but I never imagined that it was because you were getting it somewhere else. Does she know about me?' Amy demanded, her voice rising, 'this... this other woman.'

'Sshh, Amy, you'll wake everyone. I'm trying to tell

you there is no other woman.'

'But you just said—' Amy stopped mid-sentence.

'I said I had met someone. Nothing has happened between us because I'm not sure it's what I want. You are the only girlfriend I've ever had and I love you, but ever since I met Tom I haven't been able to get him out of my mind. I'm so confused, Amy,' he said, burying his face in his hands.

Initially, Amy felt shock. It was one thing to be dumped by your boyfriend for another woman but to be dumped for a man? She was not sure how to feel. She had never had the slightest inkling that Jack might be gay. Was it something she had done? Had she turned him off women?

The silence stretched on in the dark room until finally Amy whispered, 'Does Hugo know?'

'No, just us,' replied Jack, his voice muffled by his hands.

'Where were you tonight?'

'We went to dinner and then a club. I couldn't face another night of you looking so sexy and me not fancying you. I told Hugo I'd texted you. Amy, what's wrong with me? Why can't I just be normal?'

Amy put aside her own feelings of hurt and embarrassment and even anger. The person she had shared her life with for the past eighteen months was in crisis. She had to be strong for him.

'There is no such thing as normal, Jack. There's an expectation that boy meets girl and they live happily ever after but that's not right for everyone. Have you talked to…' she paused, trying to keep her own emotions in check. 'Have you talked to Tom about your attraction towards him?'

'Yes,' he said, in a voice so quiet it was almost impossible to hear.

'And what did he say?' she asked, reaching out to take Jack's hand in a gesture of reassurance.

'He said he'll wait for me to find myself. I'm scared, Amy. And I'm so so sorry that I've done this to you. You are the kindest...'

'Sshh, Jack, this is not about me, it's about you. I'm not inside your head or your heart so I can't feel what you feel. All I know is there should be no place in anyone's life for regret. We'll keep this to ourselves until we get back to England and then we'll split up. I'll find a flat share with some other girls and that will give you some space to decide what you want. But Jack,' she took a deep breath, 'this is it for us. Whatever you decide, we're finished. It could never be the same again for me knowing that maybe you've chosen me out of some out-dated sense of expectation. Every argument, one or other of us would bring it up. I don't want to end up hating you, Jack. You do understand, don't you?'

Jack's shoulders had slumped forward while Amy was speaking. 'I will always love you, Amy.'

'And I will never forget you, Jack.'

CHAPTER 36

Philippe caught the Gatwick Express to the airport. Robert had suggested that he drove to Woldingham, as Harry had, and then he would take them both to the airport on Monday morning, but Philippe couldn't really see the point. It was much quicker for him to get a cab from Battersea to Clapham Junction and then the train.

He spotted Harry standing by the foreign exchange booth immediately. He was amazed at how different he was in looks from his mother. He was also amazed that Holly could have a son of that age. She simply didn't look old enough.

On his journey down, he had wondered at the wisdom of taking Harry up on his idea to surprise Holly in Barbados. He was desperate to see her, of course he was, but he wanted the reunion to have the best possible chance of working. Harry seemed to think that the exotic location would bring back memories of Mauritius and initially he had agreed, but now he was wondering if taking advice from a twenty-year-old was sensible. It's too late to change my mind now, he thought, striding up to Harry.

'Sorry I'm a bit late,' he said, 'I'm afraid I missed the train I intended to catch by two minutes. It's a good job they run so frequently.'

'No problem,' said Harry, glancing at his watch, 'but we should probably go straight through in case they are queuing at Security.'

'Good point, but I just need to change some money. Did you get Barbados and American dollars?'

'Yep.'

'I'll just get American then. They'll probably take them most places and you've got cash for tipping and the like.'

There was no queue at Security, which was just as well as, by the time Philippe had changed his money, there was only an hour to go before take-off. Once through the security checks the two men had made their way to WHSmith's; Harry to buy a magazine and a bottle of water, and Philippe to make sure that his book was on display. While Harry was waiting in line for a self-service checkout to become free, he noticed Philippe in a somewhat animated conversation with someone in a store uniform.

'What was that all about,' he asked, when Philippe finally joined him outside the shop.

'Bloody idiots hadn't updated the Bestsellers chart. I rang my publisher this morning to tell her I was taking a few days' holiday in Barbados and, once she'd calmed down, she shared the news that my book *Tiffany* is now at number one. That stupid lot in there had still got me in last week's position. Lazy sods. I tore them off a right old strip!'

Harry glanced back over his shoulder into the shop, where he could see that the staff were in the process of moving all the chart books into their new positions. 'I'm sure they'd have got round to it, Philippe. I expect Monday morning is pretty busy for them.'

'Well they should have got in to work earlier then. There are plenty of unemployed people who'd jump at the chance of their job if they can't be arsed to do it properly. God knows how many sales I've lost because of their incompetence. Come on, Harry, let's get ourselves to the VIP lounge. I need a drink.'

'A bit early isn't it, Philippe,' Harry said, glancing at his watch again and noting it was only 9.30 a.m., but Philippe was already pushing through the crowds, oblivious to the looks of disgust thrown in his direction as he barged people aside.

Philippe had managed to down three large scotches, while Harry sipped his orange juice before their flight was called. Once on board, he took advantage of the free champagne on offer to Business Class customers.

'No such thing as free,' he said to Harry. 'We pay for this in the extortionate ticket prices. I'll have yours if you don't want it.'

'Be my guest,' Harry said, wondering if maybe he had been a little hasty in suggesting that Philippe joined him on this trip. I really know very little about him, he thought, except that my mum fell in love with him. I wonder if she knows about his drinking and his temper? In one brief hour at the airport, Harry had learned a lot about Philippe and none of it was good.

CHAPTER 37

Even from a distance, Holly could see Amy's beautiful strawberry-blond hair as she sheltered from the midday sun, sitting on the soft sand under a manchineel tree. She hoped the younger woman had read the sign that was on every one of these trees, warning people not to touch the tree or eat the fruit, known locally as death apples. It was even advised to keep away from them during a rain storm as water running off the leaves could be contaminated with the caustic sap and result in irritated skin. They had been very lucky with the weather so far. August was unpredictable in the Caribbean as it was right in the middle of hurricane season, but they hadn't been troubled by a drop of rain. Holly raised her arm to wave to Amy as the boat neared the shore but there was no response. She mustn't have seen me, thought Holly, gathering up her beach bag from the slatted bench at her side and stumbling towards the front of the boat to disembark.

'Mind your step,' Winston the boatman said, taking hold of each of his passengers by the elbow and helping them to jump down into the shallow water. Holly had enjoyed the boat trip but had been disappointed not to see any turtles, the main purpose for going. She was the last to disembark and Winston jumped off the boat so that he could lift her down, rather than having her jump. 'We don't want baby coming early on account of me not helping you off,' he said, kindly.

Once they were all assembled on the beach, Winston informed them that the courtesy bus from the hotel would be picking them up at the roadside very shortly, then he pushed the boat back out through the waves to go and collect his next lot of passengers.

Holly trudged up the beach with the rest of the group. As she neared the manchineel tree she called out to Amy, 'I'm so pleased you could come, although I guess that means Jack and Hugo have been a bit thoughtless again.'

Amy's head jolted upright. 'Holly. Sorry, I think I must have dozed off. How was your trip?'

'Uneventful for the most part, although I did enjoy seeing the coral formations that we passed over.'

'Maybe Rodney can take you out in his boat another day. He seems to know exactly where to find the turtles. I thought maybe we could get the bus to Alleynes Bay. Jenneen says there is a really nice beach bar there, although she is still cross at me for refusing the packed lunch she offered to prepare.'

Holly thought she could detect a flatness in the usually bubbly Amy. The holiday clearly wasn't panning out as she had hoped. She felt a flash of irritation towards Jack and Hugo for their selfishness in choosing to do things that excluded Amy. 'Where have the boys gone today?' she enquired.

'They wanted to go on the mini-submarine and I don't

like the idea of being submerged, so I told them to go on their own.'

'Right,' said Holly, wondering if maybe there had been an argument about it, hence Amy's demeanour. 'Well, let's go and find ourselves this beach bar for lunch and cocktails, although mine will have to be a virgin one, of course.'

Lunch at Roy's Place had been a delight. Some people might have been put off by the plastic chairs and plastic tablecloths but, as Holly pointed out while they sipped on their drinks after treating themselves to a dessert of Mount Gay rum cake with ice cream, they weren't eating the furniture. After paying the extremely reasonable bill they dropped down the three rickety wooden steps on to the beach and were almost immediately hustled by beach hawkers asking them if they wanted a sun-lounger.

The going rate seemed to be twenty Barbados dollars, plus an extra two dollars for a parasol, but Amy wasn't having any of it because Jenneen had told her to haggle.

'That's the price for the cruise ship passengers,' she said. 'We're staying on the island. You can do better than that.'

At first no one seemed interested in offering a lower price. They were clearly all working together and no one wanted to go against the crowd until a man with a heavily scarred face approached them.

'I can give you the local rate,' he said, 'fifteen Barbados dollars including the parasol.'

'That's very fair,' Amy said, reaching into her bag for her purse, before handing over the money.

'And if you come here again tomorrow, just ask for Spider.'

'We will, thank you.'

'Poor man,' Holly said in a hushed tone, after Spider had moved away, 'I wonder what happened to his face. A car accident do you think?'

Amy shook her head. 'No, the scarring was too symmetrical. It looked like a spider's web, and it looked like it had been done deliberately. Maybe it was some kind of punishment or perhaps a show of strength.' She shuddered. 'Either way that must have hurt a lot. I'm not good with pain.'

'Don't have a baby then,' Holly said. 'Even after twenty years I can still recall the agony of childbirth.'

'Yes, but look what you got at the end of it,' Amy said, spreading her brightly coloured beach towel over the sunbed cushion, and sitting down to twist her hair into a knot on the top of her head. 'You're not telling me Harry wasn't worth it.'

'You are funny, Amy. I sometimes think you can see no wrong in Harry. I'm surprised you and he didn't get together rather than you and Jack.'

As though someone had opened the floodgates, Amy started to cry. Not huge sobs, just an endless stream of tears rolling down her cheeks, punctuated by the occasional sniff.

'What's wrong, Amy, what did I say?' asked Holly, immediately moving over to Amy's sunbed and putting her arm around her shoulders to comfort her.

Amy couldn't speak and she couldn't stop crying, tears dropping off the end of her nose on to the turquoise and pink playsuit she was wearing.

'Please,' appealed Holly, 'you have to tell me what's wrong.'

'Nothing. It's nothing,' Amy said, struggling to control herself. 'I'm just feeling a bit emotional. It's probably hormones, my period is due any day.'

Holly was doubtful. What on earth had brought about this deluge? It had started just after she mentioned Harry. Oh my God, she thought, maybe Amy and Harry had a fling, before she got involved with Jack, and he dumped her. Holly had never pried into her son's private life but had to admit that she was a little disappointed that he didn't seem remotely interested in having a girlfriend. Perhaps Amy moving on to his best mate had put him off girls for the time being. Hang on, Holly reprimanded herself, this is all just conjecture.

'Tell me it's none of my business, but you and Harry never, you know, got together, did you?'

'Harry's never shown any interest in me that way. I can't lie to you, Holly, I had a major crush on Harry in my first year at uni, but he didn't want to know. In fact, I've never seen him with a girl at all. You know, some of my friends even started rumours that he was gay, because he paid them no attention.' Amy gave a hollow little laugh at the irony.

'I've occasionally wondered that myself,' Holly confessed.

'Really? Would it bother you if he was?'

'I wouldn't love him any less, but I would maybe feel sad for him that he could miss out on the chance of being a dad, unless he adopted of course. He's fantastic around young children. When we went on holiday together last year he never had a minute to himself around the pool.

He's a natural with them. You don't think he is, do you?'

'No. I don't. But then you never can tell what people are hiding from you,' she said, the merest hint of bitterness creeping into her voice. 'I'm sorry about the waterworks earlier. I'm fine now. Shall we go and paddle?'

CHAPTER 38

When the bus reached Mandy, Amy waved her goodbyes to Holly and once again headed round towards the side gate to let herself in. She could hear the sound of laughter coming from the pool area, so clearly Jack and Hugo were home. A small part of Amy wanted to creep in the front way, unobserved, and hide in her room until dinner but she had promised Jack that they would keep up the boyfriend/girlfriend pretence until they got home. Reluctantly, she turned right down the path towards the pool, plastering a fake smile on her face. Moments later the smile turned from fake to real.

'Harry,' she cried, rushing towards him and flinging her arms around his neck. 'When did you arrive? I've just left your mum on the bus back to her hotel. Should we get Rodney to chase after it and intercept her at Speightstown?'

Harry returned the hug. 'No rush, Amy. I'll ring and invite her to dinner tonight. We only just got here about twenty minutes ago. You didn't mention that you'd run into my mum,' he said, in the direction of Jack and Hugo.

'They haven't,' Amy said pointedly. 'They've been too

busy hanging out together doing boy things. Holly's been my saviour,' she added, shooting a look at the boys. 'Did I hear you say "we"?'

'Yes,' Harry replied. 'Hugo very kindly said I could bring a friend.'

'True,' said Hugo, 'but I wasn't expecting another man. I thought you'd finally got yourself a girlfriend,' he added, shaking his head in despair.

Amy was certain that her heart had missed a beat. Oh my God, she thought, perhaps the conversation with Holly at the beach hadn't been too far from the mark.

'You'll never believe it, and Harry hasn't explained why yet,' Jack said, 'but he's brought the author that you had at the bookshop last week.'

'Philippe?' Amy exclaimed, in total confusion.

On cue, the French doors opened and Philippe emerged wearing shorts and a linen shirt.

'Did someone mention my name?'

CHAPTER 39

Harry closed the bedroom door. He needed to make sure that the conversation he was about to have with his mum wasn't overheard. When he and Philippe had arrived at Hugo's house an hour earlier only one room had been made ready for them. Hugo had assumed that he was bringing a girlfriend.

Jenneen had been very accommodating in preparing the fifth of the six bedrooms in the house, and Harry had gallantly volunteered to move rooms, even though the new room didn't have a spectacular view like the one he'd left. It was still a magnificent space and he could always move back when Philippe left on Thursday.

There had been plenty of time on the plane journey over to concoct a plausible story as to why Harry had invited Philippe to Barbados. They had told Amy, Jack and Hugo the truth: that they knew each other through Robert. They simply said that the pressure of the book launching to such critical acclaim, hot on the heels of losing his friend Rosemary to cancer, had overwhelmed Philippe and that he needed a few days of complete relaxation. There had been a sticky moment when Amy had asked why they hadn't brought Robert too, but Harry had covered it by saying he couldn't remember how many rooms the house had and he didn't fancy sharing with Hugo.

He had excused himself from the gathering by the pool, telling them that he needed to unpack and call his mum. Amy had gone on and on about inviting his mum to dinner so that she could meet Philippe. To his credit, Philippe had gone along with the pretence that he didn't know her and said he always liked to meet people who enjoyed reading his books. Harry didn't want his mum at dinner that evening. He needed to speak to her in private first. He had a lot of explaining to do.

Holly answered his call on the second ring.

'Harry! I tried to FaceTime with you last night but it wouldn't connect. How are you?'

'Oh sorry, Mum. I saw that I had a missed call from you. I was at Robert's and had left my iPad in my room. How is Barbados?' he asked, a smile playing at the corners of his mouth.

'Gorgeous. But then you'll find out if you come over to stay at Hugo's house. Why didn't you tell me he had invited you all out here? I bumped into Amy on the bus by chance. It was such a shock for both of us.'

'Well, I didn't want to disappoint you if I couldn't make it. The trip to LA was really successful, in fact, we won the contract to do the refurbishment, subject to cost, but Robert thinks that won't be a problem.'

'Oh Harry, that's fantastic news. What a shame you aren't here! We could have gone out to celebrate your first commission. I'm so proud of you.'

'What would you say to going out to celebrate tomorrow?' Harry asked.

Holly squealed. 'Are you flying in tomorrow? You are going to love Hugo's house, it's absolutely stunning. I'm so looking forward to seeing you. What time does your flight get in?'

'I'm already here.'

'Then we can celebrate tonight. I've arranged to have dinner with a couple I've got friendly with but I'm sure they won't mind if I cancel. Or you could join us?'

'And how exactly would you explain who I am? I'm presuming you are still using the same cover story?'

'You're right. In my excitement, I hadn't thought about that.'

'Well, in truth, I'm a bit knackered after all this jetting around, so I was going to get an early night. I don't know how you do it, Mum. Huge respect. I was wondering if we could meet up during the day tomorrow if you haven't got anything planned?'

'Actually, that would be perfect. I've hired a car for a couple of days to go and explore the east coast. It will be much more fun to do it with you rather than on my own.'

'That sounds great, Mum. I'll get Rodney to drop me at your hotel around ten if that's okay?'

'More than okay. I can't wait to see you. Get a good night's sleep and I'll see you tomorrow.'

'See you tomorrow, Mum,' Harry said, disconnecting the call. He was relieved he hadn't had to lie to his mum. He genuinely was tired and planning to get an early night, straight after dinner. There's no way I could have had a conversation with Mum about Gareth and Philippe tonight, he thought.

Thirty minutes later, freshly showered and changed into shorts and a T-shirt, Harry joined everyone on the terrace.

'Is she coming?' Amy asked.

Harry looked beyond Amy to Philippe. They had agreed that Harry needed to speak to his mum alone before dropping the bombshell that Philippe had accompanied him to Barbados.

'She can't tonight, Amy. She had already made dinner arrangements. I'm seeing her tomorrow though. Sorry,' he added, noticing the look of disappointment on Amy's face.

'Oh, that's a shame, well at least for you, after all, I spent the afternoon with her. Jack's taking me to the wildlife reserve tomorrow but maybe we can all get together for dinner?'

Everyone turned as the French doors opened.

'Well this is quite a gathering,' said Natalia, looking every inch a model in a long gold dress cut down to the waist front and back. 'Exactly how many more of your school chums did your father say could join our family holiday?'

'We don't go to school, Mother,' Hugo said, 'we're university students. This is my friend Harry and this is his friend Philippe, who obviously isn't at uni with us, although I guess he could be a mature student. This is my mother Natalia.'

'Thank you for allowing us to stay in your beautiful home,' said Harry, but Natalia wasn't paying attention.

She was making a beeline for the only other person over the age of twenty.

'Enchanté,' Philippe said, brushing the back of her hand with his lips.

'Are you French?' she asked, fluttering her false eyelashes at him.

'Only half French, on my mother's side.'

'You can tell me all about her over dinner. You will sit next to me won't you? I haven't had any proper adult company in days,' she added.

The conversation throughout dinner was punctuated by Natalia's fake laughter. Perhaps Philippe should have been a comedian rather than a writer, Harry thought, judging by Natalia's reaction to virtually everything he said. In fairness, Philippe looked quite embarrassed by the constant attention and might well have been regretting his decision to sit next to her.

At one point, Philippe excused himself to go to the men's room. Hugo leaned in very close to his mother and hissed, 'For God's sake, Mother, you're embarrassing me in front of my friends.'

'Oh grow up, Hugo,' she hissed back. 'We're all adults here. I don't see why Jack and Amy should be the only ones getting any action.'

Jack concentrated on eating, and Amy went the colour of the beetroot risotto she had just enjoyed. Harry had had enough.

'I'm really sorry, guys, but I'm going to have to call it a night. I hadn't quite got over the jet lag from LA and now this on the back of it. Plus I need to be up in the morning to meet Mum. Enjoy the rest of your evening.'

Philippe was coming out of the downstairs toilet as Harry went into the house.

'I'd lock your bedroom door tonight if I were you,' Harry said, 'unless of course Hugo's mum is your type.'

'Couldn't be further from my type, Harry. Fake and skinny and with a really annoying laugh. I'll make my excuses from the safety of the French doors I think.'

'Smart move.'

'Good luck talking to your mum tomorrow. I hope she won't be too mad at you for bringing me out here and telling me about the baby.'

And that's not the half of it, Harry thought, taking his own advice and locking his bedroom door from the inside. Natalia seemed to be some kind of nymphomaniac and, if Philippe showed no interest, he was the only other male in the house who wasn't related or attached.

CHAPTER 40

At precisely ten o'clock, Rodney drew the limousine to a halt in front of the Cane Hill hotel. Holly was sitting on a bench to one side of the entrance and as soon as Harry opened the door of the car, she leapt to her feet and rushed over to give him a hug. 'Harry, it's so good to see you.'

'You too, Mum,' he said, hugging her back, 'although it does feel a little strange to be meeting up like this, four thousand miles from home. Let's get out of here before someone spots us together and thinks I'm your toy boy.'

'The car is in the car park, although I'm not sure I've made the right choice of vehicle,' she said, indicating the grey skies overhead. 'You seem to have brought the UK weather with you.' She stopped in front of a mini-moke which, although it had a soft top, was completely open to the elements at the side. 'Do you think I should try and change it?'

'We'll be okay, Mum, it probably won't rain much, if at all.'

Holly looked doubtful. 'Well, I suppose we can always go inside for lunch somewhere if we do get caught, although I managed to get the hotel to do a picnic lunch for two,' she said, indicating the cool box wedged securely behind their seats. 'I had a look at the map last night after dinner and I thought maybe we could head for Bathsheba. Apparently the east coast is very different from the west, more like Devon and Cornwall's surfing coast, but with bigger waves.'

'Whatever you think, Mum, you're the boss.'

'I'm so looking forward to today, Harry, you and me going to the seaside for a picnic, just like the old days.'

He shot a sideways glance at his mum. She seems to have forgiven me for not mentioning that I might be coming out here on holiday, he thought, but how is she going to react when she finds out who I've brought with me?

Harry was wrong about the rain. They had been driving for almost an hour, taking a few wrong turns due to lack of sign-posting, when the first spots of rain hit the windscreen. By the time Holly was steering the moke down the steep hill into Bathsheba, the rain was lashing down, causing a fast-flowing stream at the side of the road. At least the direction of the rainfall was downwards rather than sideways so they were predominantly dry, apart from when the car splashed through puddles.

'I don't think you would have a career as a weather forecaster,' joked Holly, bringing the moke to a stop next to a multi-coloured VW camper van with two surf boards strapped to the roof. 'Shall we try and sit it out, or do you want to make a dash for that cafe,' she asked, indicating a small wooden structure whose outdoor chairs were all sitting upside down on the tables. Clearly they had been expecting the downpour.

'We'll probably get wetter making a run for it. We're fairly dry and there's no denying that is a spectacular view.'

In front of them, waves the height of a London bus were crashing on to the silver sands, creating a mass of white froth similar to the uncorking of a champagne bottle. The boom as each wave struck the shore was thunderous and occasionally they could feel the vibration as a particularly giant wave made contact. No wonder there were huge rock formations dotted along the beach, the result of the Atlantic Ocean pummelling the coast for thousands of years. Neither spoke for a few moments but then they both began to speak together.

'After you, Mum,' Harry said.

'Well... I was just wondering why you didn't tell me your friends would be here at the same time as me? Even if you couldn't have made the trip, you know how fond I am of Amy. Are you embarrassed because I'm pregnant? She knows by the way... well, it's pretty obvious now, isn't it.'

'I wouldn't say I'm embarrassed, Mum, but it is a bit of an awkward situation. If you hadn't have been given this last-minute assignment to Barbados I could have leisurely slipped it in to a conversation at a later date that I was going to have a new brother or sister. It's not really their business anyway.'

'True. I just don't like the thought that you're ashamed of me, that I've let you down.'

Harry reached his arm around Holly's shoulder. 'I am so not ashamed of you. I think maybe I've always had you on a pedestal because you're such an amazing mum but, in fairness, it must have got a bit uncomfortable for you up there, never allowed to relax and be you. I was upset that I heard about the baby from Robert, but that wasn't really your fault, I know you would have told me at the right moment. He does have a bit of a habit of opening his mouth and putting his foot in it,' he said, recalling the episode with Philippe. 'And as for letting me down…' Harry shook his head, 'that couldn't be further from the truth. I've grown up in this past few weeks. I've realised no one is perfect, even my brilliant mum.'

'I am so relieved to hear you say that, Harry. I've felt like a chasm has been opening up between us because of this little one,' she said, resting her hands on her baby bump. 'It's stirred up all sorts of things, like you wanting to know about your father.'

There it is, Harry thought. The opportunity has presented itself. This is where I have to tell Mum about Gareth.

'Mum, there is something I have to tell you.'

'You've been looking for him haven't you?' Holly said, without a hint of accusation.

'Yes. And I found him.'

Holly gasped, her hands flying to her mouth. 'Don't tell me, Harry, I don't want to know.'

'Yes you do, Mum,' Harry said gently, 'you really do. I did go out to LA to have a look at the hotel project for Robert, but there was an ulterior motive. I had discovered that Gareth had gone to America to study, like you said, but what you didn't know was that he didn't come home, in fact, he couldn't come home.'

Holly's eyes were wide with questions.

'He had an accident, Mum, a really bad accident. He was in a coma for weeks and when he woke up he couldn't remember anything about his life over the previous year. You see, it wasn't that he didn't want to come home to you, he didn't even know that you existed.'

'Oh my God, Harry,' Holly said, fighting back tears, 'all these years I thought he had chosen to abandon me, well us, to be more accurate, and he was oblivious to our existence. Was he all right? I mean, is he all right? Did you see him while you were in America?'

'I have seen him, but not in America. I met his parents, my grandparents, Bethan and Jim, who moved to America after the accident. They stayed, but Dad,' Harry felt Holly flinch, 'erm, Gareth, went home to Wales.'

Holly's eyes were now blinded by tears, the dramatic performance of nature outside the car paling into insignificance compared with the drama within.

'He wants to see you, Mum.'

'What's the point?' she asked, wretchedly, 'he doesn't even know who I am.'

'Yes, he does. He started to remember things. That's why he went back to the UK. He tried to track you down through your mum but…'

'But what, Harry? What did she say to him?'

'I don't know how to tell you this. She told him that you had died in the car crash with your dad.'

A strange noise emanated from Holly's mouth, a cross between a shriek and a scream that could have been mistaken for a seagull's call as it soared in the wind.

'No, no,' she cried. 'Why would she punish me like that? How could she be so evil? All I ever wanted was for her to love me, but she despised me. She blamed me for my dad's death and this was her way of getting back at me. How could she, Harry? How could she do this to her own child?' Holly sobbed.

Harry held his mum close to his chest until her sobbing subsided. 'It's okay, Mum, it's okay. When we get home I'll take you to see Gareth. He's such a nice person and you've got so much to talk about.'

'It's not okay, Harry,' Holly sniffed. 'All those years I waited, a tiny spark of hope kept me believing that one day I'd find him. And now you've found him for me and I'm pregnant with another man's child. Why must life be so unfair?'

'He still wants to see you, Mum. I told him about us, about the wonderful childhood you gave me that he should have been part of. He wants to thank you for all the sacrifices you've made that have made me who I am.'

'Are you trying to tell me that he has his own life with a wife and children? A life that I'm not a part of but that he'll allow you into? I'm not sure I can cope with that. I don't think I could bear to see him happily married when I've struggled all these years on my own. I'm sorry, Harry, I must sound so selfish. I want him to be happy, really I do, but I can't bear to see him living the life I wanted to share with him, with someone else.'

'You've got it all wrong, Mum. He doesn't have a wife and a loving family, he doesn't even have his mum and dad. Even after years of therapy he can't get past blaming them for sending him to study in America, so he barely speaks to them because when he does he can't stop himself getting angry. He can walk, but only for short periods – most of the time he's in a wheelchair. He lives alone, apart from his dog, so the nearest thing he has to a family is us.'

'Is you, Harry. You are his family. I'm just some long-lost girlfriend who stupidly got herself pregnant. Why would he be interested in meeting me, particularly as I'm now in the exact same situation?'

'I don't know, Mum, but he must have his reasons because he does want to see you, baby and all.'

'You told him I was pregnant? That's not really your decision to make.'

Harry fiddled with his fingers. 'I don't understand. A few minutes ago, you were questioning why I hadn't told my friends that you're pregnant. Now you're telling me it's not my decision to make. How am I supposed to know who I'm allowed to tell?'

There was a sudden belligerence in his tone that Holly couldn't fathom, unless…

'Harry, who else have you told?' she demanded.

'Look, Mum, he just turned up on the doorstep. It's not like I went searching for him or anything.'

'Please tell me you're not talking about Philippe,' she said, knowing as the words came out that he was.

'I think he has a right to know. He's been searching for you since he got back from Mauritius to apologise for whatever it is he did wrong, although he doesn't seem to know what that is. Maybe you should hear him out. Maybe it's all a misunderstanding.'

The rain had stopped and a glimmer of blue was breaking through the grey cloud. Harry was holding his breath waiting for the angry outburst which he was sure was heading his way. Instead there was total silence. Without saying a word, Holly got out of the car and started walking in the direction of the steps down to the beach.

Harry grabbed the keys out of the ignition and ran after her shouting, 'Mum, wait.' He caught up with her halfway down the beach as she marched towards the angry surf. He pulled her arm to swing her round to face him. 'Look, I'm not going to say I'm sorry for telling Philippe cos I'm not. But I am sorry if it's upset you. I thought I was doing the right thing. I hoped you and he could sort things out. Mum, talk to me,' he begged, as she pulled her arm away from his grasp and stormed off again. He stood watching her for a moment and then followed a few paces behind, stopping as she reached the water's edge.

They stood that way for what seemed to Harry like an eternity. The only movement from Holly was the clenching and unclenching of her fists as she looked out to sea. As the movement ceased, Harry risked edging closer. 'Mum?' he ventured.

Holly spun round to face her son. 'This is not okay, Harry,' she shouted. 'You can't go round meddling in people's lives. It's bad enough that you involved Robert in helping you search for Gareth without telling me, but this… I just don't understand what you were thinking. Life isn't a fairy tale, full of happy endings, at least it isn't for me. You went in search of the person I've spent half my life loving. I've always imagined him how he was when I last saw him, tall, strong and confident. Now you tell me he is broken – damaged mentally and physically. The dream I'd clung on to for so long smashed to pieces like the shells on this beach. But that wasn't enough for you. Oh no,' she ranted, 'you had to go one better. You had to take away my chance of having the same close relationship with my new baby that I've always shared with you. What was it Harry? Jealousy? You didn't want anyone else to have our special relationship. Well, it's not so special now, is it? Is it?'

Harry watched in horror as Holly sank to her knees in the writhing foam, clutching her belly. He could see the wave about to engulf her but couldn't reach her in time to prevent it. It flattened her, smashing her head against a large stone and then began to suck her out in the undercurrent. Harry grabbed for her arms, pulling her from the clutch of the waves with a strength he didn't know he possessed. She was unconscious and bleeding. He staggered up the beach, his knees buckling under the weight, shouting, 'Help me, please somebody help me.'

CHAPTER 41

Philippe had stayed in his room until he was sure the coast was clear. Despite locking his bedroom door the previous evening, as Harry had suggested, he had been lying in bed reading when he heard a key being inserted into the lock from the outside. Idiot, he thought, looking at the key on his bedside cabinet, why didn't I leave it in the lock? I should have realised that the housekeeper would have a spare.

The door eased open and Natalia backed into the room with a bottle of Bollinger in one hand, two champagne flutes in the other and the key between her teeth. She pushed the door shut with her bottom and sashayed over to the bed dropping the key on to the covers.

'Nice one,' she purred, sliding on to the bed next to him, 'coming to bed early. The children thought you were just exhausted from your flight. Do you want to do the honours?' she asked, offering him the champagne bottle.

This is awkward, Philippe thought. He didn't want to offend the lady of the house but he had no desire to have her in his bed either, which in itself was something of a novelty for him.

'Look, Natalia, I really am shattered. It would be a waste of a good bottle of champagne to open it tonight. Why don't we save it for tomorrow?' he suggested, making the decision to move to one of the hotels for his final two nights in Barbados.

Natalia pouted. 'I'm not used to being rejected,' she said, lying back on the pillows and arching her back to make the most of her small breasts. 'Surely you can manage a quickie? And tomorrow we could go for a more athletic session,' she said, rubbing her hand suggestively over the gold silk fabric covering her thigh.

'No, really, it doesn't feel right, particularly with your son sleeping in the next room. What if it gets back to your husband?'

'We're getting divorced,' she said. 'He was bloody useless in the sack. How we ever managed to conceive Hugo is a mystery to me,' she added, holding up her little finger in a bent position.

'Well, I'm sorry to hear that but maybe you'll have more luck with husband number two,' Philippe said, squirming out of the other side of the bed and very thankful that he had left his undershorts on to sleep in.

'You could be husband number two if you wanted. I'm going to be very rich when the divorce goes through. I wasn't stupid enough to sign a pre-nup agreement like these silly girls do these days. I might even insist on this place as part of the settlement. You could do your writing here.'

Now she had caught Philippe's attention. 'How do you know I'm a writer?'

'I read the glossy magazines. Your picture has been all over them since the big reveal. I couldn't believe it when

Hugo introduced you earlier. I've even read a few chapters of your book. Amy left her copy here today instead of taking it to the beach. Are you as sexy in real life?'

Philippe could feel a stirring in his manhood. He didn't fancy Natalia at all, but this rich bitch was laying it out on a plate for him and his head was having difficulty persuading his penis that he wasn't interested. He remained resolute.

'I'm going down to the kitchen to get a glass of water,' he said, 'if you are still here when I get back, I will knock on your son's door and ask if I can bunk in with him tonight as I've discovered a scary creature in my room. I hope I've made myself clear?'

Fortunately, Natalia had taken the hint and vacated his room before he returned. Nevertheless, Philippe stayed out of the way until he was sure she had left for her morning yoga class before he went down to breakfast.

It was a solo affair. Hugo had tagged along with Amy and Jack for their visit to the wildlife reserve, and Harry had gone to meet Holly at her hotel. He hoped Harry would break the news that he was in Barbados in the right way. He didn't want her to think he was some kind of mad stalker.

Philippe spent the morning relaxing by the pool although the grey clouds overhead were growing increasingly threatening. Pouring himself a top-up of black coffee, he carried it inside just as the first few drops of rain started to fall, and just as his mobile phone started to ring. It was a number he didn't recognise.

'Hello?'

'Hi, is that Philippe? This is Alice from Jo's office. I wondered if you'd seen her today? She's normally in the office before eight but she's a no show at the moment and she hasn't been answering my calls.'

Checking his watch, Philippe could see it was 8.20 a.m. UK time.

'Maybe she overslept? She's not exactly hours late is she?'

'No, but she's never late and if she has a breakfast meeting she will always let someone at the office know. I just thought maybe you and she...'

'I'm in Barbados for a few days, Alice, so wherever Jo is, she's certainly not with me. I hope you find her,' he said, disconnecting the call and shaking his head in disbelief that apparently Jo was kept on such a tight leash. He couldn't help wondering where she might be though. He had never known her miss a day's work in all the years he had known her.

He was settling down to read a magazine, the rain now pounding down on the terrace, when his second call of the day interrupted his relaxation.

'Philippe, it's Harry. Is Rodney around?'

Philippe could instantly tell from Harry's tone that something was very wrong.

'Rodney took Hugo, Jack and Amy to the wildlife reserve and he was waiting there until they're ready to come back. What's wrong?'

'Ask Jenneen to call you a cab. You need to come to the hospital in Bridgetown. There's been an accident.'

The blood in Philippe's veins turned ice cold with fear. 'What accident,' he said gripping his phone more tightly.

'Just get here as soon as you can,' Harry said.

Less than forty-five minutes later, Philippe burst through the doors of Accident and Emergency at the Queen Elizabeth Hospital, and demanded to know where Holly Wilson was. He was asked to take a seat but instead paced impatiently up and down until he was told that she had been moved on to a ward. He took the stairs two at a time to the second floor and rushed over to the receptionist.

'I'm looking for Holly Wilson,' he said.

'Are you family, sir?'

'I'm her partner, the father of her baby. The baby is okay, isn't it?' he asked, his voice full of panic.

'Mother and baby are both fine, sir. She is resting now in room 216. I believe your son is sitting with her.'

Philippe was puzzled for a moment. 'Oh, you mean, Harry.' He was about to explain that Harry wasn't his son but realised the futility of it. Instead he said, 'I'll just go and check on them if that's all right?'

He made his way along the corridor to room 216 then paused outside for a moment, his hand resting on the door handle. He took a deep breath. He hadn't seen Holly since March and it had been in very different circumstances. Harry hadn't elaborated on the accident, other than to say his mum had fallen and been knocked unconscious. The lad was clearly in shock, Philippe thought. Noiselessly he pressed the handle downwards and peered round the door. Holly was lying on the bed, her head swathed in bandages, her eyes closed. Harry was sat on a plastic chair at her bedside holding one of her hands between his two. He glanced over towards Philippe. Gently, he laid Holly's hand on the pale blue hospital blanket and crossed to the door, ushering Philippe out as he closed it behind him.

'How is she doing?' Philippe asked.

'She's going to be okay. They gave her a mild sedative so that she would sleep.'

'And the baby?'

Harry nodded. 'Okay too,' he confirmed. 'She had a bit of a bleed but they've checked on the baby with an ultrasound scan and it's fine, as far as they can tell. It's a little girl.'

'Thank God. What happened, Harry?'

Harry gave a sketchy account of what had preceded Holly's fall on the beach. He didn't mention Gareth, but he did say that his mum was angry with him for telling Philippe about the baby.

'Thank goodness the surfers were there,' he said, 'and not out riding waves because they were too rough. They helped me carry Mum up from the beach and then drove us here in the back of their camper van. I don't know what might have happened if we had to wait for an ambulance. They were so kind and practical. They had a first-aid kit in the van because of all the bumps and scrapes they get surfing, so they cleaned the gash on Mum's head and wrapped a tight bandage around it. Shit, Philippe, I was so scared.'

Philippe was now doubting the wisdom of allowing Harry to have been the bearer of the news. He's little more than a kid really, he thought, looking at his pale face and slumped shoulders. Maybe coming out to Barbados with him hadn't been such a clever idea.

'You know, Harry, I'm thinking maybe I should change my flight and go back to England today. Holly's had enough of a shock. The last thing any of us want is for her to lose the baby.'

From inside the hospital room a weak voice called,

'Harry, is that you? Who are you talking to?'

'You're here now,' Harry said. 'It might help Mum to have someone other than me at her bedside, after all, it was me she was angry with.'

'Harry,' Holly called again.

'Coming, Mum,' Harry said, starting to push the door open. He looked back at Philippe. 'It's your call.'

Philippe stood for a few moments, indecision keeping him rooted to the spot. He didn't want to upset Holly but he was desperate to find out what went wrong between them. I want to be there for her and the baby, he thought, which means I'll have to face her at some point. It might be better to do it while she is sedated and in hospital. He raised his hand and tapped lightly on the door.

'Come in,' Harry said, gripping his mum's hand tightly.

Holly gasped. For a moment she wondered if she was dreaming.

'What are you doing here?' she asked, her words slurring, her heart beating loudly in her chest.

'I've been looking for you Holly,' Philippe said, approaching the bed, 'and now I've found you, I don't ever want to lose you again.'

Holly's eyes felt heavy, she could feel herself slipping back into sleep.

'Do you really mean that, Gareth?' she mumbled, as she drifted off.

CHAPTER 42

After a little bit of persuasion from both Harry and Philippe, Holly was released into their care following the doctor's examination round at 7 p.m., on the understanding that she would have total bed rest for a few days. Harry checked with Hugo that it would be all right for Holly to stay at the house, rather than going back to her hotel alone, so that they could keep an eye on her.

When Hugo, Jack and Amy had arrived back from the wildlife reserve looking like drowned rats, Jenneen had been able to explain to three of them that Holly had been rushed to hospital but not why Philippe had been summoned by Harry. Amy was distraught. She hadn't mentioned the pregnancy to the boys and was terrified that maybe Holly had lost the baby, so it was a huge relief when she was able to talk to her while they settled her in to the spare room.

'Is everything all right with the baby?' she asked in a low voice, concern etched into her young face.

'Thankfully, yes,' said Holly, still drowsy from the sedatives. 'I had a terrible cramping pain in my stomach that made me fall to my knees and that's when the wave hit me. It was all so sudden.'

'Don't talk now,' Amy said, 'get some rest. I'll come back and see you before I go to bed.'

Holly smiled weakly. 'You're a good girl, Amy.'

The others were already seated at the dinner table, with the notable exception of Natalia, as Amy made her way across the terrace. Everyone looked a little shell-shocked. It had been a hectic couple of hours with Rodney driving Hugo over to Bathsheba to collect the mini-moke, and Jack and Amy getting a cab to the Cane Hill hotel to collect Holly's things and check her out. The hotel had been reluctant at first, but a phone call to the hospital confirmed their story after which the hotel even waived the extra fee for Holly's use of the Internet. Amy had packed as quickly as she could, anxious to be back at the house for when Holly arrived.

'Is your mum not dining with us tonight, Hugo?' Amy asked, settling herself into the wicker seat.

'No. She's eating at The Cliff with some of her cronies. Did I tell you she's going back to England tomorrow? She says she's had enough of nurse-maiding a bunch of adolescents, which is a load of rubbish as we've barely seen her.'

'Is Mum sleeping?' Harry asked.

'She probably is now,' replied Amy. 'I hope the drugs they gave her won't hurt the baby.'

'What baby?' Hugo and Jack chorused in unison.

Amy's hand flew up to her mouth.

'Don't worry, Amy, I was going to tell them tonight

anyway. Mum's pregnant. The baby's due just before Christmas. That was why we were all so concerned. We thought maybe she had lost it as a result of the accident.'

'We?' Amy said.

Harry looked across to Philippe who was staring into space. The other three followed Harry's gaze.

'What's going on here, mate?' Jack asked.

The look on Amy's face suggested that the pieces of an intricate jigsaw were starting to fall into place, while Hugo looked totally confused.

Philippe said, without emotion, 'Holly and I met in Mauritius and fell in love. I'm sure I don't need to spell it out for you,' he said pushing his chair back from the table. 'Excuse me, I'm not hungry.'

There was an awkward silence as Philippe strode across the terrace, then three pairs of eyes fixed on Harry.

'It's true. I only found out about the baby the day before Mum's birthday. I knew she'd met someone in Mauritius but I didn't realise things had got quite so serious so quickly. For some reason, which she has refused to explain, she ended things between them before she discovered she was pregnant. The accident today was all my fault,' he said despondently. 'If I hadn't tried to get them back together, none of this would have happened. And now Mum hates me.'

'Don't be ridiculous, Harry,' Amy said. 'She may be cross with you for interfering but she could never hate you. It'll all sort itself out, I promise,' she added, reaching across the table for his hand.

'Bloody hell,' said Hugo. 'I thought my life was full of drama. This could be a Hollywood movie. Are they going to patch things up for the baby's sake?'

'I'm not sure that's the right reason for two people to be together,' Jack said, meaningfully, looking across at Amy. 'Other people's expectations are no substitute for true love.'

'You're right, Jack. I'm not sure now that Mum truly loved Philippe as much as she thought she did. I shouldn't have stuck my nose in.'

'You did it because you love her and you want her to be happy,' Amy said. 'For what it's worth, I think you acted with your mum's best interest at heart. Philippe has a right to know that he is going to be a father and your mum wasn't planning on telling him. At least now it's all out in the open, and it's for them to sort it out. Come on, let's at least try and eat some of this lovely food Jenneen has prepared. She'll be starting to doubt her culinary skills at this rate.'

After dinner, Harry and Amy went to check on Holly. She was fast asleep. Before they went to their respective rooms, Harry said, 'So Mum told you about Philippe then?'

'Not exactly. She told me about falling in love in Mauritius and then how the man did something awful that made her finish with him.'

'Did she say what it was? She won't tell me.'

'She hasn't told me either. I don't know about you, but I'm shattered. See you in the morning, Harry,' she said, opening the door of her bedroom to be greeted by the sound of Jack snoring.

'Night, Amy. Hope you manage to get some sleep.'

Amy hoped so too, but it wasn't the sound of Jack

snoring that she feared would keep her awake. Her mind was whirring and it was all down to a glib remark from Hugo. She had felt there was a familiar feeling about elements of Philippe's storyline and now she realised what it was. His book *Tiffany* was very loosely based on the Hollywood movie *Breakfast at Tiffany's*. It surely couldn't be a coincidence that the lead character in the film was called Holly, she thought, and, based on the detailed description he had given of his title character, the dark curly hair and curvaceous figure, Amy was pretty sure the Holly she knew had been his inspiration. And, now she came to think about it, Pierre, the struggling writer in his book, was clearly based on Philippe.

She lay on the bed staring up through the darkness at the ceiling fan which was making a valiant attempt to mask Jack's snoring. What if Holly, by some strange twist of fate, had been sent Philippe's manuscript to copy edit, she thought. If she recognised herself from the description he had given, she would most likely have been shocked and hurt to read that he had made her character into a high-class prostitute. And then there was the explicit nature of the sex scenes. Maybe that was why she had ended things, Amy thought, and who could blame her? But that was only a small part of the story. If Holly had continued reading she would have discovered that Tiffany was only doing it because she needed to raise a vast amount of money quickly. Her daughter would certainly die without a pioneering treatment being offered in America. Amy had cried when she read that bit of the book. Holly would also have learned, if she had read on, how deeply and totally in love Pierre was with Tiffany.

Amy's last waking thought was that she had to get Holly to read Philippe's book. There were no guarantees but, if she was right, maybe there would be a chance for Holly and Philippe to have a life together with their baby.

CHAPTER 43

Philippe slipped the white envelopes under Holly's and Harry's doors, picked up his Louis Vuitton travel bag and slipped out of the front door. It hadn't been easy to change his flight at such short notice, and he'd had to pay a premium, but he couldn't stay under the same roof as Holly knowing that the woman he was so besotted with was still in love with another man. The slip of the tongue at the hospital had hurt as much as if she had slapped him in the face. It didn't matter that she was drugged- up, which Harry had tried to convince him was the reason for the slip, the person Holly obviously wanted to be at her side in a time of crisis was Gareth, not him.

His note to Holly was short and to the point:

I hope that, when you feel strong enough, we can sit down, maybe over dinner, and talk about what went wrong between us. If we can't make things work for us, please will you consider allowing me to see our little girl from time to time.

Philippe x

To Harry he simply wrote:

Thanks for trying to help. You're a very caring young man and your mum is lucky to have you. Please look after her for me if she won't allow me to.

Philippe

Rodney was waiting with the car to take him to the airport. Philippe was relieved to be leaving this beautiful island where he had spent a few of the unhappiest hours of his life.

The car door closing must have woken Harry. His room was at the front of the house overlooking the driveway and he watched the limousine pull up at the gates for Rodney to activate them, assuming that his passenger was Natalia. Harry was glad to be up early. He wanted to take his mum breakfast on a tray.

It was only after he had showered and dressed that he saw the envelope that had been slipped under his door. Although he was sad that Philippe had left without having a proper conversation with Holly, in a way it was a relief. The less stress placed on his mother at the moment the better. He slipped his feet into his deck shoes and went downstairs to the kitchen.

Jenneen was already up and about. 'Good morning, sir. What can I get you?'

'Morning, Jenneen. I was wondering if we could put a tray together for my mum.'

'I'm already doing that. Some fruit and toast, I thought.

Is there anything special that she likes?'

'Can you make poached eggs?' Harry asked.

Jenneen laughed. 'Is that a real question? I can make anything.'

Ten minutes later Harry tapped on the door to his mum's room. He had a flashback to two months previously, the last time he had taken her breakfast in bed on her birthday. So much had changed since then.

'Come in.'

Harry took a breath and pushed the door open.

'Morning, Mum. I've got your breakfast and look, Jenneen has made you perfect poached eggs.'

He waited for her to sit up, then stood the tray across her legs before opening the curtains to reveal a perfect blue sky.

'My favourite,' she said, 'and tomatoes. I think somebody has been giving away my secrets.' There was a moment's silence. 'Not the best choice of words,' she admitted, patting the bed for Harry to sit down. 'I'm sorry I shouted at you yesterday. I was totally out of order. I woke up in the middle of the night and all I could think about was the terrible things I said to you. If I could turn the clock back twenty-four hours so that none of yesterday ever happened, I would. I hope you can forgive me, Harry.'

'I had a bit of a restless night too, Mum. I wish I hadn't kept secrets from you. I should have told you I was going to try and find Gareth, but I was afraid of what I might uncover. He could have been married with ten kids or a drug addict or even dead.'

'I think I would still have wanted to know. Things like that are too big for anyone to carry on their own. Shall we make a pact, Harry? No more secrets – ever.'

'Do we need to cut our fingers and exchange blood to seal the deal?' he asked, trying to lighten the mood.

'That's only if you're not already blood relatives,' she smiled. 'You know, you were right to tell Philippe about the baby. I'm going to talk to him about things today and see if we can at least be civil with each other.'

'It's too late, Mum. He's gone. He pushed a note under my door and it looks like you've got one too,' Harry said, walking across the room to retrieve the envelope that had been pushed to one side by the door opening.

Holly scanned the note then let it fall on to the tray.

'It's not too late, Harry. Philippe has gone home but he wants to talk when I'm up to it. Maybe we have got a chance to make this work, one way or another.'

CHAPTER 44

Three days of total bed rest was what the doctor had ordered and Harry had made sure that was exactly what Holly got. The only time she was allowed out of bed was to go to the loo and to shower. Harry had managed to change his mum's flight back to the UK to the same one that he and Hugo were on, and Hugo had very kindly organised for his father to pay for an upgrade to Business Class, although Harry wasn't absolutely certain that his father was aware of it. They still had a few of days' holiday remaining and today Holly had been allowed to sit outside, so long as she remained in the shade.

'Are you sure you'll be okay if all four of us go, Mum?' Harry asked, adjusting the parasol to cast a shadow over her baby bump.

'Of course I will. Jenneen will be here fussing around me and I'll probably just have a snooze. I feel like I've spoilt your holiday so it will make me happy for you all to go off and enjoy yourselves. What time have you got to be at the stables?'

'Rodney is dropping us at five o'clock. Apparently, it's better for the horses a bit later in the day when it's not so hot. We'll be back around seven thirty for dinner, assuming none of us fall off,' he laughed. 'Hugo's the only one that has ever ridden before and I'm not sure he is that proficient.'

'It will be fun,' Holly said, her mind flashing back to her only experience on horseback. 'Riding on the beach is just amazing.'

Harry waited for a moment for Holly to elaborate but, when it was clear she had no intention of doing so, he said, 'Well, if you're sure. I'll just go and round the others up. See you later.'

Amy had been waiting at the top of the path to the side gate. She needed a few minutes with Holly alone. Clasping her copy of *Tiffany* she hurried down the path.

'Harry's looking for you,' Holly said.

'I know. This will only take a minute. You'll probably think I'm interfering but please hear me out. I think you should read this,' she said, placing the book on Holly's side table. 'All of it.'

'What do you mean, "all of it"?'

'I may be way off mark here, Holly, but I think maybe you had already read the first few chapters before it was published.'

Holly could feel the warm flush staining her cheeks.

It was all the confirmation Amy needed. 'You may be surprised at how the story turns out. Please say you will.'

Holly rested her hand on her rounded tummy.

'How did you work it out?'

'It wasn't hard. Knowing both of you and where you met. He's a really brilliant writer, but then, you know that already.'

Holly nodded. 'Yes,' she said.

CHAPTER 45

The limousine had dropped Harry and his friends at the address they had been given in Holetown. There were no stables as such, just an open-sided shelter in one corner of a large field with five horses tethered to a rail.

'Are you sure about this, Hugo?' Jack asked.

'I know it doesn't look very professional but, according to Mother, the guy that runs it is an ex-jockey and he has some of the best cared-for horses on the island,' Hugo replied.

'That'd be me you're talking about, fella,' said a small, sandy-haired man with an Australian accent. 'I'm Steve and your ma's right,' he said. 'I look after my animals. So, have any of you ever ridden before?'

Harry, Jack and Amy shook their heads.

'Only me, I'm afraid,' said Hugo, extending his hand to Steve. 'I'm Hugo, and this is Amy, Jack and Harry,' he said, pointing them out as he spoke.

'Okay. Well we'd better go through a few basics then before we get you on the horses and when we get down on the beach, I'll lead and Hugo here can bring up the rear.'

Fifteen minutes later, the five of them were sat astride their mounts and were waiting in line to cross the main coast road.

'I'll stop the traffic,' Steve said, 'and you lead them across, Hugo. Remember just a gentle dig in the ribs to get them moving, we don't want you to go galloping off.'

'Geez, Hugo, who thought this was going to be a good idea?' moaned Jack. 'It's a long way down if I fall off.'

Suppressing a laugh, Steve said, 'Well, don't fall off then, fella. Here we go,' he added, riding into the middle of the road to stop the traffic.

Once on the beach everyone relaxed a bit, knowing that the sand or the sea would be a softer landing than the tarmac road. They followed in a line behind Steve as he guided them around the rocky outcrops jutting into the sea between sandy bays. The horses were very sure-footed. They had clearly done the journey hundreds of times before, so all the riders needed to do was grip lightly with their knees and keep hold of the reins. The occasional stumble on unseen rocks caused a few expletives from Jack and Harry but for the most part it wasn't as hard as they'd feared it might be and they were all enjoying the experience.

Because they were all such novices, it had taken longer to reach the turnaround point than usual. The sun was already making its descent over the horizon as they made their way back along the coastline, the failing light making it slightly more hazardous and, to make matters worse, the tide was higher so the water was deeper around the protruding rocks. None of the non-riders felt confident enough to remove their feet from the stirrups to prevent them from trailing in the water and consequently they were all starting to feel chilly when they got back to the beach in Holetown.

'Hugo, you deserve a medal, mate, but the best I can offer is a canter along the beach for helping me get your mates back safely.'

Hugo had been a little frustrated by the slow pace. He wasn't the greatest rider in the world but five minutes of freedom with the wind in his face would round his day off nicely.

'You don't mind do you?' he asked his friends.

'Of course not,' they all agreed.

'I'll just be five minutes then,' he said, urging his horse into a trot before cantering towards the far end of the beach.

'It's nice for Hugo to be able to show off a bit,' Amy whispered to Harry. 'I sometimes think he's got a real inferiority complex, despite all his money.'

Harry was only half listening. 'Is he okay, Steve?'

Hugo had turned the horse and was now moving back towards them at a terrifying speed.

'Bloody idiot. Get off the wet sand,' he shouted, gesticulating wildly, to try and get Hugo on to the soft sand at the top of the beach. 'It's a retired race horse, but the horse doesn't know he's retired. We gallop them on the hard sand to train them. I would have thought your mate would have known that,' he added, flailing his arms like a demented windmill.

Eventually Hugo managed to regain control of the horse and brought it skidding to a halt a few feet from where the others were waiting for him. His face was red and sweaty and with his dishevelled blond mop of hair he bore a striking resemblance to the London mayor.

'Did I win?' he asked.

The four friends burst out laughing but Steve just shook his head muttering, 'Bloody tourists.'

It was past 8 p.m. by the time the friends had changed out of their wet things and joined Holly on the terrace for dinner.

'I'm sorry we're late, Mum,' Harry said, 'it was a longer trip than we thought and then Hugo decided to go for a lap of the race track. Blimey, I can already feel the muscles in my bum and legs aching. Did you have a decent afternoon?'

'Lovely, thanks. Jenneen kept me hydrated with delicious fruit drinks and water, and I got my nose stuck into a book,' she said, glancing across at Amy.

'Good book?' he asked, reaching for the dish of rice and peas.

'Enlightening,' she answered.

CHAPTER 46

Harry shivered. Although it had been a beautiful early September day in Wales, it was chilly out of the sun as he stood on the platform of Swansea railway station awaiting the arrival of his mum's train. He'd spent the previous five days staying at Gareth's house and, although their relationship was still in its early stages, he felt confident that they would now always be a part of each other's life. He was filled with admiration for the determination his father had shown, which had played a large part in his recovery. Harry felt as though a missing piece of the jigsaw puzzle of his life had slotted in to place. He didn't love his mum any less than he always had, he'd simply made room in his heart for another person, just as he would when eventually he found a partner of his own and they had children together.

During his time with Gareth, he had managed to persuade him to have a Skype call with Jim and Bethan in America. They had been overjoyed when the camera on his computer had captured him standing up from his wheelchair and walking across the room. Part of Gareth's anger towards them seem to wash away with Bethan's tears of joy and he had ended the call by inviting them to stay with him in Oxwich for Christmas.

Harry smiled. He had achieved part one of his objective. Now to tackle part two, he thought, as his mum made her way down the station platform.

'Good journey?' he asked, kissing her on the cheek and taking her overnight bag from her.

'Really easy,' said Holly. 'I quite like train journeys. Much less hassle than driving. I even managed to start jotting a few ideas down for the book you're always telling me I should write.'

'Really? What's it going to be about?'

'It's at a far too early stage for me to start trying to explain, but I thought it would be handy to have some ideas in place before I go on the writing course in Tuscany next summer. I'm so pleased they were able to move me to a later course, at least you'll have finished your degree. Thanks for offering to babysit for me. Are you sure you will be able to manage?'

Harry looked at his mum in disbelief. 'You will have absolutely nothing to worry about,' he said, 'particularly as Amy has offered to help. By the way, did I tell you she and Jack are having a trial separation? She's moving her stuff out of the flat and sharing with some other girls.'

Holly raised her eyebrows. She wasn't surprised, but she didn't want Harry to know that she and Amy had discussed it in Barbados.

'Maybe it's for the best,' she said. 'Perhaps they rushed into things too quickly.'

'You're a fine one to talk, Mum,' Harry said laughing. Holly blushed.

On the drive from the centre of Swansea to Oxwich, Holly was very quiet. All the way down on the train she was trying to imagine what it would be like seeing Gareth again. She had longed for and dreamt about it for twenty years but nothing could prepare her for the actual moment. Obviously they had both aged and she had had to come to terms with the idea of Gareth spending most of his time in a wheelchair, but there had also been so much tragedy in both their lives and they hadn't been there for each other. The Gareth she had known was a larger-than-life character who enjoyed being the centre of attention but, according to Harry, his existence now was much more solitary. The man she had been so in love with was a different person now, and so was she. He had been the love of her life for so many years but someone else had forced his way in to Holly's heart. Her mind was in turmoil.

She had yet to meet up with Philippe since arriving back from Barbados but they had spoken at some length on the phone and decided they were going to give each other a second chance. In some ways, she could have done without the distraction of meeting with Gareth but she knew that if she didn't, a little piece of her heart would always belong to him and she would always be thinking of what might have been.

'It'll be okay, Mum,' Harry said, reassuringly.

'Will it? I'm not even sure why I'm here?'

'In part, I think you're doing it for me. By meeting with Gareth at least I'll feel comfortable talking to you about him. But I think it's for you too. You need to find closure to a piece of your past.'

'Maybe you're right. It just feels so strange that the only reason I'm making this journey is because I finally fell in love with someone else and became pregnant again. When I think of all the years I waited for him to come and find me, and all that time he thought I was dead. I don't think I'll ever be able to forgive her.'

'Don't even think about her, Mum, she doesn't deserve a moment of your time. She's the one that has missed out on having us in her life.'

'I know you're right, Harry, but I can't help wondering what happened in her life to turn her into such a bitter and twisted human being. The mother-and-child relationship is supposed to be the closest connection and yet I feel like I never knew her at all. She never wanted to be close to me, Harry, maybe that's why I've been so selfish with you.'

Harry shot his mum a sidelong glance. 'Selfish?'

Holly nodded. 'Perhaps the reason I didn't make more of an effort to go out and meet people when you were growing up is because I didn't want to share you with anyone.'

'Mum, don't dwell on the decisions you made. At the time they were right for you and I haven't turned out too bad. It's history, Mum, you need to move on and that's why you're here.'

Harry had pulled the car on to the tarmac driveway.

'Thank you for finding Gareth,' Holly said, her voice thick with emotion. 'I have no idea how I'm going to feel when I see him, or what he'll make of me being unmarried and pregnant, but I think we're both grateful for the chance you've given us. I'm so proud of you.'

'Don't get all tearful. You want Dad to see you looking your best don't you? Come on, he's as nervous as you.

Let's get this over with, shall we?'

Gareth heard the car pull up outside. He had been rehearsing in his head what he was going to say when he laid eyes on Holly again, but the words had all gone from his mind. He sat at the dining table almost breathless with anticipation. The door opposite him swung open and the years fell away as Holly stood, framed by the doorway, her swelling belly outlined against the warm orange tones of a beautiful sunset.

'Hello, Gary,' she said, shyly.

'Hello, Holly,' he replied, his words catching in his throat. 'You'd better come in.'

She took a few faltering steps into the room. The door closed behind her but when she turned to look, Harry had not followed her in.

'He's a good lad. He thought we should have some time to ourselves. You've done a grand job in raising him, Holly.'

Slow tears started to trickle down Holly's cheeks.

'Hey, don't cry. We've got nothing to cry for. At least, not now we haven't.' Gareth pushed himself up to a standing position and moved over to where Holly was. 'You haven't changed a bit. You're still just as beautiful as I remember,' he said, opening his arms. She leaned her head against his chest and he wrapped his arms around her and her unborn child. For a few moments Gareth allowed himself to imagine how it would have felt to have to have been embracing her twenty years previously, when she was pregnant with his son, Harry. 'I've always loved you, Holly,' he whispered into her dark curls, 'and I think I always will.'

When Harry returned to the house two hours later he was met by the wonderful smell of the casserole that Gareth had put in the oven prior to Holly's arrival, and the sight of his parents curled up on the sofa together, with Ben at their feet.

'It's only me,' he had called out to announce his arrival.

Instead of springing apart like adolescent teenagers caught out by their parents, they remained where they were, Holly's head comfortably resting on Gareth's shoulder.

'How's it going?' Harry ventured.

'Well, there would have been a lot to talk about,' Holly said, 'but it seems you've told your dad most things already.'

'She's joking,' Gareth said. 'We've barely scratched the surface. Clearly your mum is going to have to come and visit again, if she wants to of course?'

'Is that even a proper question? It's lovely here, so calm and peaceful. No wonder you came to live here after what happened in America.'

'I don't want to talk about America, remember? Not tonight, not ever. As long as we get that straight we'll be okay,' he said, a note of warning in his voice. Gently he pushed her away from his shoulder and eased himself to his feet. 'Megan should be here any minute. She's joining us for dinner, I hope that's okay? I wasn't sure how we were going to get along and I didn't want it to be awkward. I could always cancel her if you prefer.'

'No, of course I don't mind. I'm looking forward to

meeting her. She sounds like a saint from what you've said, coping with your moods.'

'What's that supposed to mean?' Gareth said, spinning round to face Holly, his eyes dark with anger.

'Hello, I'm not too early am I?' Megan asked, peering round the front door.

Gareth visibly relaxed. 'Of course not. Come in. You're just in time to set the table.'

'I don't know how I put up with you,' she said amiably, 'and you're forgetting your manners. You haven't introduced me.'

'This is Holly,' Gareth said, 'Harry's mum.'

'And you must be Megan,' Holly said smiling, relief rushing through her where moments earlier she had felt real fear.

Later that night, Holly lay in bed in Gareth's spare room, reflecting on the events of the evening. Now she thought about it, all the talk while she had been alone with Gareth had been about her and Harry, or Gareth's life since he got back from America. Harry had told her that Gareth blamed his parents for sending him to study in LA, but it was clear that he also apportioned some of the blame to her, despite the fact that she had never wanted him to go. She had felt frightened by the expression on his face when she had light-heartedly mentioned his moods. The carefree Gareth she had known all those years ago was gone forever.

Silent tears rolled down her cheeks in the darkness. Tears for the life they had had snatched away from them.

CHAPTER 47

I'm really nervous about tonight,' Philippe said, fiddling with his tie in the reflection of his bathroom mirror, an action made all the trickier with the phone cradled between his chin and his shoulder.

'The reason being?' Jo asked. 'It's not as though it's a blind date. You already know each other pretty intimately, if your descriptions of her in your book are anything to go by.'

Philippe cringed. He had had plenty of time to reflect on writing about his and Holly's most intimate moments in his novel. What had seemed like a good idea at the time now transpired to have been the reason Holly broke off their relationship and Philippe was deeply regretting going into so much detail about their intimacy.

Holly had contacted Philippe as soon as she had returned to the UK from the ill-fated trip to Barbados. Although it had been an uncomfortable conversation, they both agreed that it was easier to discuss the reasons for the break-up over the phone rather than face to face. There had been an awkward moment for Philippe when Holly had asked him why he thought she had finished with him. He had been about to confess to the evening of drunkenness and his subsequent belief that she had found out that he had spent the night with an exotic dancer, but instead had answered lamely, I really don't know. Maybe that was why he was feeling nervous about tonight. He still hadn't been completely honest with Holly, despite his best intentions.

'There is more than the physical act of sex to consider in a relationship, you know.'

'Well, there's something I never thought I'd hear you say.'

'I'm a different person now, Jo. I've been telling you for months that Holly has changed me. The moment I saw her I fancied her, but even spending the little time together we did, and I mean out of bed, I knew she was the person I wanted to spend the rest of my life with. I can't wait for you to meet her, I think you will really like her.'

'She does know tonight is a double-date doesn't she? I know you want Geoff and me there for a bit of moral support, but maybe she would have preferred a quiet candlelit dinner for two?'

Philippe was still coming to terms with the idea of his city-girl-about-town editor dating the very parochial Geoff from Chapters bookshop. It seemed an incongruous pairing but Jo was clearly happy, even taking annual leave so that she could spend a couple of days with him in Bath, which was very unlike her.

'I'm hoping there'll be plenty of time for that,' Philippe responded. 'Tonight is about reacquainting ourselves with one another. It will be a bit like when we first met in Mauritius in the company of Robert and Rosemary. I know now that she broke off our relationship because of using our intimacy in my book but I think she realises that it was meant to be an homage to her because I think she is so wonderful.'

There was a pause on the other end of the phone.

'Jo, are you still there?'

'When exactly did Holly break up with you?'

'Don't remind me. It was just after I'd sent you the manuscript for *Tiffany*.'

'That's what I thought. What puzzles me is how she could have seen it.'

'You know, I hadn't even thought about that. I was just so relieved to find out that her reasons for splitting were only to do with my book and to know that, with a lot of grovelling from me, she is prepared to give me another chance. We'll ask her tonight over dinner.'

'That could be quite an interesting conversation,' Jo said. 'What time is the table booked?'

'Eight o'clock.'

'Don't be late,' Jo said. 'I'm looking forward to seeing Holly's face when she sees me.'

'Us, you mean, Jo. You're part of a couple now.'

Jo didn't bother to correct Philippe. She had said what she meant. Holly had quite a lot of explaining to do if Jo's suspicions were right.

At precisely 8 p.m., Holly stood by the railings at the entrance to Mosimann's restaurant in Knightsbridge, waiting for Harry who was having trouble finding a parking space. She had butterflies in her stomach. She hadn't been in any fit state to talk to Philippe when she had seen him at the hospital in Barbados, and besides they had not been left on their own, so, in some respects, this felt like a first date. The decision to bring Harry as a kind of chaperone was twofold. She couldn't trust her heart not to want to go back to Philippe's place and spend the night with him and that was something her head didn't want to happen. I need to take things slowly, she thought. I need to be sure that this is someone I want to share my life with before I jump into his bed again. Just the thought of sharing his bed brought a familiar flush to her cheeks and a stirring deep inside.

She also wanted Harry there for a more practical reason. There were still a few secrets that she hadn't discussed with Philippe in their phone conversation. He might not take too kindly to her not revealing her other job as a copy editor. He had been very understanding about the need for secrecy surrounding her Liberty Sands work but she had deliberately passed up on the opportunity to tell him about working for the publishing company he was signed to. The last thing she needed was to be abandoned in the middle of Knightsbridge, heavily pregnant, potentially with a hefty restaurant bill to pay and no transport home. Holly and Harry had made a deal. He had agreed to accompany her on the understanding that he would be able to enjoy a few glasses of wine. She wasn't drinking so she would drive them both home. Although she hadn't told Philippe that she was bringing Harry, she reasoned that they knew each other already and, if he was going to be a more permanent fixture in her life, they would need to build up an amiable relationship. She hoped the restaurant would be able to accommodate a third person at their table for two.

Holly had been very impressed by his choice of restaurant after checking it out on their website while trying to decide how she should dress. Mosimann's was an Italian restaurant converted from a nineteenth-century church. There was the main dining area but also a choice of seven private dining rooms and Holly was interested to find out which room Philippe had chosen for their rendezvous. She had selected an emerald green, loose-fitting silk shirt to wear over her maternity leggings and the comfort of black patent ballerina pumps, which she hoped would be suitable.

'That was a bit of a mission,' Harry said, hurrying towards her, 'we'd better go in, I know how you hate being late.'

'Wow, this is beautiful,' Holly said, gazing up in awe at the wooden gallery that ran around the room filled with diners and others enjoying a pre-dinner aperitif.

Harry was equally impressed. 'How the other half lives, eh? Mind you, you've had your fair share of that over the past few months. I bet you'll miss it now you're grounded.'

'Not really. I was so uncomfortable on my last trip and I don't think Rosie liked it much either,' she said, resting her hands on the top of her belly.

Since the scan in Barbados, where they had found out that the baby was a girl, Holly had got into the habit of referring to the baby bump as Rosie. It made Harry uncomfortable. There was still two months to go before the baby was born and things could go wrong, especially in an older mother.

They followed the maître d' to the back of the room and up a flight of stairs.

'The other guests are already here and I've notified your waiter that he needs to lay an extra place,' he said.

Holly and Harry exchanged a quizzical look.

'Philippe must have invited Robert,' Harry said, 'although he didn't mention it when I spoke to him earlier.'

'How thoughtful,' Holly said. 'But what a shame Rosemary couldn't have been here too. She would have loved this place.'

The maître d' pushed open the door to the Davidoff room and said, 'This is one of the very first "chef table" dining rooms in the country. I hope you will enjoy your evening with us.'

Holly gasped. Instead of the convivial Robert, Philippe was sat at a table with her old friend from university, DD, and a man she didn't recognise.

'How odd,' said Harry, 'that looks exactly like Geoff from the bookshop where Amy works.'

Holly's pulse was racing. Why the hell would Philippe have brought DD to their reunion dinner? Philippe had pushed his chair back and was walking towards her, but she was rooted to the spot.

'Holly, you look absolutely radiant. You should have told me you were bringing Harry, I would have booked a bigger table,' he said, kissing her on the cheek.

She felt weak at the knees but, surprisingly, it wasn't due to his kiss.

'Let me introduce you to my editor from Ripped,' he said, linking his arm through hers and propelling her towards the round table, where a waiter had already laid the fifth place. 'Holly, this is Jo, and her boyfriend, Geoff. Jo, this is my Holly and her son, Harry.'

Holly sank into the chair that Philippe had pulled out

for her, unable to speak.

'So this is the Holly you've been searching for?' Jo said, the surprise in her voice real despite knowing that it would be her. 'What a small world it is. Holly and I were at university together, and she does some work for me occasionally. I had no idea you had a son,' she added.

CHAPTER 48

'Are you sure you're okay to drive, Mum?' Harry asked, looking anxiously at Holly's ashen face. 'I've only had a couple of glasses of wine, and that was with food, so I won't be over the limit.'

'I'm fine,' Holly replied, although clearly she wasn't. 'I don't want to risk you losing your licence because of me.'

The evening couldn't have been much worse. Not only had Philippe found out about her job as a copy editor before she had the chance to tell him, totally removing her from any high moral ground with regard to keeping secrets from each other, she was now fearful that DD wouldn't put any work her way because she hadn't been truthful about her relationship to Philippe when she had withdrawn from copy-editing *Tiffany*. With no money coming in from Soleil Resorts for the foreseeable future, she had been relying on Ripped Publishing to keep her going financially until she could resume her blogging trips.

'I didn't realise you hadn't told DD – Jo – whatever you want to call her – about me,' Harry said.

'It wasn't necessary. I didn't want her to think that

I wouldn't be able to make deadlines because I had a young child, but I also didn't want her to put two and two together and realise that Gareth was your dad.'

'Why was it so important for her not to know Gareth is my dad? What difference would it have made?'

'None, I suppose. My stupid hurt pride has made me make a lot of mistakes and now it looks like I'm going to have to pay for them.'

'What do you mean?'

'Well, Philippe wasn't exactly all over me after Jo dropped her bombshell was he? He didn't try to encourage us to stay for dessert after I made my excuses for leaving early.'

'Maybe you're reading too much into it, Mum. You are looking pretty pale. He was probably just concerned for the baby. I'm sure he'll ring you tomorrow and you can talk it through then.'

'We'll see,' she said, in a resigned tone of voice, 'but I'm pretty sure I won't be hearing from Jo any time soon. Publishers have pretty strong ethical rules and I'm worried that maybe I should have just been honest about knowing Philippe from the outset. I have no idea what I'm going to do for money if she stops sending me work.'

'I think you're fretting over nothing. What would she gain by losing one of her best copy editors? Once the dust has settled it'll be fine and if not I could speak to Geoff for you. He's a really nice chap.'

'Yes, he is, but I doubt he would have any influence over Jo. She doesn't mix business with pleasure. I just can't believe I've made such a mess of things again.'

'Lights, Mum!' Harry cried.

Holly slammed her foot on the brake. She had been

so engrossed in the conversation that she hadn't noticed the traffic lights turning red and had nearly run into the car in front.

'Geez, that was close. I can't let you drive, Mum, you're too upset. Pull over to the side of the road and we'll swap over.'

Holly didn't argue. The emergency stop had forced her seatbelt to restrain her and where it had dug in, she was now experiencing a sharp pain. By the time the lights changed, the pain had subsided so she was able to pull across the junction and into the side of the road but, in the short time it took for them both to undo their seatbelts, walk round the car to exchange places and buckle up again, Holly had begun to feel another sharp stabbing pain.

'Harry,' she whispered, 'I think I might be going into labour.'

'Are you sure?' Harry asked. 'You're not due for another couple of months.'

'Pretty sure,' she replied, trying to breathe through the pain. 'Has your sat nav got hospitals listed on it? I don't think I'm going to make it back to Reading.'

Harry scrabbled in the glove box of his old Corsa, retrieved the sat nav and plugged it into the cigarette lighter. As he did so he said, 'You'd better try and ring Philippe. He said he wanted to be there for the birth.'

Holly dialled his number but it went straight to voicemail. She left a brief message.

'Philippe, I'm in labour. We're going to the hospital. Harry will call you later.'

CHAPTER 49

Once Holly and Harry had left Mosimann's restaurant, Philippe turned on Jo.

'Was that really necessary?' he asked.

'What?' she answered, innocently

'You'd already worked out that your Holly and my Holly were one and the same, hadn't you? Why couldn't you just tell me and not put us all in such a difficult position?'

'I wasn't sure,' she replied, shrugging her shoulders. 'The Holly I went to uni with was very prim and proper, not the sort to go around having illegitimate children with a variety of partners.'

'That's not how it is and you know it. She hasn't had a boyfriend in twenty years.'

'Well, that's what she would like you to believe. How do you know it's true after all the lies she has told you?'

'Actually, it was Harry who told me but I would have believed her anyway, because I have faith in human nature. I thought Geoff was making you a nicer person but clearly I was mistaken,' he said, pushing his chair back and throwing his napkin down on the table. 'I was going to treat everyone to dinner but you can put it on your big fat expense account instead. If I hurry I might just catch up with them and apologise for your appalling behaviour,' he said, heading for the door.

The cool October air rushed to meet Philippe as he pushed open the double doors of the restaurant and hurried down the steps on to the street. He looked in both directions but there was no sign of Holly and Harry. He walked up to the corner, reaching in his pocket for his mobile phone. He was about to turn it back on and dial Holly's number when he remembered that she had said she was driving home because Harry had been drinking.

'Damn,' he cursed, thrusting the phone back in his pocket and kicking out at a pile of orange leaves that had gathered beneath a tree. 'What a bitchy thing to do.'

To Philippe, it felt as though Jo was deliberately trying to come between him and Holly. Or maybe it was just a case of if she can't have me no one can, he thought. He flagged down a black cab. 'The Met Bar, please,' he said, slamming the cab door and slumping on to the back seat. I need a drink, he thought, a bloody big one.

CHAPTER 50

Harry screeched to a halt in the ambulance bay in front of accident and emergency at St Thomas's Hospital. Before anyone could tell him he couldn't park there, he ran into the hospital and up to the reception desk.

'I need some help. My mum is in labour. She's not due for another two months,' he said as calmly as he could. 'I'm parked in the ambulance bay.'

Within minutes an orderly had arrived and they both helped Holly, who was in the middle of another contraction, into the wheelchair.

'You'll have to move your car into the car park, lad,' the orderly said, 'but don't you worry, I'll look after your mum.'

'Harry,' Holly said, as she was wheeled away, 'please try Philippe again.'

'I'll keep trying, Mum, and I'll be with you in a few minutes.'

Harry tried Philippe's number several times but it still kept going to voicemail. In the end Harry sent him a text message to say they were at St Thomas's just before the battery on his phone died.

Taking the stairs two at a time, Harry followed the signs

to the maternity wing and then asked the receptionist there for his mum's whereabouts.

'She's gone straight into the delivery room. Does she want you to be with her?'

Harry suspected that his mum would rather have had Philippe in attendance but as they couldn't contact him Harry was the next best thing. When he pushed open the door, the room was a hive of activity but everyone was very calm, including Holly.

'You don't have to stay if you don't want to, Harry,' she said.

'Don't be silly, Mum, I'll be fine so long as I stay at this end,' he said, taking hold of her hand. Holly's face contorted as another contraction started. 'Squeeze as hard as you like, Mum, if it helps.'

'We're nearly ready for you to push,' said a voice from the other end of the bed. 'I can see baby's head and you're fully dilated.'

Holly was sweating. She was trying to breathe as deeply as she could through the contractions. 'Please let Rosie be all right, please let Rosie be all right,' she kept repeating over and over, like a mantra. She could feel another contraction starting.

'And push,' said the midwife, 'keep pushing. Good girl. This little one's in a hurry. It won't be long at all.'

'Where's Philippe?' Holly managed to ask, before the next contraction overwhelmed her.

'He must have his phone off. You just concentrate on pushing,' Harry said, sad for his mum that, once again, she was going through this experience without the baby's father.

Less than thirty minutes later, Holly gave a final

big push and her little girl was born. There was a tense moment before the baby let out a whimper. The midwife clamped then cut the umbilical cord and then laid her on a flannel blanket on the scales.

'It's a little girl. She's a good weight for a premature baby. Just over five pounds. She would have been a nine pounder if she'd gone to full term,' the midwife said, wrapping the blanket around the baby and laying her in Holly's arms.

'She's tiny. Is she all right?' Holly asked, gazing in wonder at the doll-like being in her arms.

'We'll need to check her over but I just wanted you to have a couple of minutes with her first. She's breathing on her own, which is always a good sign.'

Harry was wiping his mum's face with a damp cloth.

'Well done, Mum. You were brilliant. Did I arrive that quickly?'

Holly smiled up at him weakly, the memory of the only other time she had given birth flooding her mind. 'It took you eight hours to make your appearance, Harry. I'd begun to wonder whether you'd changed your mind.' She looked down at her daughter. 'Not like Rosie here, impatient to make an entrance,' she said, stroking the rosebud lips with a finger that looked huge by comparison. The tiny baby opened her cloudy, deep blue eyes and seemed to stare intently at her mother before her lids flickered closed again, as though the effort of being born had exhausted her.

Harry had wondered if he would feel jealousy when the new baby arrived but instead he was filled with awe at the miracle of nature, and relief that everything seemed normal.

CHAPTER 51

Philippe's mouth tasted of sawdust and his tongue felt like sandpaper. One drink had turned into several when he had run into a few of his former newspaper colleagues in The Met Bar. He had finally staggered out of the bar at 2 a.m., drunker than he had been at any time since the episode in Mauritius. *So much for my promise never to drink again*, he thought, easing himself gently into an upright position. *No wonder Holly has reservations about spending the rest of her life with me. I didn't stick up for her in front of Jo and then I go and get off my head on Jack Daniel's. What a great catch I am*, he thought, *I simply don't deserve her.* He padded down the steep stairs of the terraced house to make himself a strong black coffee, picking up his phone from the hall table en route.

In the few seconds it took for the water in the Nespresso machine to heat up, Philippe turned on his mobile phone and keyed in his code. He selected the strongest blend of coffee and dropped the pod into the machine. As the bitter frothy liquid was spewing into the waiting cup, his phone alerted him that he had messages. He read the text from Harry before dialling his voicemail. The glass espresso cup he had just brought up to his lips fell to the floor, shattering on the cream travertine tiles and spilling scalding liquid on his bare feet. He hardly noticed. All he could think about was getting to St Thomas's hospital as quickly as he could. He raced up the stairs, dragged on a pair of chinos and a shirt and was out on the street within five minutes, frantically searching for a black cab.

Less than a mile away, someone else was trying to flag down a taxi. Geoff had gone back to Jo's Chelsea flat after the debacle at the restaurant the previous evening. Neither of them had spoken much on the short journey from Knightsbridge but as soon as they were inside the front door, Jo rounded on Geoff.

'Come on then, spit it out. No doubt you agree with Phil that I should have told him that I thought I might know his Holly.'

Geoff hated confrontation. 'How long have you known? Surely you haven't let him keep on searching for all these months, knowing the desperation he was feeling?'

'Well, thanks for the vote of confidence. Just how nasty a person do you think I am?'

'You didn't answer my question,' Geoff said, calmly.

'Nor you mine but, for your information, I had no idea that the two Hollys were one and the same until my phone conversation with Phil earlier this evening.'

'So why didn't you just tell him your suspicions like most normal people would have done?'

'Are you saying I'm not normal?' Jo asked, her eyes

darkening and her voice rising.

'Don't be ridiculous. I'm saying that most people would have said something to Philippe to avoid the situation you put us all in. What you did was plain cruel. And the way you kept hinting throughout the evening that you're not going to give her any more editing work. She's pregnant, for God's sake. You were like an animal toying with its catch.'

'She broke the rules. Why didn't she just tell me she knew Phil when she rejected working on his manuscript, instead of inventing some story about a friend dying of cancer? It seems as though little Miss Victim has you all wrapped around her little finger. Well, not me. I've got a business to think of. I need to be able to trust the people I employ.'

'You can't mean that? Surely even you must realise that it was an extraordinary set of circumstances that led to her having to make an excuse not to work on Philippe's book. She was embarrassed. You've done nothing but talk about the titillating sex scenes in *Tiffany*. Imagine how you'd feel if the author had written about you.'

And therein lies the problem, thought Jo. Phil would never have written about me in his bloody book because he never loved me like he loves his precious Holly, and now she's having his baby!

'You've missed the last train to Bath so you can sleep on the couch, but please be gone before I get up in the morning,' she said, slamming the bedroom door behind her so forcefully that the whole flat vibrated like a minor earth tremor. She leaned back against the door, her heart thumping and her mind racing. What have I done? she thought. Why am I destroying my chance of happiness with Geoff?

Jo lay awake for a long time hoping that Geoff would tap on the bedroom door and that she would be able to apologise for shouting at him. The knock never came and the last thing she remembered thinking, before drifting into a restless sleep, was, he would have tried to make this up with me, if he really loved me.

CHAPTER 52

Holly had been moved from the delivery room to a ward with three other new mums at around 2 a.m. once baby Rosie had been returned after her medical checks. The nurses said that Harry could sleep in the deserted relatives' room but, after an hour of trying to fall asleep stretched across four plastic chairs, he decided to go back and grab a nap in Toby. He was very grateful for the fleecy blanket that his mum always insisted he kept stashed in the boot of his car for emergencies. He slept fitfully until 7 a.m. then decided to make his way over to the hospital coffee shop. Harry felt a bit weird. He wanted to tell the world about his new baby sister but was there really anyone, apart from the baby's absent dad, who would be interested? Don't be stupid, he reprimanded himself. Robert had asked him about the baby every time he had spoken to him in the past few weeks, and he would need to text Amy, Hugo and Jack later. And then there was Gareth. Although Rosie wasn't a blood relative of his, he had asked Harry to let him know when the baby arrived. There was going to be a lot of love surrounding this little girl.

Harry ordered a cappuccino and a croissant and picked up a Sunday paper. He guessed it would be quite some time before he was allowed back on to the ward so reading the paper would help pass the time. Harry scanned the back pages first. He wasn't particularly interested in sport but, since meeting his dad, Harry liked to check and see how the Ospreys had got on. He smiled. They had thrashed their opponents 36–7.

Harry flicked idly through the magazines that accompanied the Sunday papers and then started on the paper itself. He glanced at his watch. It was almost nine o'clock. He was pretty sure that breakfast on the ward would be over and he was desperate to see his mum and baby sister to make sure everything was all right. He took a final sip of his second cappuccino of the morning and folded the paper to tuck under his arm. A photograph caught his eye. It was of three men staggering drunkenly out of a bar under the headline 'A DROP TOO MUCH OF THE WRITE STUFF'. Harry could barely believe his eyes. While his mum was enduring the excruciating pain of labour, Philippe had gone on a bender. Harry was filled with disgust. Maybe his mum had been right after all. Perhaps Philippe wasn't husband and father material. He gathered up the paper and headed up to the ward.

At just past 10 a.m., Philippe approached the reception desk on the maternity ward at St Thomas's.

'I think my girlfriend has gone into labour prematurely,' he said.

'Name?'

'Philippe Marchant.'

'Do you mean Philippa?' the receptionist asked, running her finger down a list of patients.

'What?' Philippe asked, his brain still fuddled by the over-consumption of alcohol the previous night.

'Your girlfriend. Is her name Philippa? Although I can't see anyone by that name on the list.'

Philippe thought he saw a flicker of recognition on the nurse's face. Not now, he thought. The last thing I need right now is to have to be nice to an adoring fan. 'Oh sorry, my misunderstanding. My girlfriend is Holly Wilson.'

'Right. Here she is, a late admission last night. She's just down the hall, third door on the right. Visiting is normally after 2 p.m. but, under the circumstances, I'm sure it will be fine.'

Circumstances? thought Philippe, what circumstances? But he didn't want to engage the nurse in conversation, so he thanked her and headed in the direction she had indicated. He stood outside the door, memories of a similar situation in Barbados filling his head. He realised his hands were shaking and that was nothing to do with the whisky he had been drinking. He had no idea what he was going to find on the other side of the door. Had it been a false alarm? And if not, had Holly had the baby and was it okay? He knocked and pushed the door open.

The room was divided into four separate areas by curtains encircling each bed. It was surprisingly quiet apart from a murmur of voices he could hear from the bed closest to him. 'Holly?' he ventured, in a voice little more than a whisper.

The voices stopped and a curtain was pushed back. Harry stood facing him, with a face like thunder.

'You've got a nerve,' he hissed at Philippe.

Philippe was taken aback. Harry had been so welcoming towards him until now. Clearly what had happened in the restaurant the night before had not pleased him. Philippe knew he should have taken Holly's side and protected her from the vitriolic Jo, but he had been shocked to the core by Jo's revelation.

'Look, Harry, I'm sorry about last night. Is Holly okay?'

'Sorry? Is that all you can say? Mum could have lost the baby and all you can do is go off and get pissed. You really are a loser.'

'Harry, that'll do,' said Holly. 'This isn't the time or the place. I don't want Rosie to be hearing anger in her first few hours.'

'Rosie? You mean our daughter has been born?'

Harry reluctantly stepped to one side to reveal his mum holding the sleeping baby close to her chest.

'She's so tiny,' Philippe said, a look of wonderment on his face. 'May I hold her?'

'I don't really think that's a good idea, do you? I can smell the alcohol on your breath from here,' Holly said, wrinkling her nose.

Philippe accepted the reprimand. 'Yes, yes you're right. I shouldn't have gone out drinking but I was so upset by the way Jo treated you. Straight after you'd left I gave her a piece of my mind and followed you out, but you'd already gone. I had no idea this was going to happen.'

'True. But it's a bit of a concern if you always turn to alcohol at the first sign of trouble.'

'And you didn't exactly do it privately,' added Harry, thrusting the newspaper at Philippe.

'Holly... I...'

'Philippe, I'm tired and emotional and I don't want to say anything I might regret. I needed you last night and you let me down. I think it would be best if you left. Once I'm back at home and settled with Rosie I'll call you, I promise. We've got a lot to discuss.'

'I know I've messed up, Holly, but please give me another chance.'

'Mum said she'd call you, so she will. She needs her rest now,' Harry said, ushering the distraught Philippe from the room.

Philippe looked back towards Holly and his baby daughter before Harry closed the door in his face. All the feelings of elation he had felt on hearing that he had become a father had been crushed. He dragged his feet back down the corridor as if they had ton weights attached to them.

As he passed the reception desk the young nurse behind it asked, 'Would it be possible to have an autograph please, Mr Marchant?'

Philippe ignored her as he made his way back towards the stairs, his heart heavy and his head full of regret.

CHAPTER 53

Holly had forgotten how all-consuming it was being a new mum. The first six weeks of Rosie's life sped by in a flurry of feeds, nappy-changing and seemingly endless sleepless nights. It was made all the harder because Rosie was so small and needed feeding on demand, but Holly wasn't complaining. Every time she held the tiny baby to her breast she felt the connection between them grow stronger. The hospital had been so pleased with Rosie's progress and weight gain that they had allowed mother and baby home after just a week.

Throughout Holly's stay at St Thomas's, Harry had been constantly on hand. He had rung his university to explain why he would be missing from his lectures for a while and was staying with Robert in Woldingham so that he wouldn't be too far away from the hospital. Robert had visited with Harry the day after Rosie was born. He sat and cradled the tiny girl, tears flooding down his cheeks. The baby had stayed awake for the whole time, regarding him with her blue eyes, not making a sound.

Amy had been their first visitor once they arrived back in Reading. At first she was nervous handling the baby but before long she was winding her after feeds and rocking her to sleep to give Holly a few minutes of precious time to take a shower or a bath. She and Harry had taken Rosie for her first walk in the newly acquired buggy, a present from Robert. Holly watched from the bedroom window as they walked along the street pushing the pram. They made a beautiful couple and she wondered if Harry would ever realise just how much Amy adored him.

True to her word, Holly had rung Philippe. He was filled with remorse and still hopeful of a reconciliation, but she needed time to think. Philippe had disappointed her by not standing up for her when Jo was pointedly making her feel like some kind of loose woman. She had eventually been able to forgive that but the drinking was a different issue. There was no way Holly was going to have Rosie's childhood blighted by alcohol as hers had been. She made excuses about being too tired to see him at home because of the constant demands of the baby but had instead suggested that he came to Rosie's christening, which was being held at St Agatha's church in Woldingham the week before Christmas. Holly reasoned that the neutral territory would make it easier for them to talk and Robert was more than happy to accommodate if it meant the possibility of bringing his two friends back together.

Robert was being a total brick, visiting Holly in Reading twice a week once Harry had gone back to Bath. He knew there wasn't much he could do for her practically, apart from making her cups of tea, but he guessed she might be feeling a bit isolated. It was on one of these visits that Holly broached the subject of Christmas.

'You know, Robert, I would love to have you here for Christmas but we simply haven't got the room. I know it's going to be difficult for you, the first year without Rosemary.'

'I think I'd rather just stay at home. We'll have had the christening the week before so I will have seen everybody. I don't think I'll be very good company.'

Holly looked across at Robert relaxing comfortably on her duck-egg-blue sofa, her baby daughter nestled in the crook of his arm. She couldn't bear the thought of him being alone and upset. 'I hope you don't think I'm being too forward, Robert, but I wondered if maybe we could come to yours?'

His eyes lit up but then he said, 'That's so kind of you to offer, but you've got your hands full with your own family. It's not fair to have you all walking on eggshells because you're afraid of upsetting me.'

Holly had spotted Robert's initial reaction and that was all the encouragement she needed. 'Actually, you would be doing me a massive favour. Harry loves Christmas. He loves decorating the house and stacking presents under the tree, not to mention buying way too much food for the two of us. I don't know if I can give him the kind of Christmas he enjoys while trying to look after Rosie. I don't want him to resent her. I know there will be moments where you just want to be alone with your thoughts but I think it would make Rosemary happy if you have loving friends around you.'

'I would love you to come. Valley View was always filled with people at Christmas time and I was dreading it. I'd even thought of going out to Mauritius to escape it but I think I would be even more miserable there. How about if you and Harry come over a couple of days before the christening and stay until New Year? If we're going to do it, let's do it properly, particularly as it might be my last Christmas there.'

'Have you sold the house?'

'There's an offer on it, but I haven't accepted yet. It's a bit under the asking price and I'm in no rush. If they want my home they are going to have to pay for it.'

'Will you buy something else in England or will you just move out to Mauritius? We'd miss you terribly.'

'I would definitely keep something here. Maybe a flat in London, or perhaps I'll buy somewhere near here. I've always liked the idea of living next to the River Thames in Berkshire.'

'I like that idea too, then we could come and visit more often. You can be Rosie's honorary grandpa. She loves being with you. I don't think I've heard her cry once when you're cradling her.'

'My little angel doesn't cry,' Robert said, looking down at her with adoring eyes.

'Only at 4 a.m.,' replied Holly, yawning.

In the end, Robert's Christmas house-guest list doubled. Harry had forgotten to mention to Holly that Gareth had invited them to Wales for Christmas. It would have been a bit of a squeeze because he had also invited his parents from America and the farmhouse only had three bedrooms. Holly didn't think it would be fair on everyone if Rosie woke in the night crying and besides she had already promised that they would go to Woldingham and she couldn't let Robert down.

It was Robert who came up with the solution. Valley View had five bedrooms and the master bedroom was located away from the other four. He would move out of the master bedroom so that Holly and Rosie wouldn't disturb anyone.

It was snowing as Harry drove his mum's VW Golf up the hill into Woldingham village two days before Rosie's christening. He wasn't keen on driving Holly's car but they had no choice with the amount of stuff they had to bring for Rosie who was contentedly sleeping in her car seat. Holly was squeezed in between Rosie and piles of brightly coloured presents, bags of clothes and the travel crib. The snow was only light but it had started to settle on the roads and footpath creating an eerie feeling in the early evening gloom.

The gritting lorry had done its job on the major roads but it had yet to visit the village and Harry felt the Golf losing traction on a couple of the bends, even though he was driving very slowly.

'I hope it's not going to get much worse,' Harry said, relieved to be pulling up in Robert's driveway. 'You know what public transport is like in this country, it grinds to a halt at the least little thing. If it's not leaves on the line in autumn, it's frozen points in winter. It does make you wonder how they cope in places like Siberia.'

'I suppose they're more used to it. Don't worry, it'll have all melted by the time Gareth and his parents are due to travel. I'm feeling a bit nervous about meeting them.'

'They're really nice, Mum. Two people whose lives got turned upside down by a freak accident. I'm so pleased Dad invited them for Christmas. Maybe they'll even think about moving back now that he seems to have forgiven them,' Harry said, lifting his baby sister out of the car.

'Get her inside quickly, Harry, she's still only a couple of pounds heavier than most newborns, we don't want her catching cold.'

Harry strode the few paces to the front door and rang the bell. Moments later the door opened, throwing an amber glow on to the glistening snow, to reveal Robert wearing an apron over his clothes, his hands covered in flour.

'You just caught me putting a batch of mince pies in the oven,' he said, wiping his hands down the apron. 'I'll take the little angel and you help your mum with the rest of the stuff.'

Harry smiled as he headed back to the car. Rosie's arrival really had brought so much happiness to so many people. 'You go in, Mum, I can manage the rest.'

Several trips later and the contents of the car were strewn across the landing at the top of the sweeping staircase. Harry stamped the snow off his feet on the doormat and locked the door behind him with fingers that were already feeling numb from the cold.

'Oh my God, Robert,' Harry said in delight, 'that is the biggest tree I've ever seen, apart from Trafalgar Square, of course. How tall is it?'

'I don't know. We always get it delivered from the garden centre because they know the room and they put it up for us too. I told them to leave the decorations though because your mum said you liked doing it.'

A broad smile spread across Harry's face. This was going to be the best Christmas ever, he thought.

CHAPTER 54

Contrary to Holly's prediction about the weather, the snow had kept falling and by the morning of Rosie's christening everywhere looked like a winter wonderland. It was pretty to look out on from the cosy warmth of Valley View, but Holly had real concerns about whether Robert and Rosemary's friend, Melody, and her family, would be able to make it.

Amy had called at the crack of dawn to say that she wasn't going to risk driving because of the atrocious conditions, but would get on a train which, surprisingly, were running a near normal service. Harry had intended to pick her up at the station in his mum's car but decided against it once he saw how virtually impassable the roads were. Instead, he left on foot to meet her at the station.

Holly was in the kitchen making final preparations for the buffet lunch. She glanced anxiously at the clock. Harry had left over an hour ago. Surely they should be here by now? The front door banged closed and she heard Harry's voice. Relief flooded through her.

'It's carnage out there,' Harry announced from the landing. 'There are cars stuck in the snow all the way up the hill. Amy and I managed to push a few near the top of the hill but there's no chance for the ones further down. I have just had my faith in human nature restored though. There's a guy in a posh Range Rover Sport towing the people who have stayed with their cars. How nice is that?'

'Well, it is nearly Christmas,' Holly said, 'the season of goodwill. Come in and get warm by the fire, Amy. Thank you for making such an effort to come, not everyone would.'

Amy was standing transfixed at Harry's side. 'This place is amazing,' she said, 'it's like something out of one of those posh interior design magazines. Look at the size of the tree! How on earth did you manage to decorate the top of it?' she asked, reaching the bottom of the stairs and making a beeline for the crackling log fire, after giving Holly a big hug.

'It was a bit precarious,' Harry said, laughing. 'I was up on the landing, leaning over the balustrade for the stuff at the top. It was worth it though.'

'It certainly was, it looks gorgeous and I love all the real holly you've dotted around. I just love Christmas. You guys are going to have an amazing time,' Amy said, a tinge of envy in her voice.

'If the weather gets any worse, you may well be spending it with us,' Robert said walking into the lounge from his office, a contented Rosie, resplendent in her christening gown, nestled on his arm.

'She looks adorable,' Amy said. 'That gown must have cost a fortune.'

'It's an antique. It's been in my late wife's family for generations. Her mother gave it to her in the hope that we would have babies but I'm afraid we failed in that department. It's a little bit big for Rosie,' he continued, unaware of the awkward glances around him, 'she's still such a tiny little thing.'

'We should probably leave for the church. It's going to take us a bit longer to walk through all this snow,' Holly said, tactfully moving the conversation away from Rosemary.

'Is Melody meeting us there?' Harry asked.

'She just rang to say they can't make it,' Robert said. 'They can't even get their car off the driveway.'

'So, it's just us then,' Holly said, 'unless Philippe has managed to find a way through the mayhem. I'm not waiting here for him because he's always late. I told him to meet us at St Agatha's.'

The snow had not been too bad in Battersea, and the roads were well gritted but, as Philippe headed towards the Surrey Hills, conditions were rapidly deteriorating. He had been determined to show Holly how seriously he intended to take his role as a father by arriving at the church early. Now, thanks to Mother Nature, it was looking unlikely that he would make it at all. The traffic through Purley and Kenley was painfully slow but at least it was moving, however, once he turned on to the Woldingham road, he began to realise the hopelessness of his task. The road wasn't gritted and cars had been abandoned making it very difficult to keep to the tyre tracks of the cars that had made it through. With dogged determination, Philippe pressed on, the wheels of his new Audi A5 spinning. How he wished he had gone for a four-wheel drive option.

The clock on the dashboard read 10.45 a.m. and the christening service was due to start at 11 a.m. The Audi finally gave up the ghost on the bend by the station, at the bottom of the big hill. Philippe slumped forward on to the steering wheel, his head in his hands. There was no way he was going to be able to walk in the deep snow to the tiny church at the other end of the village in fifteen minutes. There was a tap on his side window, startling him.

'Do you need a tow?' asked a man in a pea-green puffa jacket that had clearly seen better days, his voice muffled by the scarf wrapped round his face, snowflakes settling on his navy woolly hat.

Philippe couldn't believe it. Finally, lady luck is on my side, he thought, getting out of his car into snow that was almost knee deep. 'That would be amazing. I'm trying to get to my daughter's christening at St Agatha's. It starts in fifteen minutes and I really didn't want to be late.'

'Well, I can hook you up and try to tow you up the hill or you could leave your car here and I'll take you. The second option will get you there quicker if you don't mind risking someone skidding into your car. It looks pretty new.'

'It's a car and it's insured. I can always get another one. But I'll never have another chance to see my baby christened. Thanks so much,' Philippe said, climbing in the passenger door of the Range Rover Sport.

Holly had been surprised but secretly delighted when they had arrived at St Agatha's church at five minutes to eleven to find the solitary figure of Philippe waiting outside. They had walked together to the front of the small church with Philippe holding his baby daughter for the first time.

The service hadn't lasted long and although Rosie had been quiet throughout, she predictably started to cry as her head was wet with water. Robert immediately reached for the baby and within seconds she was smiling up at him, as she always did.

After thanking the vicar for turning out in such inclement weather, the small group trudged back through the snowbound village to Valley View, Harry and Amy leading the way, followed by Robert carrying Rosie, and Holly and Philippe bringing up the rear.

'I'm so impressed you were here on time,' Holly said, 'particularly with all this snow. Did you get a train?'

'No, I drove, but I wouldn't have made it if some chap in a four-wheel drive hadn't offered me a lift. I abandoned my car down by the station. I'll have to move it before it gets dark.'

'I'm sure Harry and Amy will give you a push after lunch. They've got to go down to the station for Amy to catch her train home anyway. She's beautiful isn't she?'

Philippe looked puzzled. 'Who, Amy? Well, I guess so. I hadn't really given it much thought,' he lied, remembering his comments to Jo after the book signing.

'No, silly. Rosie. And I don't think it's just because I'm her mum.'

'I don't really know much about babies but she looks pretty perfect to me, as do you, Holly. Being a mum suits you.'

'Really? Even with the dark circles under my eyes?'

'Your eyes are shining with happiness. I just hope

you'll let me be a part of it?' Philippe said, reaching for her gloved hand.

She didn't resist. 'We haven't really had the best of starts have we but I'm prepared to let that all be water under the bridge and try again, on one understanding.'

Philippe stopped walking and they turned to face each other. 'Anything,' he said. 'I'll do anything to have another chance.'

'You have to stop drinking,' Holly said, trying to gauge the reaction in his pale green eyes. 'I've lived through the devastating effect an alcoholic can have on a normal family life. I don't want that for Rosie.'

'Stop altogether? As in, I can't even have a glass of champagne today or a glass of wine with dinner ever again? That's a big ask, Holly. Even if I said I would, I'm not sure I could stick to it, no matter how much I want to.'

'I'm glad you said that, Philippe, because I don't think you can stop either and I wouldn't have believed you if you'd said you could. I'd like to start seeing you again, for dates and stuff, taking it slowly even though we've already got Rosie. How do you feel about that?'

'Honestly? I just want to move in with you both and be part of a happy family. You are the only woman I have ever felt this way about, but I know that's not true for you, so I'm prepared to do things your way, if it means we have a chance of eventually being together.' Philippe bent forward and kissed the snowflake off the end of Holly's nose before brushing her lips with his.

Her heart was doing somersaults in her chest, but Holly stuck to her resolution. 'So, regarding the drinking. Social drinking is okay, but not around Rosie. If you ever come to my house with the smell of alcohol on your breath, then we'll be finished, regardless of my feelings for you. I hope you understand?'

CHAPTER 55

Christmas at Robert's had been as perfect as Holly had hoped. The heavy snow had melted away as quickly as it had arrived, so there had been no disruption on the train service from South Wales. Although initially nervous to meet Gareth's parents, any awkwardness was soon overcome when she saw how delighted they were to be in Harry's company. It was strange to think that the catalyst for reuniting the Caswell family was the tiny baby that everyone had spent the past five days fussing over, that was no relation to them at all. Rosie had played up to all the attention, chuckling and grabbing fingers when offered and barely crying. Because she had been kept so busy during the daytime with all the adoring adults she had even started sleeping through the night, for which Holly was eternally grateful.

On Christmas morning, Holly had called Philippe to wish him a Merry Christmas. She felt sorry that he couldn't join in the festivities at Robert's but she didn't want there to be an atmosphere between him and Gareth, so decided it would be best to keep them apart. Holly hadn't bought a Christmas gift for Philippe but during the phone conversation he told her he had slipped hers under the tree. Harry was handing out the gifts for everyone and they all watched with anticipation as he handed over a small sparkly gift bag. Holly undid the seal on the top and could see a Tiffany ring box nestled in the bottom of the bag on a bed of tissue paper. 'What is it, Mum?' Harry had asked. Holly promised herself it would be the last lie she ever told her son when she answered, 'A pen.' Even in the privacy of her room the Tiffany box remained unopened.

There had been no sudden mood swings from Gareth. Holly was relieved as it had really shaken her in Wales. They'd all been amused by the present that Megan had bought him. Pants and socks are quite a personal gift from the girl who delivers your groceries, Holly thought. She hoped that maybe one day Gareth would realise that Megan would like to be more than just his friend.

Holly's only concern over the past five days had been Robert. He had been almost too happy. In his efforts to entertain his house-guests he hadn't allowed himself any down time, and this morning, after Harry had left to take his family to Clapham Junction for their train back to Swansea, Holly had asked him if he was all right.

'Holly, you've made this Christmas the best it could possibly have been. I can't lie. There's a gaping hole in my heart which will never be completely filled, but you and Harry and baby Rosie have come as close as will ever be possible. Are you okay to keep an ear out for Rosie while you're making lunch? I'm just going to have a walk down the garden.'

'Of course, Robert,' she said, pretending she hadn't seen the tear slip out of the corner of his eye. 'She's sleeping. She'll be fine.'

Robert walked the length of the garden and sat on the bench near the wooden summerhouse, where he and Rosemary had shared so many summer evenings admiring the sunset over the valley. He pulled the crumpled sheet of paper out of his pocket that he had read hundreds of times since he had found it in the large white envelope in his wife's desk, shortly after her death. The words always reduced him to tears. He traced Rosemary's flowery handwriting with the tip of his finger, an action that always made him feel closer to his soulmate.

'Oh Rosie,' he mumbled, 'how could you ever think anyone would replace you? We had our second chance at happiness and we took it. I just hope Holly and Philippe will be as lucky as we were, although I'm still not sure they are right for each other. I miss you every single day, my darling, but being able to cuddle baby Rosie has brought me such comfort. Watch over us and wait for me...' his voice trailed off. He carefully folded the paper and put it back in his pocket, at the same moment as he heard a baby cry. He rushed up the garden as quickly as he could, careful not to slip on the wet grass so recently encased in snow.

As he reached the French doors the crying abruptly stopped.

'Hi Robert, the front door was unlocked and I could hear this little mite crying. I hope you didn't mind me barging in.'

'Nick, you're early. Harry's not back yet. You've clearly got a way with babies. Go ahead and pick her up if you like. She enjoys a cuddle.'

'I had plenty of practise when the twins were small,'

Nick said, lifting Rosie out of her cot, taking care to support her head.

The kitchen door opened and Holly stopped dead in her tracks. A stranger was cradling her baby and Robert was letting him.

'Holly, this is Nick. Nick this is Holly, Rosie's mum,' Robert said, indicating the baby.

'Oh, erm, sorry. Would you rather I put her back in the cot? It's just she was crying and there didn't seem to be anyone around,' Nick said, pulling his wool hat off his head with his free hand allowing a mop of dark curly hair to fall into his eyes.

'I've got the extractor fan on in the kitchen. That's why I was coming to check on her. No need to put her down, she prefers being held and you've clearly done it before,' Holly said, watching her daughter clasping the green fabric of his puffa jacket with her tiny hand.

'Not for a few years. My twins have just had their nineteenth birthday, but I guess it's something you don't forget, a bit like riding a bike. She's beautiful. How old is she?'

'She'll be ten weeks tomorrow.'

'Really? I'm sure my boys were bigger at that age.'

'She was two months premature,' Holly said, 'but she's doing really well. Robert didn't mention we had an extra guest for lunch.'

'I'm not stopping. I've got to pick the twins up from the station in a couple of hours. They've been at their mum's for Christmas so they're spending New Year with me. I just popped in to meet Robert's young apprentice, Harry. We might be doing some work together.'

'Nick's a fellow architect,' Robert explained, in answer

to Holly's raised eyebrows. 'The LA project is going ahead and I don't want to overload Harry with his finals coming up. That sounds like him now.'

The front door slammed. 'Mum, I'm back,' Harry called.

Nick's face registered surprise.

'Whose is the Range Rover Sport in the drive? It looks like the one that was towing people up the hill in the snow.' Harry stopped halfway down the stairs when he noticed Nick holding his baby sister. 'Oh, it is you. I'd recognise that jacket anywhere. That was such a kind thing to do.'

'It was nothing,' Nick said, flushing with embarrassment. 'You must be Harry. Robert's told me a lot about you.'

'He has?' Harry said, looking questioningly at Robert.

'Don't worry, it was all good.'

'Are you sure you can't stay for lunch?' Holly asked. 'It's only homemade soup but there's plenty to go round and it seems like you three have quite a lot to talk about.'

'Well, if you're sure it's no trouble. I am kind of sick of turkey sandwiches.'

'No trouble at all. I'll take your jacket if Rosie will let go of it.'

Nick gently uncurled the baby's fingers. 'What have you got there Rosie? It looks like a piece of down has worked its way through the fabric,' he said, retrieving a tiny white feather from the baby's grasp and holding it out to show Holly.

She stared at it for a moment before raising her gaze to look into Nick's light green eyes.

Acknowledgements

Firstly, thanks so much to everyone who read *Life's a Beach and Then…* and provided me with such positive feedback. I was thrilled that you all cared as much about my characters as I did when I was writing about them, and I hope you have enjoyed the second instalment in their lives.

Thank you to Justine Taylor, my copy editor, for your continued patience, knowledge and guidance. I have learnt so much from you and hope you will agree that the sequel was a little easier to knock into shape than book one. I'm looking forward to working together again for the conclusion of the Liberty Sands Trilogy.

Yvonne Betancourt has once again turned my manuscript into a book. Not so many decisions this time round but thank you for helping me make them.

I had so many compliments about the cover of *Life's a Beach and Then…* and I accepted them all on behalf of my cover designer Angela Oltmann. I absolutely love the cover of the new book – the position of the white feather is inspired.

To everyone at Ripped thank you for your support, belief and tweeting.

Once again friends and colleagues at QVC have offered their help and support. Kathy Tayler was the first person outside of my family to read this book. You are never sure how people will react to your work but, 'WOW – I think it's probably even better than the first,' was a real confidence booster. Thank you, Kathy. Thanks also to Alison Keenan for volunteering to proof read, drawing on her experience from many moons ago when she worked for a publisher, so that the book could be as mistake-free as possible.

A big thank you to my daughter, Sophie, who was the first to read this book and gave me valuable feedback on the way young people speak. I loved being in the room with you and hearing your reactions to certain twists and turns… 'I didn't see that coming!' Thanks also for coming up with the brilliant shout line when I couldn't make the words I wanted to use fit! To my son, Daniel, who generously allowed me to stay with him at his flat in Swansea on numerous occasions when I needed peace and quiet to write, and also for introducing me to the stunning Gower peninsula which, as a result, featured in the book. And to my partner of thirty eight years, Chris, thank you for being the wind beneath my wings. I'm sorry I can't promise you that I won't be scribbling notes, or reading through draft manuscripts, on our next holiday… and the next… and the next.

OTHER BOOKS BY THIS AUTHOR

Life's a Beach and Then…
The Liberty Sands Trilogy Book 1

Holly Wilson has landed a dream job but there is one provision… she must keep it secret, and that means telling lies. Holly hates telling lies. Her latest assignment has brought her to the paradise island of Mauritius where she meets a British couple, Robert and Rosemary, who share a tragic secret of their own. The moment they introduce Holly to handsome writer, Philippe, she begins to fall in love, something she hasn't allowed herself to do for twenty years. But Philippe has not been completely honest and when Holly stumbles across the truth, she feels totally betrayed.

One Hundred Lengths of the Pool
Preface *publishing*

One Hundred Lengths of the Pool is a memoir exploring Julia's extraordinary life, including surviving the killer disease polio and against all odds becoming a professional dancer. That was the start of a long and varied career in the entertainment industry. In a unique book, each of the hundred lengths is associated with a special moment or memory from her life. However, there is an extra length of the pool that she didn't expect to swim and it has changed her life completely, testing her belief in her favourite saying, 'That which does not kill us, makes us stronger…'

Available on **amazon.co.uk**

Holly has to dig deep in her heart to find forgiveness and understanding after long-buried secrets are revealed. She deserves her happy ending in the final book of the Liberty Sands Trilogy, but who will it be with? Read on for a preview of

It's Never Too Late to Say …

CHAPTER 1

Carol shivered beneath the pile of blankets on her bed. They were heavy but provided little warmth as they pressed her slight body into the sagging mattress. January and February had been mild and damp in the UK and had lulled everyone into thinking that spring was in the air, but in late March an arctic wind had swept across the country depositing heavy snow. The single-glazed, ill-fitting bedroom windows rattled and did little to keep the cold at bay and the flimsy curtains occasionally flapped in the draught, allowing light from the street-lamp to spill into the room and create strange-shaped shadows in the corners.

Carol felt her heart beating loudly against her ribcage. Someone was in the room with her, she could sense it. Easing herself up, she drew her knees into her chest to make herself as small as possible and pulled the covers up to her chin. She peered fearfully into the dark, unaware of the whimpering noise she was making, like a neglected dog. The wind gusted again, causing the curtains to billow inwards and, in the flash of illumination, a figure standing next to her bedroom door became clearly visible. She gasped.

'It's all right, Carol. No one's going to hurt you.'

The figure began to advance towards her.

'Mummy! Mummy!' she tried to cry out, but no sound came.

Two strong hands pushed her back on to her pillows. 'Shh, shh. It'll be over soon.'

Carol closed her eyes to block out the face but it was no good, it was imprinted on her mind. She could feel hot breath on her cheeks. 'Please, not again,' she begged in an almost inaudible whisper, 'I don't want to.' She opened her eyes as a hand was being lowered towards her face. It was a risk, but she had to take it. She grabbed the hand and bit down on it hard.

'Shit! What did you do that for?'

Carol squirmed out of the bed and, gathering all her strength, hurried towards the door. Footsteps closed in on her as she stumbled across the dark landing. If I can just reach Mummy's room and prove to her that I wasn't telling lies, Carol thought, then maybe she will love me again. A hand gripped her shoulder but, with an almighty effort, she pulled away, tripping on the hem of her nightgown. Terrified, she staggered forward, reaching out for the handrail of the staircase but her hands were so cold she couldn't grip and she plummeted headfirst down the stairs, landing at the bottom with a sickening thud.

'Carol, Carol, are you all right?' a woman's voice asked.

That doesn't sound like Mummy, Carol thought.

The last thing she heard before slipping into unconsciousness was the woman's voice saying, 'Ambulance, please. There's been an accident.'

CPSIA information can be obtained at www.ICGtesting.com
Printed in the USA
LVOW07s2136231115

463852LV00007B/335/P